THE WORKING LEADER

Other Books by Leonard Sayles

Leonard R. Sayles

THE WORKING LEADER

The Triumph of High Performance over Conventional Management Principles

Foreword by Henry Mintzberg

THE FREE PRESS
A Division of Macmillan, Inc.
New York

MAXWELL MACMILLAN CANADA
Toronto

MAXWELL MACMILLAN INTERNATIONAL
New York   Oxford   Singapore   Sydney

SIMON & SCHUSTER
Rockefeller Center
1230 Avenue of the Americas
New York, New York 10020

First Simon & Schuster paperback edition 1999

SIMON & SCHUSTER and colophon are trademarks
of Simon & Schuster Inc.

Manufactured in the United States of America

10 9 8 7 6 5 4 3 2 1

The Library of Congress catalogued this edition as follows:
        Sayles, Leonard R.
The working leader / Leonard R. Sayles.
p.   cm.
Includes bibliographical references and index.
1. Leadership.   2. Executives.   3. Industrial management.
I. Title.
HD57.7.S3   1993
658.4'09—dc20   92-34089
                         CIP
ISBN: 0-02-927755-8
        0-684-87103-3 (pbk)

In memory of my parents,
Rose and Robert Sayles

Contents

Foreword

In the early 1970s, when, with considerable difficulty, I was trying to publish *The Nature of Managerial Work,* Jim Campbell of Harper and Row sent the manuscript to Leonard Sayles for review. *The* Leonard Sayles, whose pathbreaking book, *Managerial Behavior,* had so influenced me. He not only recommended its publication: he actually volunteered to write a foreword!

My response here in kind, in answer to Free Press editor Bob Wallace's request to do a blurb for the back cover (the kind of thing, with forewords, I have always been loath to do), is not merely meant to reflect my gratitude for that offer so long ago. It is an effort to support, not just a critically important book, but a lifetime of critically important work.

Leonard Sayles has been championing one vital message for decades, persisting as American management practice has gone the other way, to its great discredit. He has never written about managing in a minute, and so he has not sold millions of copies. Instead, he writes with dignity, rare in this field, about managing as a serious art, rooted deeply in action—in making tangible things happen, getting real things done—based on a profound understanding of what is being managed. This is management practiced by thoughtful and devoted men and women—especially in that dreadfully mistreated place called "middle management"—often up against awfully difficult circumstances. It may be the "slow track" to the top, but it is the sure one.

Thoughtless managers won't like this book. It takes effort, like serious management. My hope is that it will reach the others, and like people who develop and select managers, so that the careful words of a wise observer can be heeded. For this is a truly revolutionary book in the field of management: it makes a case for the hard work of common sense! When a thoughtful book like *The Working Leader* begins to reach the bestseller lists, then we shall know that American management has turned the corner.

If you share these sentiments, do your bit and read this book. Vote with your eyes for a coming to senses in the practice of management.

Henry Mintzberg

1

Waltz Faster—They're Playing a Tango

The culture of the United States can produce strong individuals—eager to challenge conventional wisdom, flexible, and improvisational. Americans learn very early to talk up and talk back, to take initiative, and to try new things (often to the consternation of those around them). Increasingly, business requires managers who can solve the intractable problems created by the pace of change. As we seek to catch up and surpass Japanese and European competition, it would be a serious mistake to seek to mimic group- or clan-based work cultures. For one thing, it wouldn't work for us. More importantly, we would be ignoring one of our great strengths: these strong individuals.

This book demonstrates how many of the most pressing challenges of modern business require *not* more Japanese management (or other quick grafts) but the fostering of a more vigorous, individual-based leadership style. It is leadership focused on work issues, not just people issues, and it is very different from the method and style of managing that have evolved from our traditional management principles.

WHY IS LEADERSHIP BEING REDISCOVERED?

Anthropologists assess the anxieties and passions of a society by interpreting its myths, wise sayings, and folk wisdom. The same process can help uncover some of the hidden dynamics of the world of

1

the manager. Why are so many companies now seeking more leadership and more teamwork?

In the last half-dozen years, the subject of leadership has been rediscovered by business as a critical factor in organizational performance. Books and courses proliferate as companies recognize that there is much more to gaining commitment and performance than investing in automation and robots or in better compensation plans (although the quest for the right "magic bullet" still continues). At the same time, the subject of teamwork has assumed growing importance in the perspective of operating managers. Improving the cooperation that takes place among interdependent managers, professionals, and employees is the primary focus of a great deal of management training.

Underlying this rediscovered significance of leadership and teamwork is a gnawing sense among American business managers that they have been doing something wrong. The self-assurance of the post–World War II era that American business knew the answers has been replaced by the growing perception that they probably don't, and that Japanese and European managers may do many things better than U.S. managers do.

For the most part, though, the teamwork and leadership issues are jumbled and tangled in webs of ever-changing jargon, or one or another kind of improvement program. They have appealing names—total quality management (TQM), time-based management, high-performance work systems, to mention just a few. The development of attractively titled new approaches to management is indeed a growth industry all of its own. Little attention, however, is paid to the underlying worldview of managers; therefore, basic management actions and reactions tend to remain fixed.

No one can claim to look inside the heads of managers. Even so, there is a great deal of external evidence in how they talk and behave that many managers have a view of their jobs and their organizations that doesn't check out with reality but is, instead, a throwback to dated management principles and models.

Scientific management still represents the core values of most managers. American business is in a time warp; it talks "modern" but acts as though traditional mass-production industry was still the mode. Management theory doesn't copy very well with the reality of today's external business environment, in which volatile markets, fast-paced technological change, and the need for increasing customization are the rule, not the exception.

These managers fail to notice that the predictability and controllability of the work itself has changed dramatically in the past decade. What managers do and what professors of management study may not be as relevant as they once were. But since neither look very closely at the challenge involved in getting work accomplished, the mental images they carry around are not challenged.

This book, then, is an effort to look more deeply at what I think are basic failures in how American managers manage that are inconsistent with the needs of the real work of modern business. By seeking to explain where those failures came from (ironically, their source lies in efforts to make management more scientific), the case data provide very different management principles than those that have been dominant in U.S. business and business education for almost a century.

The case data that will be examined focus on managers who ought to be on the cutting edge of change. It is the middle managers who should have the responsibility for making things happen, for achieving integration and coordination among tasks and functions and overcoming the defects in plans and systems.

THE HEAVY HAND OF THE PAST

Most of what managers think of as the heart of their jobs has little or nothing to do with these problems, which weren't envisioned by either the fathers (or fathers and mothers) of scientific management or their offspring. They thought more of hierarchies than lateral coordination and integration challenges, hierarchies in which clear and fixed plans would get passed down and results passed up (with certain contingencies to take effect when results were especially good or bad).

The result is that American managers for the most part think of their job in hierarchical terms: pleasing the boss and satisfying subordinates. There will of course be occasional work problems requiring involvement, it is assumed, particularly if one is a manufacturing manager (given how equipment and suppliers can misbehave). But most managers believe that involvement with work is a major defect reflecting either unsatisfied needs to give up managing (and go back to being a worker) or a distrust of subordinates. Worse yet, involvement demotivates subordinates.

Most managers are never taught, or fail to learn, that the heart of their job as managers is work leadership, facilitating coordination and integration in order to get work done. This neglected but critical responsibility involves change, but a very different kind of change than is envisioned by those who assert that leaders have to be transformational (that is, have a vision of some consequential discontinuity and seek to bring that to fruition).

THE FUTURE IS NOW

The leadership of the coming decade will diverge from concerns with personality and satisfaction to a focus on work systems and technology. But these concerns do not make relationships and interpersonal effectiveness less relevant. Quite the contrary, continuously improving work effectiveness requires even greater leadership skills than old-fashioned, compartmentalized "people" problems. Almost every modification in technology, no matter how trivial, requires a good deal of information, communication, and persuasion, not to mention persistence and perseverance, all of which derive from leadership capabilities.

Organizations will demand much more value added from their managers.[1] The recurring cutting out of managerial levels and slimming down of overhead and staffs are sharp testimony to the increasing recognition that many managers have not been earning their way. What could the managers of a company have been doing when, under market pressures, they can cut almost half their people, square footage, and inventory and still produce the same volume of merchandise? Organizations often become bloated with extra layers of management and accompanying staff when coordination problems fester and managers "run to stand still."

To be sure, as the reader will see, the fault is often in the inducements, rigidities, and role models provided by senior management. But that aside, managers will have to be able to demonstrate their ability to create more self-maintaining work systems, instead of constant fire fighting. Ironically, as many cases will illustrate, the need for individual leadership skill increases even though business appears to be dominated by impersonal, technology-based systems.

The chapters that follow provide an explanation of why today's managers have to be much more involved in the management of work than Americans have presumed (as well as what form that involvement should take). Otherwise, given a high level of change, uncertainty, and the need for continuous improvements in quality and efficiency, companies become littered with temporary "patches" and new one-shot (but expensive) improvement schemes.

Neither the annual plan, the systems, nor the hierarchy work any more to keep everyone and everything in a "straight line." The reason is not politics or sloth or stupidity; it is because the interrelationships among functions, jobs, and departments are now so complex and dynamic that there can be no real coordination among the parts without continuing, astute managerial inputs. Citicorp's CEO, John Reed, said in 1991 that he expects far fewer meetings and less emphasis on plans, with "judgment replacing a lot of three year plans that no one ever looked at."[2] This is a far cry from what CEOs such as Reed were saying only a year or two earlier.

Thus, this is a book about what managers need to do to make organizations stay organized; to make things work. It describes a view of managerial jobs and roles in which effectuating work, handling teams, and work flow relationships are more important than the traditional hierarchical boss-subordinate relations. This is what is both truly important and immensely difficult—and what American management hasn't known much about doing.

For American business effectiveness to improve, managers have to add value. They have to do those things that directly affect productivity. In the past, most companies have been content to have managers contribute *indirectly* by their planning, standard setting and controls, and motivational skills. This ignores the enormous work leadership needs of modern business.

2

A New Leadership Perspective

For the most part (and surprisingly, given all the criticism of American business management), the major issues of management and the functions of the executive are viewed in much the same way as they were fifty years before. The classic assumptions related to management are accepted almost without question in both boardrooms and MBA classrooms (although the wording keeps getting updated):

- Executives face their most profound problems in the decision-making arena, setting goals and converting these into soundly executable plans. The primary managerial activities are those of *command* and *control*.
- Although there is some overlap, problems of efficiency, excessive overhead, customer service (and customization), product quality, and innovation are essentially distinct and require unique solutions. Managerial responsibilities can be compartmentalized and programmed effectively by means of the hierarchy.
- Leaders have two kinds of work—"people" work and "work" work. Motivation issues are very separate from work or technology issues.
- Managers primarily need to learn to "manage upward," gaining credibility with their boss.
- Good management is almost synonymous with clarity; issues, jobs, responsibilities, and authority need to be defined clearly.

There also should be a clear line separating the work of a manager from that of her subordinates.

- Just as there is reasonable separation between jobs, between levels, and between technology and people issues, managers can be separated into two distinct groups: *administrators* (those who follow prescribed, programmed managerial directives) and *leaders* (those who introduce transformational change).

- Among both nonleaders and leaders, the managers who do best are those who delegate most. They manage by results and don't get involved directly with work and technology.

- Management itself represents generic skills (particularly of command and control) that can be transferred quite easily from one organizational setting to another with minimal start-up costs.

The research and company case studies presented in Chapter 3 challenge all of these comfortable presumptions.

THE AUTHORITY CORE

Most of management theorizing deals with the preservation and application of authority. Designing the hierarchy, handling delegation, deciding who is responsible for what, and many leadership improvement programs all have issues of authority as their core. Some years ago, interest focused on how much managerial authority should be shared with subordinates (that is, how participative a style was optimal). Good managers were those who balanced a focus on work issues with an interest in people and their needs and problems.

Conceptions of command and control have changed. Control is now sometimes called *transactional* management. This is a market or exchange view, in that managers are seen as maintaining control by trading good working conditions, various kinds of rewards, and decent supervision for a good day's work. Command has now become *transformational* leadership—leadership that focuses on introducing change. Transformational managers have a vision and a conception of future organization attainments that not only impose ambitious change goals but also inspire subordinates. Their commanding vision of what the organization can become should inspire consensus and the commitment of followers much more than do the fair exchanges of transactional, control-oriented leaders.[1]

Even with these more modern versions, however, managers are told to emphasize the hierarchy. Rather than gain cooperative subordinate behavior by the naked use of power, they should find ways of leading that appeal to followers' minds, especially their imagination and desire for achievement. This advice, of course, is very sensible.

NAGGING QUESTIONS:
WHY AMERICAN MANAGERS "LOST IT"

Left unanswered is why managers need special (and costly) programs to tell them that quality and efficiency and continuing improvements are all part of their managerial jobs (and how to achieve them). Aren't these what management is supposed to be largely about? Aren't these the very heart of managerial work? If managers weren't addressing these problems in the past, what were they doing? (Ironically, as will be described in chapter 13, all these "new" improvement programs were being taught in some progressive U.S. university business programs almost fifty years ago.)

The basic flaws in conventional management practice (and in many of the currently popular academic theories central to organizational behavior) were hidden when American business could focus on old-fashioned mass production of fairly straightforward products and simple services.[2] Work involved fixed, almost unvarying routines that were easy to count and assess (for feedback) and that could be programmed from the top down. Careful planning, tight controls mixed with the proper dose of motivational technique (conveniently apart from the work) to reduce the sting of authoritarianism—all of it worked, aided by old-fashioned economies of scale and a protected and huge internal market.

The extraordinary success of U.S. industry in World War II and the decades immediately following would explain a good deal of the self-confidence, even arrogance, of those managers. How can one argue with clearly documented success? Halberstam, in a recent book concluding that this past experience is no guide to the future, lists some of these extraordinary achievements of what he calls "the American century":

> With our great assembly lines and our ever-expanding industrial core . . . we became the industrial arsenal of the mightiest of war efforts. In 1942 and 1943, America alone produced almost twice as many airplanes as the entire Axis. In 1943 and 1944, we were producing one ship a day and an airplane every five minutes.[3]

American management, once the envy of the world and even feared for its omnipotence, has been on the defensive for the past decade, if not longer. It may be difficult to remember, but in the 1950s, one of General Motors' greatest concerns was its own success. GM feared that if its market share became too great, it would encourage government antitrust initiatives. Throughout the world, corporate names like DuPont, Esso (now Exxon), and U.S. Steel inspired enormous respect. Never mind that some of the success was due to the decimation of the war, or that Japan and Germany would rise mightily to challenge U.S. business supremacy by the 1980s; U.S. business was a powerful economic force.

It is not surprising that there was almost a mystique surrounding the managerial skill base for this earlier success. Europeans in particular worried that they could not expect to compete until they had learned to give and get MBA-type education, which they viewed as the wellspring of American business preeminence.[4] American executives were good at decision making, were not adverse to risk taking, and encouraged employee involvement and participation (although there would always be those who said not enough was encouraged). In addition, Americans were inventive and creative, and a steady stream of inventions flowed to industry.

But failures came in the 1970s and 1980s in managing complexity, ambiguity, and the challenge of ever faster and more demanding change. Halberstam says it more cogently: "We have dissipated the enormous head start we had, and other nations have caught up with us. Some of that is inevitable; it was unrealistic to expect any nation to remain as dominating and powerful as America was."[5]

American companies have waged an uphill fight to maintain markets against the best of the Japanese and European multinationals. Economists blame business management ineptness, in part, for the failure to compete effectively and the resulting cost in American's standard of living. (The rate of increase of after-tax real income per worker declined 75% in the period 1973–90 from what it had been during the first three quarters of the twentieth century.[6])

TECHNOLOGY IS NOW THE MANAGER'S PROBLEM AND CHALLENGE

The flaws in management systems could *not* be hidden when:

- the products were complex goods (such as large software programs)
- these products were forever changing, with continuing new generations in the pipeline
- selling to sophisticated customers with attractive alternative sources and who demanded ever-changing customized adaptations
- senior executives required ever shorter development cycles
- adept foreign competition became a reality

In the current environment, with these technological issues in both manufacturing and services, it has become apparent that the critical problems of management involve coping with the incredibly profound issues surrounding coordination and systems; that is, getting managers continuously and adaptively to rearrange work routines, communication patterns, and performance standards. As the reader will see, the challenges of quality performance, efficiency, responsiveness to customers, and effective (in other words, timely and successful) innovation are essentially the same challenge: getting discrete, semiautonomous jobs, work groups, tasks, and departments to fit synchronously into an integrated whole, be it accomplishment, finished work, a customized product or service adaptation, or effective innovation.

The critical difference between yesterday's business and managerial effectiveness and today's anxieties about organizational effectiveness is the decreasing leverage provided by economies of scale. American management skills were honed on mass production; today the critical element is flexibility in terms of quick change, short product runs, and customizing for good customers.

Every line manager has to cope with change on almost a daily basis, because the new "parts" (however the term is defined) don't fit easily into integrated wholes. One long-neglected reality is that the interface or boundary between given jobs, departments, and functions is hardly ever a simple, neat one. There is an incredible wealth of fine and increasingly elaborate detail in the method and process by which both work and critical functions get performed that makes it unlikely that separate jurisdictions will coordinate easily or comfortably. One only has to look at the literally thousands of issues that arise when two software systems have to intermesh to get some feel for the interaction of complex interfaces, each of which is a moving target. But the same occurs when black box A has to fit with black box B, or when sales work has to integrate with marketing work.

These technical complexities are accentuated by "suboptimizations," complex group norms, and contradictory (but legitimate) functional goals, among other factors. All ensure that the typical manager doesn't confront a finely tuned, assembly-line-like work organization. For the same reason, the manager has no reason to expect neatly bounded jurisdictions separating "my" from "their" responsibilities. Inevitably, there are profound ambiguities as to who should change what and when if "our" work is to get done properly.

To make matters worse, the number of interdependencies, given ever-increasing specialization in management, guarantees a lack of equilibrium. In other words, small disturbances create large problems. To cope with one misfitting element, the manager must seek to jiggle or rework a dozen interfaces with relevant staff and line groups that are sequentially affected by the issue. Thus, problems ricochet from one organizational unit to another, with responsible managers, seeking to make something work, chasing just behind.

Managerial life would still be relatively simple if these interface complexities stayed relatively fixed. No such luck, of course. Each unit in real, contemporary organizations keeps changing what they do and how they do it in response to recently uncovered internal imperfections or external dynamics (new problems or opportunities in the marketplace, with vendors, or in technology).

Another dynamic factor affects top management's efforts to implement new programs. New strategies and new technologies require profound changes in the interrelationships of key functional and product heads. Once-dominant units may retain some of their initiative but cede some of their "power" to formerly less prestigious and more deferential functions. Decision making is itself a kind of work flow requiring the orchestrated participation of various functional heads and experts analogous to how lower-level production operations get performed. Success depends on the sequencing and interrelating of these functional inputs over time.

But, again, these are not one-dimensional interrelationships, as among marketing, manufacturing, R & D, and finance. Marketing, for example, even in a firm emphasizing a new core technology, will still need to be consulted early on some issues, whereas it has to be more deferential on others.

EFFECTIVE LEADERSHIP REQUIRES INVOLVEMENT

There is just no way for the uninvolved, broadly delegating hands-off manager to cope with the dynamic interplay of overlapping jurisdictions and the contradictions in subgroup work routines. Similarly, the manager cannot hope for clear, unambiguous direction; absence of clarity is one of the costs of increased specialization. Work, technology, and people issues are almost one and the same thing because of the inherent ambiguities in technical interfaces.

In other words, many intergroup conflicts and boss-subordinate disputes have their source in technology and the work process. Usually the issues being debated reflect differing views of who should do what with whom, when, where, or how often. These differences can flourish because the intersections of jobs and functions are complex, ambiguous, and ever changing. Of course, these differences also provide a rich broth in which personality differences can grow to gargantuan proportions, particularly when managers are technologically naive.

From one point of view, good leadership is synonymous with being able to cope with the problems of the human condition. Everything gets involved, from family and health issues to matters of discipline and economic theory. But this is a hopeless morass. Reasonable parsimony is required if U.S. management is going to cope with the extraordinary competitiveness of the 1990s.

Management will never be effective if one new technique or another keeps being layered on through management training and consulting. At present, self-managing teams, walking-around management, a customer-focused organization, and so on are discrete techniques. For many managers, these are new "toys" that do not change their basic view of management principles.

Management doctrine and actions continue to focus on authority, plans, and morale. (Interestingly, the subject of work, in the sense of coordinated effort, is almost never mentioned in management or organizational behavior texts except when reviewing the rather narrow issues of production management.) I would argue that attaining high levels of efficiency, quality, service, and the ability to innovate embody almost the same tough coordination issues, which are also composite people-technology relationships. If so, managing coordination becomes a much more parsimonious way of treating the complexities of management.

Thus the focus on what needs to happen if both worker work and managerial work are to get done efficiently, with high quality and adapting to continuous fine-tuning changes and periodic strategic changes, provides a very different set of managerial imperatives than that provided by plan-focused management principles. Companies that are still struggling with the realities of staff/line conflict on the one hand or debating whether to be centralized or decentralized are not going to be able to make it in a world of enormously complex hardware and software and rapid change and ever-rising customer expectations. Managers will be coping with systems that are centralized *and* decentralized, with peers who are staff *and* line.

Working leadership involves the capacity to make fast-paced trade-offs (each involving embedded people and technology issues) focusing on the ever-changing needs of coordination and the overall system, regardless of whether one is dealing with a quality, service, innovation, or efficiency problem. Unfortunately, outside of special arenas like project management, these system issues get short shrift or are not even understood by managers concentrating on motivation and the big picture presented by "the plan" and its apparent programmed work requirements. Learning both the nature of these system issues and how to cope with them is what leadership and management are really all about. In turn, this can represent a coherent and parsimonious approach (or theory, if one wishes to be a little pretentious) to management and leadership.

Without this kind of involved, hands-on working leadership, there is almost no chance that a company will be able to compete in world markets that simultaneously demand high efficiency, high quality, innovativeness, and customer service. All of these have the same root: work systems that work. And they don't work because of good policies or good intentions; the inherent centrifugal forces in most organizations are too powerful. A work system doesn't function effectively without leadership—in fact, it self destructs! But what it requires is not leadership for inspiration or for astute decisions, but leadership that integrates the disparate elements of the system.

One now can explain why all the behavioral studies of managers show those extraordinarily peripatetic, interactive workdays. The explanation is that a significant share of leadership is not what it appears to be (that is, motivating, delegating, planning, and implementing plans). It is both making things work and making them work better, because nothing really works in the dynamic reality of modern organizations without constant retrofitting and realigning of the technology (or system). Jobs and functions and departments are tending to fly apart at worst or failing to mesh at best, and it is only the manager/leader who can make the system work by integrating the elements dynamically (in real time, not by plans and structure).

With all the talk—and consulting and behavioral theorizing— management as practiced and the models that managers carry in their heads have changed almost not at all in fifty years, except for greater sensitivity to the needs of people. I think the reason for this is the failure to comprehend how very difficult it is to integrate work and management systems, given the inherent complexity of interfaces and the reality that these interfaces are in constant flux because of imperfections, improvements, and innovation. What happens when managers learn to focus on continuously reassessing, reworking, and adapting these is this book's primary theme.

3

U.S. Management Principles

A Step Back from the Future

T he business press and many business books of recent years
are filled with horror stories about the failure of U.S. management. Americans invent the basic technology of the video
camera and recorder but can't manufacture consumer models to
compete with the Japanese. The U.S. auto industry, one of the stand-
bys of the American economy and a technology in which U.S. companies have extensive experience, finds it difficult to compete with
Japanese plants set up almost next door using the same technology
and employees. Almost all consumer electronics come from offshore,
and the Japanese now are almost the sole source for certain critical
electronic components.

Has American business management acumen declined? Did American management grow soft with its easy post–World War II suc-
cesses? Or more likely, did American management never have the
skills to operate in a world of turbulent change (frequent product
change, demanding customers who want unique features or service,
ever higher standards of quality, and continuous pressures from competitors for lower costs and improved features)? Perhaps American
management's strengths were uniquely relevant to mass production
involving absolutely fixed routines. For these technologies, profits
were derived almost purely from volume, exceeding the break-even
point.

At the opposite end of the continuum, American culture produces smart, aggressive, and flexible entrepreneurs. In small organizations the owner/CEO, by being directly involved and controlling all the elements, can turn his or her organization on the proverbial dime. Teamwork builds more easily in a small organization. Also, the entrepreneur can encourage specialists to emphasize coordination and larger goals and resist the temptation to "do their own thing." Regrettably, most modern technology and a good deal of world-class marketing, manufacturing, and development require large organizations.

THE MYTH THAT U.S. BUSINESS WATCHES THE BOTTOM LINE

One of the most careful and damning studies of U.S. management deficiencies compared the performance of Japanese and U.S. room air-conditioner manufacturers. The researcher, David Garvin of the Harvard Business School, was able to get detailed data on manufacturing costs of all but one of the companies in that industry. All used very similar technology to manufacture a very similar product. Although Garvin focused on quality, it should be noted that the quality of production translated directly into lower manufacturing costs. Here are some of his startling findings:

- Japanese companies had an average assembly-line defect rate almost seventy times lower than their American counterparts.
- U.S. companies with low-quality production had failure rates that were as much as five hundred to one thousand times greater than the product failure rates of the best Japanese companies.
- The best American company had warranty costs (primarily the result of their manufacturing quality) that were three times greater than the average Japanese company. The worst U.S. company had warranty costs that were almost nine times greater.
- Total costs incurred to ensure high-quality production on the part of a typical Japanese company in this industry was less than one-half what it cost the typical U.S. company to pay for the extra costs associated with low quality. The latter included

the costs of scrap, reworked production, and warranty repairs and replacements.[1]

What is so revealing about these data is that American companies suffered immediate lower profitability as a result of their inability to manufacture effectively. In other words, ignoring the risk that they would lose market share because they were producing lower-quality products (which would erode longer-run profitability), they also accepted short-run reduced profitability. In his study, Garvin cites other research that supports these findings:

> Other studies . . . have demonstrated a further connection among quality, market share, and return on investment. [For example] among businesses with less than 12% of the market, those with inferior product quality averaged an ROI [return on investment] of 4.5% . . . those with superior product quality an ROI of 17.4% [and] it also leads directly to market share gains.[2]

A consultant who works with companies to improve quality performance cites the case of a U.S. auto manufacturer who for many years tolerated an 80 percent defect rate in the "first-time yield" (that is, before rework) of their transmission assemblies. Another of his examples is a company, pressured to improve performance, that was able to cut its changeover time when having to shift tooling from thirty-five hours to twenty minutes! For some years this company had tolerated the costs inherent in thirty-five hours of down time, just as the auto manufacturer had lived with the costs associated with reworking more than three-quarters of their transmissions.[3]

It is worth emphasizing that these are not examples of companies making a trade-off between higher quality and lower costs or obtaining better labor relations for higher costs, but rather managements who seem unable to do their production work effectively. As a result, they are less profitable than they would be if they had learned to manufacture properly.

Another compelling example of ignoring profitability appeared in the business press. Investigative reporters found that some companies, forced to change their manufacturing methods by environmental protection rules and standards, actually lowered their costs of production!

The Carrier division of United Technologies, in seeking to reduce the quantity of pollution it produced, realized that it needed to deal with the degreasing line. This process cleaned oil and other debris that accumulated during machining and soldering from finished metal parts prior to assembly; it also produced a major share of the division's hazardous waste.

Company engineers discovered that they could adjust cutting machines so that they would produce less waste. They also found that they could adjust the process so that there was less friction produced. Therefore, less lubrication would be needed, and the oil itself was a source of pollution. The engineers then found that they could simplify the design of the products being produced, thus using less parts (and, in turn, less machining).

Overall, these various changes cut production costs by reducing scrap and the need for degreasing. They also increased the quality of the product. And this improved performance was the result of being pressured by state and federal environmental regulation authorities, not management initiatives, to be more efficient or to produce higher quality products.[4]

The question is, why weren't these improvements that would flow through to the bottom line made without external prodding?

Another account by business journalists recounted the high cost (to complacent companies) of poor service in international markets for capital goods. They cite a number of instances in which large Korean importers of sophisticated machinery who preferred U.S. sources found U.S. managements deficient in providing follow-up service after delivery. The buyers reported large numbers of problems with faulty installations, "stingy service," and "lackadaisical" installation engineers who wouldn't work overtime or would leave before the job was completely finished. As a result, contracts gradually were shifted to Japanese suppliers.[5]

An unpublished study of the Xerox Corporation's successful struggle to improve the manufacturing quality and efficiency of its copiers suggests the magnitude of the problem. In 1980, before Xerox initiated a major and successful revamping of its methods of manufacturing and

managing copier production, management discovered
that Japanese copier manufacturers could manufacture,
ship, and have their product pass through distributors
and dealers and have a selling price that was lower than
Xerox's U.S. cost! In part, this reflected the reality that
Xerox had about 1.6 indirect workers supporting every
production employee, while its Japanese counterparts
had 0.7 indirect workers.[6]

American managers in charge of divisions that are perceived as not
having consequential growth prospects by senior management (and
therefore as unworthy of new resource allocations) often lose their
interest in maintaining effectiveness. Soon quality declines and costs
rise, and customers become increasingly disenchanted with the service as well as the product. What is often interesting here is *not* the
self-confirming prophecy (predict poor growth and the prediction
turns out to be a reality). Rather, it is the evidence that without substantial managerial inputs of interest and energy and initiative, work
inevitably degrades. It is not simply that no capital may be forthcoming to add new products or new processing, but existing routines
become less effective. In the words of a seasoned manager, "There is
no such thing as a static technology. Something is always changing
or breaking or needing modification, and if you have a disinterested
management, performance is going to decline even if you think you
have a facility and employees that are fixed."

In my own research, we have interviewed many plant managers
who admit quite openly that until competitive pressures became extreme, they accepted poorer quality and higher scrap losses than they
now tolerate. "There was no reason to change," went the typical
explanation, as long as profits were good. One interview with a senior executive of a very large specialty chemical manufacturer compared its U.S. operations with the European competition:

> Our most pressureful competition in Europe comes from an Italian
> company. They use the same equipment as we do, but they have
> fine-tuned it so perfectly that they have just about zero scrap. Every
> employee knows exactly how to respond to countless problems with
> infinitely subtle machine adjustments, and as a result their actual
> costs are 5 percent under ours. But we haven't been pressured as
> much by competition to spur us to do the same. And it would take a
> great deal of managerial effort to equal their operating performance.

All these examples illustrate that managers aren't encouraged to optimize; they "satisfice," to use Herbert Simon's most descriptive verb.

The business press in the 1990s contains many examples of major U.S. corporations engaging in "downsizing." In some cases, more than 20 percent of the work force (managers and employees) is cut, although the organization continues to perform the same functions and to produce the same products and services.[7] The cutbacks were motivated by recessionary pressures on margins and vigorous, often global, competition. But why did these organizations carry along surplus personnel for years, with a direct and negative impact on their sacred bottom line?

COMPANIES ARE PLAN ORIENTED, NOT PROFIT ORIENTED

In the data to be presented, a plausible explanation of these examples of profit-defeating behavior is this: many (probably most) companies have little understanding of how effectively managed their operations are. As long as managers meet their "plan," the performance goals that have been established for their departments, there are no pressures to manage better. It is only when profits take a sharp drop and top management begins to have serious worries about the future that steps are taken to improve efficiency. Regrettably, these steps are usually blunt, indiscriminate actions, such as across-the-board cuts which fail to distinguish which managers are truly effective from those who have not improved their operations.

Many explanations have been provided to explain the failure of many U.S. companies to attain high enough standards of performance to be world-class competitors. For the most part, however, these deal with exogenous factors. Most often cited are "disabilities" created by factors such as the following:

1. American managers grew complacent and flabby because of the ease of making profits in the postwar world prior to the resurgence of Japanese and German industry and the growth of world markets. Also, the moderate inflation of those years helped hide inefficiencies and inflated profits. A protected and very large domestic market that allowed non-export-oriented firms to do very well added to the myopia.

2. American industry is handicapped by institutional constraints. These include heavy debt loads that are partially the result of tax laws favoring debt over equity and of the takeover, leveraged buyout (LBO), and merger mania of the 1980s. Also, the U.S. stock market is much more short-run oriented than, for example, the Japanese stock market. Concern with share price narrows managers' focus to what it will take to look good in the next quarter, not the next decade.

3. More individualistic employees are less responsive to authority and direction than those raised in cultures that are more authoritarian, or much more deferential to the authority of managers as parent surrogates. American employees hence lack as strong a work ethic as many Asians.

4. Several major industries were subject to government regulation that in practice led to semiprotected monopoly positions (for example, banking, air and rail transportation, and telecommunications). Until this regulation was removed, many companies were "protected" in their inefficiencies. Such a culture can be slow to change.

No question that these are consequential for American management, but they do not provide a sufficient explanation.

THE OTHER EXPLANATION: INTERNAL FACTORS

Since the early 1980s, American managers have been deluged with suggestions for improved practice. Many are excellent; some are faddish. The ex-McKinsey consultants Peters and Waterman, studying a sample of what they felt to be excellently managed companies, came up with a list of widely cited improvements.[8] These few are representative:

- Move to action more rapidly, with less effort and time spent on analysis. Learn by doing, not just by thinking.
- Establish isolated and protected departments (so-called "skunk works") where innovative technical people can undertake development work free from the normal constraints of organizational forms and procedures.

- Managers should get out of their offices and move around their operations more to see with their own eyes what is occurring and to be more accessible.

The list of management techniques that have been proposed to deal with the "malaise" of American business, and are a boon for consultants, is a long one. Rarely questioned, however, are the models or basic principles that U.S. managers carry around in their heads that dictate "good management practices." As the reader will see, these form a very integrated and coherent (and logically reasonable) basis for decision making that *excludes* most of the issues central to effective performance.

But how could this be? Doesn't American business take pride in being bottom-line oriented, even to the exclusion of attending to critical social responsibilities? Aren't executives promoted largely on the basis of being hard-nosed about meeting performance targets? Hasn't one major source of industrial-relations strife been the struggle between work-oriented managers seeking higher performance and their employees who want lighter work loads or additional compensation (or both)?

My answer to all of these is that managers give speeches and interviews that make them appear performance oriented, but these words disguise reality. The reality is that managers are oriented toward designing and meeting the requirements of plans, and this is far different from struggling to attain high levels of performance. For many executives, getting better performance is synonymous with simply mandating that costs shall be cut (and, where possible, with raising prices).

As the reader will see, the model of good management that has been created both by executives themselves and by the preparation provided to neophyte managers (the business schools and corporate training programs) either discourages or ignores the kind of leadership necessary to produce innovative, high-quality goods and services that meet the ever-changing needs of demanding customers and accomplish truly effective performance.

THE CASE OF AMERICAN BUSINESS PRODUCTS

Although it is just one case, the example of "American Business Products" (not the company's real name) is one of the best indications that American managers have a more profound problem that is not being solved by learning new techniques or skills.

American Business Products (ABP) is a huge, diversified corporation that over many years has taken great pride in its ability to produce both mundane and technologically advanced products profitably and to develop excellent managers by a consistent and sophisticated internal development program. In fact, the company has supported a very extensive (and expensive) management education program and regularly invites leading management professors to teach in its programs. The company has a dynamic CEO who gives speeches on the importance of tough-minded leadership.

There is some evidence that this training and exhortation gets translated by middle managers in ABP into a management style that is not oriented towards taking responsibility for a dynamic, effective organization.[9] To improve profitability, the corporation has been seeking to reduce overhead by cutting out staff at middle management levels. As the cuts began to hurt, many managers complained that they couldn't do their jobs properly: "We are understaffed and overworked." The CEO's sensible reply was that they could get their jobs done with leaner staffing if they improved their operations— for example, getting rid of effort-draining problems by introducing improved methods.

To the chagrin of the CEO, his middle managers seemed unwilling or unable to exercise the leadership necessary to initiate such improvement programs. They focused their jobs on producing the right numbers, constantly collecting data to ensure that anticipated results would be forthcoming and pushing and pulling people to get those numbers. But they didn't involve themselves in operations.

In response to this discrepancy, the CEO hired a large corps of consultants at an annual cost of many millions of dollars. Their function was to assess the problem: why don't these expensively, well-trained middle managers appear to be exercising any leadership in their departments, and what can be done about it?

A consultant with experience as a senior line executive has been working in one of the major divisions of this large corporation. He reports that the CEO is indeed correct: Managers, at least at middle levels of the organization, don't really lead. They don't believe that improving work flows or technology is their business. His observation:

> They spend most of their time collecting, assessing, and "worrying" the numbers that they must report up the line. They have learned that usually it is easier to continue doing something "wrong" than

to seek to get it changed. To identify something as "wrong" means you are also criticizing someone and implying that a senior executive has made a mistake. Middle managers have learned not to take that kind of career risk.

When a serious effort is made to improve an operation, it can take many months to get approval, and most managers get discouraged. As a result, the most obvious work problems often aren't addressed until a consultant comes in to rethink the organization of work.

For example, Manufacturing staffs used a different kind of engineering drawing for new parts than did Engineering. As a result, all of Engineering's drawing for a new part had to be redone. Change only occurred when this wasteful failure to coordinate was pointed out by a consultant. Seeking to improve the way work gets performed and coordinated is perceived as a high-risk, low-reward kind of activity.

What is so surprising about these events is that the corporation has a reputation for being relatively well managed, and it has certainly been quite profitable. Some of the profits have come from setting higher and higher "hurdles" each year and making sure that executives know that they or their units will be eliminated from ABP if performance does not improve.

But there was no indication that ABP's enormous investment in management training was producing managers who were able or willing to take the initiative in continuously improving their organizations. Management training did not seem to result in increased managerial acumen and ingenuity focused on work and technology. Clearly, ABP and its managers were making the assumption that the work was already well programmed, and that managers were there to push it through, not to fine-tune or to innovate.

As the former head of management research in a comparably large, famous company with an extensive and costly internal management development program noted, "I find it surprising, even shocking, that no one in these companies [with enormous management development budgets] asks the question, why are we spending so much money on management training without getting managers who can cope with today's more demanding managerial jobs?"[10]

As the reader will see, the failure here is not one of being hard on people. Rather, it is that day-to-day efficiency (including quality and safety), just as much as innovation and customer service, depends on the willingness and ability of middle managers to be leaders. There is no way for high-quality, innovative work to be done without these managers intervening to manage downward as well as laterally. But their training tells them to manage upward; their job is to produce the numbers that will satisfy the plan.

THE TRADITIONAL MANAGEMENT MODEL

How managers manage and fail to lead grows out of a very specific set of historical circumstances. Much of what are called "good management principles" (whether explicitly stated or implicitly believed) were very relevant to mass-production technology as it existed for the first six decades of the twentieth century. With exceptions, of course, that technology consisted of large capital investments in fixed assets; managerial effectiveness consisted of efficient utilization of those assets. Efficiency, in turn, was provided by continuous high levels of production and sales that would push volume substantially above a fixed break even point. The greater the volume, the greater the profitability. It was that simple.

Successful management meant maintaining adequate sales levels, efficient machine schedules, high enough work loads for employees, adequate maintenance, and watchfulness to be sure that the plans for all of these were working out. Of course, there were also those protected industries and near-monopolies where there was little need to demonstrate excellence or continuous improvement.

The managerial thinking that went with this economic reality was equally simple and straightforward. It is derived from simple models of rational thinking as applied to running a business (or any other organization, for that matter). Managers learn a catechism or canon of what constitutes good management from their bosses or in business schools. For simplicity, I call it the Generally Approved Management Principles, or GAMP for short. Below are a few of its precepts:

- Start with the problem you want to solve or the goal you want to attain. (As the cliché has it, you'll never get there unless you start off with the goal clearly in mind.)
- Evaluate alternative paths (and obstacles) and assign costs and benefits to each (and perhaps probabilities of their being relevant, as well as the level of risk you are willing to assume).
- Construct a plan that will allow you to exploit the most desirable choices, including the appropriate structure (the cluster-

ing of people and tasks that will be required). Program the work.

- Assign responsibilities and performance goals to all the managers in charge of these clusters. Evaluate them on a go–no go basis: did they or didn't they meet their goals? Base rewards (or punishments) on these results.
- Every task, function, and managerial cluster should be clearly differentiated from others so that there is no overlap or ambiguity about who should do what.
- Just as there is a clear horizontal line between jobs and managerial units, there should be a clear line between what a manager does and what his or her subordinate does.
- Assure the accomplishment of goals by consistent and constant monitoring. Take "appropriate" action when plans are not met. This can involve changing the plans or more vigorous implementation.
- When a new problem or issue keeps recurring, hire a specialist. If the problem (or opportunity) involves many groups in the organization, create a specialized department to do that new kind of work.

LEADERSHIP IN GAMP ORGANIZATIONS

Leadership, in contrast to management, is embodied in senior management. That is where the action is. It is assumed that operations are not dynamic, and change is not expected (at least in the short run). Senior executives are the ones who conceive of imaginative, sometimes bold change strategies and who set ambitious goals. Tough and high-risk decisions are needed periodically (cutting staff, buying another company, selling off a troubled division), and these require the kind of leadership associated with self-confidence (or self-esteem) and a willingness to assume both risk and responsibility.

There is also leadership in exciting the organization about the worthwhileness as well as the feasibility of a new strategy and its accompanying goals. Not all senior managers either have this competence or even consider it important. Many senior managers, however, pride themselves on their ability to represent the future in ways that motivate commitment.[11] Recently, the leadership skills associated with the ability to envision an ambitious (but, it is hoped, realistic) future state for the organization and to excite and gain commitment from subordinates regarding this challenging goal has gotten a new name: *transformational leadership.*[12]

In recent years, there has also been a high incidence of "wheeling and dealing," a somewhat less exemplary type of leadership behavior. Many senior leaders, perhaps bored with the apparently dull and usually highly frustrating problems of getting a business to run well, began to focus on buying and selling assets. After all, most internal problems involve tough, almost never-ending people problems, and it must be tempting to turn to the excitement of high-stakes negotiations and "landing a big one." (Regrettably, as recent history has shown, many of these big deals, far removed from the mundane realities of the business, soon sour at great cost to the organization.)

Below the senior executives are the managers who implement the plans that make up the blueprints describing how the plans should be fulfilled. Implementation involves occasional restructuring decisions (mandated from on high, usually in response to failures to meet the plan) and clear sales, production, cost, and/or profit targets, usually embodied in the numbers that make up the annual budgets and plans of each unit. The plans were usually simply logical deductions from the goals set from above. That is, each unit was given targets that, when summated across the organization, would lead to the attainment of the goals set by senior management.

Staff (in contrast to line employees) are employed largely, but not exclusively, for two functions related to implementation. Some are guardians of important values or functions that are likely to be slighted by managers seeking to excel at meeting their goals. These staff seek to force managers to pay attention to quality, legal, and human resource standards, among others. Staff are also used to spot early signs that goals and targets won't be met. This assumes that many managers will be loathe to report bad news and will hope that the "news" can be made better before it has to reach their superiors. These staff reports can create additional pressures on lower management to work harder on performance attainment.

WHAT KIND OF MANAGERS ARE CREATED BY GAMP?

My view is that American business organizations, in part consciously and in part inadvertently, have created a distinctive but not very functional managerial perspective. There is a high degree of consistency between what management and students of organizational behavior say and what managers think and do. They have a neat, concise and appealingly "sensible" model that is a comfortable amalgam of traditional management principles (and folkways) and more contemporary human sciences. The principles component and the people component are not only compatible, they are synergistic.

If I am right, it makes sense and provides much more leverage in getting adaptation to the more competitive, dynamic world of today to seek to change this worldview that managers carry in their heads about what management is. The alternative, which American business consultants and academics have been pursuing for the past decade, is to get managers to accept as useful and then learn to employ an ever-changing array of new techniques, overlays, and course corrections. These leave the core (GAMP) untouched; it is this core, however, that is the handicap to functioning in the extraordinarily competitive, rapidly changing world of today.

THE WORLDVIEW OF THE MIDDLE MANAGER

In my talks with middle managers[13] in dozens of service and manufacturing companies, I found a very clear pattern. Almost without exception, managers perceived their role as one of maintaining the status quo: keeping output high and their boss's anxieties low.

Clear and Fixed Goals and Technology

One executive in what is considered a highly prestigious, successful manufacturing company summarized well what many had said:

> My boss or boss's boss makes the real decisions: about the technology and structure and goals; what my unit should do and how it should be done, with occasional but rare exceptions. The goals come down in the annual plans and budgets, to which I have some input, of course. If I think of something that needs changing, my boss has to approve it—and maybe her boss, too—and in general, senior management is not enthusiastic about people who "rock the boat."

Thus, the manager's job consisted of taking as given the technology, the organization, and the rules of the game. Within that neatly circumscribed world, the manager sought to allocate tasks and to meet the output and performance goals the boss had established. As one division head described her managers:

> Clarity is everything to them. They want to know precisely what is expected of them; they like you to put the proverbial stake in the ground that they can see . . . so nothing is ambiguous or not spelled out. And they have learned to ignore any problems that are not in their own job description or in their department or for which there is no immediate payoff.

It is taken for granted that there is an intelligent master plan that has carefully divided up the total task (for example, selling insurance or making satellites) into neat compartments (that is, the work of teams, departments, and divisions) and taken into account most contingencies. If everyone does their part faithfully, it is assumed that the sum total of what engineering and marketing and production do will add up to excellent performance.

Rely on Centralized Specialist Groups

Managers assume that many of the important decisions about how they should accomplish their goals will be made by finance, legal, purchasing, technology, and human resource groups, among others. If they need to have some training done, human resources probably designs and gives the program. If they need new equipment, an internal technology and/or purchasing group will have major input into the decision. One manager described her dependence on technical and support groups:

> When we need some new piece of technology or software, the systems group provides it. Since they are the only ones that know that work, they then have to maintain it. If I need improvements, they have to be called to improve it. And when we need to update how my people use the equipment, they have to be involved in the design of the training. I also count on them to design the feedback that helps me track the performance of the equipment.

As a result, changes are introduced in a standardized fashion, consistent with the technical group's rules and routines. They are not introduced so as to mesh best with existing processes and with the objectives of the line manager.

> One manager of a communications group wanted to use a new low-cost, high-performance terminal that had been developed by a new vendor. The initiation was summarily rejected on the grounds that the technical group had predefined a standard terminal.

Further, even small changes are costly as precise work orders have to be negotiated with and costed by high-overhead staff groups. Just communicating the issues to outsiders takes a high toll of management time.

Focus on Your Numbers: Budgeted Targets

As mentioned already, the critical focus of attention of the manager is the boss and the latter's performance targets. In most organizations, there is relentless pressure for results. Again, the apparent unquestionable presumption is that those results, when summated across the organization, are what matters.

A great deal of effort goes into collecting, massaging, and interpreting the numbers to avoid, if at all possible, any shortfall and otherwise to justify the deficiency. (Of course, the latter is a poor second, if one is hoping for a successful career.) As many have observed, much energy is devoted to what used to be called "balloon squeezing": finding a way of shifting costs and blame to other units of the business and, if necessary, making your goals by taking advantage of peer departments.[14]

Be As Autonomous As Possible; Ignore the Work System

Meeting those standards and having the ability to jump higher and higher hurdles each accounting period (for lower costs and higher output) are facilitated by obtaining as much autonomy as possible. When other departments or managers can interfere with work routines and priorities, usually the manager's own unit's efficiency suffers (even though what is requested may be desirable for the organization.)

As the manager expects others to respect his or her turf, he or she is willing to respect the autonomy of peers: live and let live, you do your thing while I do mine. (This norm is consistent with the expectation that there will be neatly bounded managerial jurisdictions.) Thus, managers spend as little effort as possible facilitating the work of others (and for which they don't get credit). They often forget to inform later stages of the work flow about changes they are making that will soon affect the latter. At the same time, they are quite unresponsive when another group asks them to modify what they are doing for some perceived larger good.

Delegate As Much As Possible; Manage Solely by Results

Managers manage best who manage least. (For many, a relatively clean desk is a convenient symbol of this.) Decades of human relations and "management by exception" exhortations have convinced most managers to assume that they will only have to be involved with operating problems when something truly exceptional occurs or when a subordinate is failing. "Don't get your hands dirty" (literally as well as figuratively) is given value even outside unionized situations where an overeager boss could be taking work away from a union member.

To get involved threatens the quality of delegation, the opportunity for the subordinate to have a real sense of responsibility for results. Further, there are other advantages of analytic detachment and managing by numbers: the manager gains the status of being above the fray and thus an impartial, unemotional judge of subordinate accomplishments (or failures). Most managers, like nearly all management textbooks, implicitly believe there is a hard and fast line separating the manager from those who report to the manager; the former gives assignments and monitors (and rewards or punishes); the latter does the work.

People Issues and Technology Issues
Clearly Compartmentalized

There is a clear distinction between the "hard" and the "soft" side of management. The hard side comprises the technical decisions: when to buy (or lease) new equipment; when and how many people to hire (or layoff), what a reasonable sales goal is for the Ohio office for next quarter, whether A or B will be better for the new project, and whether the introduction of a new line should be postponed in order to fill this unexpectedly large order from overseas. (These are "hard" presumably because they involve objective data that can be arrayed and assessed using well-accepted rational decision-making techniques.) The soft side involves handling people problems: creating empowerment and coping effectively with complaints of inequity, communications difficulties, personality conflicts, and disciplinary issues.[15] (Harold Leavitt first gave voice to this sharp contrast between what he called analytic, systematic, and rational decision making [the hard side of management] and the skills associated with getting things done through people [the soft side].[16])

To summarize, the management canon that I believe explains much of what one sees in contemporary organizations has these elements:

1. A presumption that managerial responsibilities can be well compartmentalized and programmed by means of the hierarchy. The structure of the work (the technology, the work system, and goal) is a given and is programmed to work.
2. A major emphasis on meeting or exceeding targets from senior management.
3. A recognition that attaining those goals is facilitated by looking inward: maintaining clear boundaries between yourself and "outsiders" and maintaining subordinate empowerment.
4. A belief that good managers rarely get involved with the operations below them, as this would injury delegation and diminish the status of the executive.
5. Clear separation of "work" issues and "people" issues.

Elements of this management canon have usefulness and validity. For example, modern managers do gain substantial benefits from their knowledge of the sources of motivation, commitment, and credibility and of the importance of empowerment.

THE FATAL FLAW: GAMP DOESN'T WORK

But there is a fatal flaw in this neat, classic model of what managers and organizations are all about. The flaw is that "you can't get there from here." As will be discussed in the next chapter, *the work of one department rarely integrates with that of other departments effortlessly and regularly for very long. In fact, there is an almost built-in centrifugal tendency in organizations that causes departments to become less and less coordinated (or in sync) with each other over time.* (It is pure myth that there is a fixed and benign division of labor that guarantees effectiveness if everyone does his or her part.) Very few things work without managerial involvement in modern business.

For these destructive trends to be overcome, managers cannot be impartial judges awaiting the results to come in from loyal subordinate groups to be summated and sent up the line. *They must instead get into the messy fray of who should be doing what; in the process, the "soft" people issues become entwined with the "hard" technical decisions.* They are almost one and the same, as the reader will see.

What is most surprising is that with all the serious research and writing and speaking about the management profession, the models of good management that managers carry in their heads have hardly changed in the past fifty years. These models (the management canon) served us well when companies did the same thing day after day and year after year—when technology was fixed, the market's demands were stable, and products almost unchanging. Ask for quick responsiveness to changing customer demands and frequent and profound innovation in both products and process, and those models don't work.

Just as surprising, though, is the failure of most companies to ask why must they keep introducing a continuing chain of new management improvement programs. In the late 1980s quality improvement programs appeared, and now there are various kinds of programs telling managers that they should continuously improve their operations (GE calls its version "workouts"). There are many more such programs for improving management. All are given great fanfare in business periodicals as innovations, but all deal with initiatives that ought to be the heart of managerial work. If a special program is required to convince managers that they should perform such core management tasks as attaining quality and improving the work process, there is indeed something wrong with what they have learned about managerial work.

4

Efficiency, Quality, Service, and Innovation

The Same Work Leadership Challenge

I n an effort to remedy past mistakes and inadequacies, management (in both the real world and academia) has gone on a binge of improvement programs. There are programs for efficiency (emphasizing continuous improvement and work flow continuity), quality (TQM and quality circles), customer service (for both external and internal customers), and abbreviating the product development cycle, to name just the more obvious. Many are useful, but altogether, each with unique terminology and methods, they can be overwhelming to line managers. In addition to the pressure to cut costs and improve performance, managers are expected to learn new jargon and new techniques whenever top management buys a new program "solution."

The introduction of diverse specialists, of course, is encouraged by GAMP, the management canon. Each of these problem areas has a separate name, distinctive terminology, and principles of how to do it. Naturally then, each should have its own set of specialists to help the organization improve in that speciality.

Many of these direct and hidden costs might be reduced if organizations understood or attacked directly their core systems issue. *Integration, coordination, and systems are at the heart of all these management concerns.* These represent a common leadership challenge to the manager, a different leadership challenge than the ones for which managers have typically been trained.

WORK SYSTEMS ARE INHERENTLY FLAWED

All of GAMP assumes that high-quality, efficient, and even innovative work will get done if everyone does the job that he is supposed to do. This is false. The kind of coordinated effort that produces desirable outputs *only* occurs as a result of extraordinary managerial leadership. *Effective performance is the exception because jobs and functions do not easily interlock with and complement one another; conflict and contradiction are more likely.*[1]

As noted in the previous chapter, it was only under those special and favorable conditions that American industry enjoyed in the first 50 years of this century that managers could work to plan. With fixed technology, stable markets, and stable products, it was possible to employ the classical canon.

What I will be describing are systems, coordination, and integration problems and issues. These represent the "dark side" of the division of labor. I say this because traditionally, managers have focused their attention on what is the optimal way to divide up tasks and functions among departments and divisions of the organization. The often unseen or ignored other side is putting the pieces back together: getting marketing work to integrate with (to complement and fit well into) operations work, for example, or integrating new product development with manufacturing.

EFFICIENCY

As I have shown in other research, efficiency is largely a function of continuity and regularity, how well and consistently work operations move between steps and stages without interruption or conflict.[2] (It is not, as naive managers sometimes assume, a function of how hard or fast individuals or groups work). Conflicts (as to what is desired or what has been received from a preceding or succeeding work flow stage), breaks in the flow, work at one stage not fitting easily into the next, stops and starts, interruptions, and the like are what injure efficiency.

Of course, this is the basic logic of automation and computer-driven work processes: one stage flows automatically into the next, thus eliminating systems problems. For the most part, it is coordination failure that injures efficiency, and it is coordination improvements (like those introduced by cross-functional work teams and "just-in-time" inventory systems) that are responsible for significant efficiency gains.

Those gains have two discrete sources. The very effort to employ continuous or just-in-time work flows acts as a whistle-blower or like a coal-mine canary. It quickly identifies the places in the work flow where there are bottlenecks or incompatibilities (for example, between stages in the flow), which no longer stay neatly pasted over by management indifference and redundant resources. The other source is the more obvious one: continuity and regularity of coordination are the foundations of all work effectiveness.

As will be discussed in the next chapter, coordination is not the same as programming jobs to fit together. Such a static design cannot work where each component is in flux (as is the case in almost all modern business). The challenge is one of continuous mutual adaptation and retrofitting; this takes managerial effort and skill, because what A needs is likely not to be what B finds desirable to give, at least not for long in a dynamic organization.

SERVICE

Service to customers depends on the ability of inside units to respond to requests for help, for new or modified products, or for some kind of adjustment or correction. All of these depend upon the responsiveness of one or more internal units to the requests from the outside—on the coordination between the insider and the outsider.

> From a customer: "We can't use the standard model, but if you could customize a more compact version it would fit in our new Series 8 that we are in the process of designing."
>
> From a customer service manager to product development: "The package you are using for the 'super' model looks too similar to the one used for the 'standard'; could you give it a more distinctive packaging so our warehouse and sales clerks won't make errors?"
>
> From a customer: "We need that spare part within 24 hours or our whole processing unit will be down. Is there any way you can expedite delivery?"
>
> From a field rep to a product manager: "Most of the supermarket chains we deal with in the South won't buy this without a different kind of seasoning; why can't we develop a special label and use different condiments for this market?"

Of course, all of these can be viewed as interruptions of more important business or even as inappropriate demands on those departments who are being asked to do something "special." Organizations that pride themselves on service are saying that customers can get quick, predictable responsiveness, *just as though the customer was another work flow stage upon whom efficiency depended.* (Interestingly, organizations are now beginning to call downstream internal work flow stages "customers.")

> An operations unit complained that a new marketing campaign promising an attractive "free" premium for customers who ordered a minimum quantity of merchandise before June 1 was going to produce an avalanche of customer complaints. The vendor who produced the premium was known for late deliveries, and the premium itself was shoddy. They were sure even loyal customers would complain when the premium didn't arrive, and again after it finally did and they saw how flimsy it was. Marketing stood firm on the grounds that advertising was their domain and, further, that the promotion materials had already been printed.
>
> A similar issue occurred in the same organization when marketing announced it was negotiating a new cooperative arrangement with another vendor, who would be allowed to solicit the firm's customers. Operations wanted to have a voice in negotiating the agreement on the grounds that they were both familiar with and responsible for many of the fulfillment issues that would arise. Marketing again insisted that these kinds of contracts were their work and that operations had no authority to mix in.
>
> In both cases, operations was overwhelmed with customer complaints, causing both delays in responding and a loss in confidence in the company's service.

As is typical of so many service problems, there was a coordination issue in the above example. Marketing was not prepared to interrelate its activities with that of another unit, operations. It is easy for the manager over these two unit heads to believe that marketing and operations have to work out their internal squabbles themselves (and that is poor delegation to get involved). The reality, however, is that there may be the need to intervene to protect the company's reputation for service and to examine what can be done to prevent recurrences. The issues also illustrate the vagueness of the boundary separating marketing work from operations work, contrary to GAMP's presumption of clarity of task and individual responsibility.

QUALITY

Most quality problems do not arise out of undetected sloppiness or ignoring of standards (although plain poor workmanship can be a problem, obviously). More frequently, they reflect poor coordination or a failure to understand the basic parameters of the technology. Most typically something happens at step A; an anomaly occurs, or the manager overseeing step A decides to modify a part or procedure. Then for step B, the change becomes a major impediment, and the B work can't be done properly. The result is inferior, below-standard quality.

The business press described a relevant example involving AT & T's long distance service. A critical cable carrying much of New York City's communication under the Hudson River was cut inadvertently by a company repair crew. Apparently, according to the published reports, both the mistake (cutting an active cable rather than the redundant cable the crew had been sent to remove) and the ensuing difficulty in getting service restored were due to coordination problems. A special crew that was supposed to guard active cables during this kind of procedure did not appear at the site. In addition, AT & T's operations center had not been notified where repairs were taking place and therefore found it difficult to locate the source of the problem when their equipment disclosed that one-fifth of the total company's telephone traffic had been interrupted.[3]

A Cascade of Failures: A Telephone Case

The inherent challenge of managing tightly interlocked systems in which small problems quickly cascade and create enormous losses can be illustrated by a very embarrassing loss of communication services by AT & T in the fall of 1991.[4]

Tuesday, September 17, 1991, was an unusually hot day in New York City, and when the local utility

(Consolidated Edison) found power demands soaring, they asked AT & T to begin using its own diesel-powered generators to power a large Manhattan switching center. (AT & T had obtained lower electric rates by accepting "interruptible power.")

The shifting over, however, was flawed. An improperly set electrical device (a "float voltage meter relay sensor") caused the system to switch to storage batteries instead of AT & T's own internal power generators.[5]

Because these batteries could only pump out power for a fixed period (in this case, about six hours), the automated system included alarms that were supposed to alert technicians to be sure that some other arrangements for getting power to the system were made before the battery-stored energy drained away. There were also visual controls, supposedly monitored continuously at the switching center's main control console. Further, a company procedure required a "visual check of the plant" when the system was operating on internal power.[6]

But according to newspaper accounts and a statement by AT & T's CEO, the conversion to batteries was not attended to; no one was watching. As a result, the batteries gradually degraded, reducing the power they could provide to the phone system. Technicians finally were alerted as the phone system was failing, but it took several hours to reconnect to the outside utility's power.

Air traffic controllers in New York airports lost contact with incoming planes, and some of the busiest airports in America had to close down. Voice calls and business data transmission between New York City and the rest of the country were interrupted as well.

In the several published accounts, there is no reference to any managers taking action during the crisis. There was no report of managers going on the alert when utility-derived power was cut off, nor when the rectifiers failed. A manager who supervised several technicians (among whose responsibilities were monitoring the system when it was on batteries) left the building *after* he received notification that the system had shifted to short-lived battery power. A training class had been scheduled for some time, and apparently he did not see any reason to cancel the training for himself and his subordinates.

It was later discovered that audio alarms had been "muffled" (for unknown reasons), and visual alarms were either inoperative or disabled. Initial reports made no mention of managers making sure that the batteries were not being overextended, nor of any manager taking initiative to see that the proper coordination was occurring. At least according to the published accounts, managers were uninvolved (perhaps assuming— incorrectly, of course—that everything was working perfectly, or that "automatic" remedies were taking over).[7]

It appears as though managers were lulled by the presumption that the system would automatically function to coordinate everything, and that they had little to do with these operations. Technicians were there to do the work, after all.

These managers in the lower Manhattan switching station were managing under GAMP passivity "rules." They delegated completely to await results. Thus, no manager appears to have checked to make sure that the internal electrical generators were operating after AT & T was cut off by the utility company. No one checked on how long the batteries could operate. And no one checked to be sure that the automatic alarm system (signaling that the system was on expendable battery power) was in operating condition. In fact, the manager responsible for the control center facility could find no record of when the alarm system had been last checked.[8]

Most *safety* problems or accidents occur because, in tightly linked systems, even slight discrepancies or anomalies get magnified as they ramify through a complex work system.[9] A major nuclear power facility suffered an accident that was supposed to activate a backup power system to control the reactor. The reactor operators, however, had neglected to change the flashlight-sized batteries that provided current to read the control panel. This rather trivial quality problem created a very dangerous situation.[10]

Quality and Know-How

Quality performance also depends on an in-depth knowledge on the part of management of what makes things work and how they work. Particularly when the product is quite technical, it is easy for management to assume that a superficial understanding of the technology will suffice. But management's lack of basic understanding represents a continuing threat to performance and quality.

> The business press recently featured a description of the problems experienced by the Pfizer company with a widely used artificial heart valve, the Bjork-Shiley Convexo-Concave (C-C) heart valve. It was estimated that about 450 of these have failed after being implanted in patients, leading to 300 deaths.
>
> In making the Pfizer C-C heart valve, it was necessary to weld one "strut" that held a disk that regulates the flow of blood. A new, improved model required welding the strut at a much sharper angle. In seeking to do the weld properly, employees sometimes had to bend the strut repeatedly. Either this bending or faulty welding could leave a crack. Inspectors looked at every piece and sought to identify cracks and then have those units rewelded.
>
> According to the news reports, management did not seem be aware of at least four critical, but subtle technology issues affecting quality production:
>
> - The new design was difficult to weld compared to the previous version of the product. Welders at times had to repeat the procedure and still weren't sure they had done it properly.
> - Inspectors often had difficulty in their microscopic examination of the completed product in distinguishing real cracks from surface imperfections where the strut was attached. It is likely that some real cracks were missed, or that non-cracks could have been rewelded. The inspection process did not allow those fine distinctions to be made with high accuracy, particularly given the substantial eye strain associated with the task.
> - The manufacturer of the metal alloy used to fabricate the struts believed that rewelding that material was not desirable and could cause metal failure (although it is not clear that Pfizer knew this).
> - The design of the disk at times would cause it to close abnormally within the patient, and this could injure the integrity of the strut.[11]

This may appear like excessive detail. How is management to learn and keep track of all of this technical information? But it is this detailed knowledge of the parameters of the system they are managing that managers in fact, need to know.[12] They didn't have this knowledge in the photolithographic alignment equipment industry case described at the end of this chapter. As a result, the efforts to copy their competitors failed.

Newcomers Complicate Quality

Another major source of quality and service issues involves the addition of new steps or participants to the system. New vendors, new outside service centers (to support customers), and contracted-out support functions all involve enormous potential to injure quality and service. Usually the newcomer to the system has agreed to a carefully negotiated price and a few obvious performance standards; however, the full requirements for doing things in a way that will precisely meet existing internal and external customer needs are almost never spelled out. In other words, the true complexity of the interface between the newcomer and existing jobs usually is not explored and resolved. For months, sometimes years, the newcomer can "botch" the system, even when performing within the contractual terms.

QUALITY, SERVICE, AND EFFICIENCY: THE SAME CHALLENGE

Many companies are busy instilling "customer consciousness" and "quality consciousness" as though these were distinct, compartmentalized activities, in contrast to recognizing that the effective management of work systems has as its outcome efficiency, quality, service, adaptiveness, and the ability to introduce product and methods changes with frequency and effectiveness.

King is a fast-growing computer company producing state-of-the-art technology and is a leader in a niche market.[13] It has an excellent reputation for producing quality products. One of the few complaints from customers about its products has to do with the difficulty of networking with the company's proprietary software. King's major product is a unique data storage device; its use requires the purchase of special King-related equipment and software. King's business has been growing rapidly, and many of its new, large corporate customers have a major investment in their peripheral equipment. King has, therefore, developed a new software package that will enable users to integrate a variety of non-King hardware and software into their King installations. (Essentially, it allows users to combine UNIX- and DOS-based operating systems.) Although King has a staff of highly trained and paid systems engineers who do the selling, they also maintain small demonstration showrooms in several large cities.

In 1989 one of King's customers was disappointed when he visited the New York demonstration room. He had purchased a very large King installation for his corporation and was bringing in a colleague from another division with some work challenges that were suited perfectly to King hardware and software. The colleague was already committed to a competitive system and would only use King if it could operate in conjunction with his other installed equipment. When that integration was simulated and demonstrated, however, the performance was terrible. Processing time was double what it would have been on an all-King network.

When the technician handling the demonstration was asked about the sluggish performance, she explained the deficiency by noting that they were using an available "286" workstation. [No one had thought to obtain a "386" workstation for this New York office, to demonstrate this new feature.] With a 386 workstation, she explained, the efficiency on the hybrid system would be just about comparable to what one would get with standard King equipment.

The colleague was turned off regarding King by the demonstration and was not ready to accept the technician's explanation. He could not rid himself of the sight of the sluggish performance, even though it was supposed to be due to inadequacies in the demonstration design. It was an example of that old expression: a single picture being worth a thousand words.

Why would King allow a demonstration that understated the performance of its equipment? Why use a relatively slow workstation when a better model would not involve a major expenditure? (The typical sale, in contrast, would be a minimum of a quarter million dollars, with many installations costing much more.) Is this a problem of customer service, a quality problem, or a work flow problem (development not integrating with sales)?

Of course, it is all of these. Management had neglected to check out the relation of the demonstration room's existing hardware to the speed with which the new software would run. As in the case below, most systems have more elements that need adapting than managers recognize.

Second Bank gave many of their checking account holders overdraft privileges, which it called "VIP Checking." When these customers wrote checks for which they did not have adequate deposits, they would be billed for the amount of the overdraft plus interest charges. In order to avoid billing customers for amounts that were less than the cost of the paperwork, Second Bank had designed its automated paper-handling system so as to "throw out" all overdrafts under $10.

Something then had to be done with these minor overdrafts, and they were therefore included in the daily batch of overdraft amounts reviewed by branch officers. Almost all of those requiring managerial overview, obviously, were from customers who did not have overdraft privileges or who had exceeded those limits. Whoever had designed the original "exception" plan assumed that the branch officer would automatically approve these small overdrafts from VIP Checking customers. In a very small number of cases, some officers were using poor judgment and charging the VIP customers interest and a substantial penalty!

This flaw, which caused a system designed to give quality service to do the opposite on occasion, was only revealed when a very good customer complained to a high-ranking bank officer that one of his checks had been

"bounced" and he had been subjected to a penalty for a
$9 overdraft when he had overdraft availability of
$1,000! The flawed system that allowed these trivial
overdrafts to be intermixed with hundreds of problem
cases had gone unchallenged for five years.

Nearly all large paperwork systems contain some such flaws, at
least until the problems begin to surface after some months or years
of service. Only when managers pursue every one of these flaws do
customers obtain consistently high-quality service. Service and quality are inextricably intertwined here.

Inefficiency and quality and service problems have their root in
the same management failure to coordinate effectively. Coordination
includes checking out all interfaces and making modifications where
necessary to assure high performance (in quality, efficiency, and service).

INNOVATION

Innovation has the identical coordination demands on management
that are the foundation of high quality and good service. It is now
common knowledge that successful innovations are not primarily the
result of a brilliant idea, insight, or unique experiment. Rather, the
management of implementation is the real challenge: converting a
good idea into products and services that can be produced economi-
cally and that are both durable and meet customer demands. Many
legitimately good ideas never see the light of day because they can't
be made to "work" (that is, they can't be routinely produced with
predictable quality and serviceability).

As development engineers and designers and market and production specialists perform their functions, there will be a continuing
need for mutually responsive exchanges, trade-offs, and compromises among them. This is the reason that conventional wisdom is
correct about small (often startup) companies outcompeting large,
much better-funded and -staffed big companies when it comes to developing innovative new products. These exchanges and trade-offs
can be made much more easily in a small, relatively cohesive organization of fifty or a hundred people than in a large, impersonal bu-
reaucracy.

The case below is a composite of typical coordination issues in development projects that seek to move an idea to routinization.[14]

> At stage 4 of a design process, it is discovered that one of the components being used by the technicians designing stage 3 is introducing some kind of electrical or chemical interference with a critical stage 4 component. Efforts at shielding that component add to the weight and complexity of the stage, which will increase the power requirements (and potentially show up negatively on a later reliability audit).
>
> For stage 3 to change that part of their design will basically require them to undo a good deal of what they had thought was finished engineering. Eventually, though, they accept that this is really a serious problem for stage 4 (and that stage 4 technicians aren't simply unwilling to devote scarce creative energies to redoing specifications). Eventually, the stage 3 people discover that they can utilize a substitute component *if* one of the final test specifications will be changed. (As the test protocol is now written, stage 3 will look deficient if there is no comparable component in place.)
>
> After a great deal of discussion, the test unit is persuaded to change its specifications, but those discussions lead the systems integrator to insist that stage 2 must now modify their work to include a supplementary circuit that had not previously been specified. Stage 2 says they can't do that unless they are allocated greater weight or space limits, preferably both. Without changing everything that has been completed to date, the systems integrator believes that the only possible way to squeeze more space for stage 2 is to take it from stage 3. But stage 3 insists that they have already "given at the office" by redoing a great deal of work to accommodate stage 4. This has handicapped them in meeting their own time and dollar budget.
>
> The supervisor of stage 3 has a creative idea involving some joint redesign with stage 5. The two groups eventually agree on a modification of the original layout. Taking the two subsystems together, this would provide the additional space and weight needed by stage 2. But

stage 5 said they could only do this *if* stage 4 could guarantee that there would be no further changes affecting their joint interface. That agreement would allow them to do more of their work in parallel with stage 4 and make up the time lost by the reworking of the layout with stage 3.

The product that emerged from this convoluted process was very successful. It exceeded the original expectations and specifications.[15]

What do we see here? There is obviously great interdependence among the stages. At the same time, there are real incentives to stay as autonomous as possible after the original designs are completed and each group is given a well-defined work unit to complete. The more any single stage (or organizational unit) has to respond to other groups, the more difficult their own job. And difficult can mean that one unit or group has to accept higher costs, injury to their schedule, and in the short run, poorer performance for their part of the innovation. All of these are serious penalties for being cooperative with another group.

But somehow the managers involved were able to build an organizational system that encouraged a great number of trade-offs. Without those, there is little likelihood that the product would have been a success. Had each stage simply sought to "work to rule"—that is, to meet the original requirements imposed on them in the most efficient manner for them—the project could never have been completed successfully.

It is revealing that in 1992, major companies are still "discovering" that having functions work together in small groups under common supervision improves coordination. Late in 1991, Chrysler began advertising on national television that it was able to develop more innovative, high-quality new cars more rapidly because it was now putting engineering and manufacturing and marketing and finance people "together" organizationally. A number of years before Ford had "discovered" the same managerial innovation and, in part, attributed the success of its Taurus to this management breakthrough.[16] In late '92 GM finally learned it!

The strong hold of functional specialization over these many decades, since the early days of scientific management, speaks volumes for senior management's disregard of integration and coordination. Getting functions to be interrelated dynamically is still not perceived as a managerial challenge by many companies.

The cliché that the whole is the sum of the parts is wrong. An effective, high-quality whole is the sum of an ever-changing, mutually adapting (to each other) set of parts. It is the dynamic evolving and mutual responsiveness that produces successful implementation. These mutual reciprocities (adaptations) in accomplishing faster and better new product development are very similar to the responses to situational exigencies that are required for the maintenance of quality or service or for efficiency.

COMPETITIVENESS

What I have called "innovation" above refers to major changes in technology: new products, techniques, and systems. But organizations also have to be able to respond to competitors who are offering improved products. These "new" products utilize the same basic technology and require many of the same skills and the application of very similar technical knowledge. Yet recent industrial history is filled with examples of well-established, highly profitable firms that could not meet their new competition. They often have years of experience with the basic technology, but can't manage the improvements introduced by a competitor.

In the 1970s, Xerox—the U.S. company that had developed, perfected, and dominated the market for plain-paper copiers—gradually lost a significant share of their market to upstart Japanese companies who made more reliable equipment.[17] It took some years for Xerox to recoup a reasonable market share.

The sad history of the U.S. auto industry over the past twenty-five years is, of course, the most powerful example. The Japanese gradually took away a significant share of the domestic manufacturers' market by slight improvements in the technology that the U.S. had essentially invented, perfected, and appeared to "own." At the beginning, Americans turned to the Japanese for better quality, often for what is called "fit and finish": doors closed better, the paint job looked better, and seams were tighter. Gradually the Japanese added improvements in engine quality and fuel efficiency and thoughtful customer-oriented touches to the driver's controls. But initially most of this represented what superficially would appear to be easy-to-match technical achievements. The challenge was improved management, and that was not forthcoming.

Management needed to exhibit flexibility in what was emphasized in their control and reward systems. U.S. auto workers for some years after the Japanese "invasion" continued to report that the pressures on them were to get cars through the line regardless of quality problems. (Those were to be fixed only at the end of the line or after customers complained.)

> A study of the Ford Motor Company reported that Ford's manufacturing development group in 1958 had perfected a very superior painting process (the "E" coat process). Though the Japanese licensed it, Ford did not bring it to all their U.S. plants for another twenty-five years![18] During this period, it was losing ground to the Japanese in part because of the superior painting on Japanese cars. And Ford was also paying high warranty costs for rust damage while they were losing customer goodwill.

It has been concluded by some sophisticated software professionals that one of the major reasons behind the IBM cooperative working arrangement negotiated with Apple in mid-1991 was to gain improved software. IBM had not been able to adapt its software capabilities to produce the degree of "user friendliness" that was the hallmark of apple.[19] Obviously, IBM software specialists had ample opportunity to assess what was so appealing to customers in Apple's software.

Many of the challenges faced by managers seeking to keep up with competitor innovations become clear in the PAE case study below. Rather than using vague and nonoperational terms like "know how," one can see in this industry precisely what leadership issues arise when a company that is lagging in technology seeks to catch up.

THE PHOTOLITHOGRAPHIC ALIGNMENT
EQUIPMENT INDUSTRY

A recent study of a small but critical industry presents the best data and the most tightly reasoned explanation of how failures in management flexibility and integration can impede dominant firms from responding effectively to competitors who introduce improved products.[20]

Photolithographic alignment equipment (PAE) has been used as one step in the manufacture of solid-state semiconductors, the basic component in most electronic equipment. These machines are used to transfer an intricate pattern representing the circuitry of the "chip" to the surface of silicon wafers.

In a study of the entire industry (six firms) from 1962 to 1986 that focused on technical improvements, Rebecca Henderson, an MIT researcher, shows how market leadership shifted dramatically from one dominant firm to a competitor when the latter introduced a product improvement.

The issue in each case was *not* one of resistance to change or failed management strategy. Rather, the previously dominant firm could not learn to manufacture the slightly modified equipment as well as the innovator. The "old" industry leader would add the new feature in response to the competitor's product introduction, but it could never integrate the innovation as well into its technology as effectively as the aggressive competitor. In a few years, however, the "winner" was likely to lose its hard-won position to the challenger who introduced the next improvement. This shift in market leadership, a sort of game of musical chairs, occurred every few years during the period of the study.

The handicaps of the dominant firm in responding to the contender were always modest: subtle failures in communications among departments in learning new ways of looking at old data and in how technical problems were to be solved. In other words, they were systems, adaptation, and flexibility problems. They were all problems of getting the work done effectively, not unlike the management problems of responding to emerging service and quality problems or learning to create more user-friendly software. (They were *not* problems of working around patents or failures of management strategy or decision making.)

The leading firms—the ones being "attacked"—believed that developing an effective product response involved attaching a new module or component to their existing equipment. Unfortunately for them, the new couldn't just be added to the old; a whole series of micro adjustments and adaptations had to take place in how work was done and coordinated.

Top management had decided that they were going to make a product that was the equal of what their competitors were producing. But they deceived themselves into thinking the new element (the innovation) could be "tacked on" to make a new system. Instead of simply adding on the new device or feature, a series of finely tuned changes and trade-offs like those illustrated in the section on innovation were required. Without this large number of adjustments and reconfiguration of what had been done, the "copy" would never work as well as the original produced by the new market leader.

Interestingly, no firm ever learned to match an improved product that had been introduced by a competitor. There was no leadership at working levels to cope with the unanticipated coordination issues. The true complexity of the interfaces that had to be reworked if the new system was going to operate efficiently (that is, predictably and consistently) was never comprehended.[21] (The next chapter details these managerial issues with a great many specific examples from companies in the industry.)

CONCLUSION

Making the parts of a work system come together in a self-sustaining, mutually accommodating whole is no simple task. A large number of human, technological, and organizational forces work in the other direction—toward disorder, internecine conflict and mutual incompatibility. Put simply, nothing fits together (or, at least, stays together) without substantial managerial effort. Most of the tough problems of managing to attain high-quality, responsive service; productivity; and effective, timely implementation of new product and process plans revolve around the inherent contradictions and ambiguities of interfaces separating tasks and functions. These are primarily legitimate technical, not political, issues.

After all these years, it is surprising that the simplistic assumptions of scientific management still prevail. When managers fail in the basics of improving performance, it is typically because they assume that tasks neatly interlock just because rational planners have programmed them that way! Thus they ignore the necessary extensive give-and-take, listening and responding, and adroit negotiating that astute managers must undertake to make something work and work well.

It is ironic that companies keep rediscovering these obvious realities of work systems. In the past, it was the "discovery" of the value of cross-functional teams to create more rapid and more successful innovations. More recently, management has found that the vendor or supplier interface is also flexible and requires managing (in contrast to simply negotiating a good contract).

The planning mode has managers negotiating the best terms they can obtain with a vendor and then making sure that the deliverables meet those standards. A leadership mode, in contrast, recognizes that there are a wide variety of relationships between vendor and customer. Successful contracting often requires bringing the vendor in early to consult during the preliminary design stages. Utilizing the vendor's expertise, early decisions can better reflect what will assure timely, economical parts or services. Vendor and customer engage in extended give-and-take to interlock their two work systems properly.

The creation of a long-term relationship built on trust and reciprocity is likely to bring more effective interrelating of the two work systems (the vendor's and the customer's) than arm's-length, threat-laden annual contracting. In the latter, vendors are simply told that if the price or quality isn't right, they will be replaced, just as an employee is told by an authoritarian boss to "shape up or ship out."

To add to the problem created when systems issues are ignored, organizations proliferate specialists who attack what is basically the same problem from their separate vantage points and with their unique tools. Rather than getting line managers to exercise better leadership when there are systems failures, new staff specialists are inserted. New controls created by these staff experts for quality, customer service, and shortening the product development cycle abound. In effect, the "solutions" then become part of the problem. More specialists and their programs, preordained by a GAMP philosophy, have to be coordinated with and integrated. Line managers spend time writing reports and implementing programs for them at the same time that they have their regular work to get done.

This multiplication of "fixes" occurs because work problems such as quality or delayed new-product introductions are perceived in a top-down fashion by senior management. They are not dealt with in work flow terms. The latter requires management to focus on the coordination and trade-off issues, on getting tasks to interlock in spite of the ambiguities and contradictions. From the point of view of the head of department A, her procedures or plans are sound and consistent with the orders she has been given. But for them to "fit" with the needs of department B (or opportunities that have arisen), Manager A must continually make painful changes. Needed too is an in-depth understanding of the parameters that shape the work system. Coordination and trade-offs (the continuing dynamic adaptation of one task or function to another) are at the heart of performance.

Managers need to learn the intricacies of all of the interdependencies that shape performance. No job description nor instruction manual will ever give a complete, up-to-date account of how and why things work as they do. New managers can't simply read up on their jobs and the work they will direct. There are too many subtle interrelationships, and these are continuously in flux. Customers have dynamic requirements, vendors change methods or materials, and other departments replace one program with another.

Learning how things work (and where and why they are not working) requires on-the-job learning and dedication. Managers in place have to get used to asking themselves questions like the following:

- If I am right, temperature, within normal ranges, doesn't affect this process. So why is quality poorer on very cold days?
- Why is performance consistently better on the night shift, even though we have less supervision at that time?
- That team working on a product modification project for that grain storage customer seemed to be doing all the right things, but they were three months late in delivering, and then the thing didn't work properly. What went wrong that we can learn from?

The manager is continuously testing the theories he or she has (regarding critical variables and their interrelationship) against real data. Where the theories fail to predict the actual results, the manager seeks to modify the theory—and develop a new theory of the case—by reconstructing the events and trying to tease out what made the difference.

Thus, management and continuous learning are synonymous in organizations that intend to maintain quality, service, and performance in a dynamic world. Managers have to stay in one place long enough to learn and, more critically, to make learning worthwhile.

How those things gets accomplished in real organizations with real people and real-time pressures is the focus of the next chapter. As the reader will see, attaining coordination represents a series of leadership issues usually not addressed by managers, nor appraised by their seniors.

5

Coordination

Why It's Hard to Make Things Work

I have described how most managers (and the management principles that nourish them) ignore the managing of systems and dealing with coordination and integration. Many managers even think of these as nonissues. After all, coordination is built into the master plan, and functions are programmed to fit together. Where they don't, supervisors ought to be able to work things out. If there are major difficulties, these become "staff" work for specialists in organization structure and technology.

Managers usually don't focus on the interrelationship of people and the work process because it isn't considered a particularly critical problem. Traditionally, managers have presumed that if correctly selected and motivated subordinates (managers as well as workers) do their jobs correctly, as the work has been prescribed, the result will be the desired total performance: the total is simply the sum of the parts, everyone doing their fair share. But is it?

Late in 1991, the DuPont company announced that it hoped to cut costs by a billion dollars by cutting its work force and restructuring operations. Interestingly, the press release stated that the company expected to save twice as much by what it called "bottom-up" initiatives. An example of the latter, the press release stated, would be getting engineering, purchasing, and distribution to work more closely with manufacturing. Apparently, there were twice the savings to be gotten from better coordination of day-to-day work than from "top-down" improvements in planning.[1]

Most managers never learn to manage work, particularly how to get consistent teamwork among functions. A CEO very critical of his subordinates observed in a private conversation, "They only manage plans and people."

Although getting work performed effectively is at the core of managing, ironically it is not considered an important management skill by most senior executives either. (At American Business Products, the company discussed in chapter 3, this skill apparently was never dealt with in its costly management development efforts. According to some of the consultants who worked for the company, ABP managers didn't think it counted in the appraisal system.)

Usually there are no obvious rewards for doing this well; management controls don't measure the "systems" competency of executives. It is rarely considered a critical leadership role, and often bosses are suspicious of those who get too involved in the work and technology under their control. It is assumed these managers aren't delegating enough and, therefore, aren't spending enough time on the big picture (that is, planning and strategy making). An experienced human resources executive in a major corporation had this explanation:

> We've all been trained in reductionistic MBO [management by objectives] methodologies which place emphasis on the task, the boundaries and accountabilities. Even the Hay System [of job evaluation] reinforces this by giving no "credit" for going beyond the boundaries of a job as part of the inherent job duties and requirements. Our appraisal and reward systems follow suit.[2]

The comfortable presumption that under normal circumstances (and with goodwill and good training), jobs and functions interlock automatically is highly unrealistic in today's organizations. It is based on the assumption that most work is like the classic view of a simple blue-collar job, where A drills a hole of a fixed size and B inserts the proper screw and nut and proceeds to tighten them so that C can do the next task. One can neatly define and circumscribe A, B, and C's work: they are reasonably independent packaged modules that are designed to fit together. They can even be rearranged and still fit snugly.

It is important to understand how unsnug the fit is among functions in modern business. Only with this understanding can the challenges of work leadership be appreciated. In the sections to follow, I will be looking at the complexity of the systems with which managers need to cope. If one of their major responsibilities is integrating and coordinating the disparate elements created by specialization, the place to begin is an understanding of that challenging task.

Not only do functions not automatically fit together (even with the best of plans), whatever fit they might have had when the work system was first developed quickly and surely erodes. Over time, perversely enough, almost all work systems degrade, and tasks become less compatible with one another. *Negative, not positive, synergy is the rule.* And this is what poses the most difficult and critical challenge for managerial leadership.

The sections to follow seek to explain both why and how the boundary between and among jobs is not the simplistic lock-and-key interface presumed by scientific management and its successor, GAMP. Generations of managers have been taught both directly and implicitly that tasks will integrate simply and directly as long as subordinates do what they are supposed to do. And the typical organization's appraisal and reward systems reinforce this binary throwback to primitive, highly routinized mass production.

Instead, tasks and functions have complex and ambiguous and even contradictory boundary conditions: the necessary interplay, for example, required if marketing and operations are each to do their respective work in such a way that it complements the work of the other (that is, so that the system requirements are met). The interfaces or interconnects have the following characteristics:

- There are many more elements that have to interlock than GAMP implicitly assumes. There may be literally hundreds of job elements, for example, in marketing that impinge on the work of operations and determine how effective the combined activities will be.
- Some of these are hidden, or at least not widely recognized by the managers responsible for individual functions or for the total system.
- Many involve significant overlap. Continuing the example, there is no neat separation between marketing work and operations work.
- Most tasks and functions, if not all, are in flux. That is, man-

agers are constantly modifying and elaborating what work is done and how it is done in response to pressures for improved performance, new external opportunities, or recently discovered internal problems requiring remedies. These changes further erode coordination with other functions.

THE INHERENT COMPLEXITY OF TASKS AND FUNCTIONS

In the real world, tasks are not neatly compartmentalized into sets of prescribed activities and responsibilities that securely fit together. When marketing is told to "coordinate" with product planning, it is almost impossible to predict what will actually occur. No experienced manager believes that job or position descriptions tell it like it is; there is a great deal of "play" in jobs and functions that easily destroys any preplanned coordination.

To be sure, there may be a small number of core activities that have to be performed, but there are many others that can be added. And managers can even subtract from their core "undesirable" functions that others have come to depend upon.[3] Even within the core, the discretion available as to how those tasks will be performed makes those core activities highly flexible. What a given job and function are in practice depends a great deal on the preferences, experiences, and even the personalities of those doing and supervising the work.

To add to the amount of play in the system (and, thus, the opportunity for poor integration among functions), the combinations and permutations of what people actually do tend to shift gradually with time. Managers learn what works for them and what doesn't, what gets rewarded and punished, and how to look good or fall on one's face, and they modify and elaborate accordingly the work for which they are responsible. More significantly, motivated managers are constantly changing what their departments do in order to get greater efficiency, to experiment with a new technology, or to adapt to new strategic thrusts of their bosses.

What Is a Job or Function?

In another context, I have called these the manager's *microdecisions*, meaning the decisions that determine what the marketing manager for X brand or the warehouse manager for Y products or the product manager for Z actually does in the name of that function.[4] Managers have substantial discretion in interpreting what functions their units will perform, as shown by the following example:

- A marketing manager, hoping to get more timely enhancements to certain critical software packages, adds a small programming group. This requires new working arrangements with a centralized software development group.
- A data systems group, convinced that a certain computer system is outdated, no longer offers internal support for that system to users. Internal users thus have to seek other sources of service or to find a budget to write off that equipment and replace it.
- In a large publishing house, the major marketing arm decides that it knows more than the editorial and acquisitions groups about what ought to be published, and it establishes its own captive publishing arm. Editorial and marketing now compete for new manuscripts.

Functional Elaboration

In earlier work, I described how functional departments reshape their activities to obtain more tasks that allow them to control or ignore outsiders.[5] They have learned the strategy that higher status and easier accomplishments accrue to those who do not have to respond to the needs of others. At the same time, they seek to shed activities that make it easy for an outsider to control them.

Purchasing groups can seek to minimize the amount of order placing they handle in favor of doing more vendor assessment, more development of standardized components and approved vendors, and assessment of current components to find ways of substituting lower-cost alternatives. Essentially, this means that they are doing more things where they are more fully in control and spending less time responding to the demands of others for service.

A critical engineering project was delayed by an unanticipated technical barrier. The project manager turned to a very specialized group of talented scientists who had been placed in the division in order to handle really tough problems. But the scientists insisted that this was simply a tedious problem requiring a lot of "grunt work," and that their mission wasn't "to pump gas." As a result, the project was much delayed, because there were no other resources to throw at the problem. Obviously, what is a legitimately tough problem and what only looks tough to the uninitiated is a matter that is easy to dispute.

A major bridge carrying subway tracks nearly collapsed in New York City because of rust and deterioration. An investigation of why the bridge had been allowed to get so weak structurally discovered that "because the Transit Authority, which inspects the bridge's track system, is not responsible for the supporting structure of the bridge and the Transportation Department bridge engineers do not inspect the track system," responsibility for significant elements of structural integrity fell between the two functions.[6]

A famous military commander is supposed to have said, "Regrettably, the most important battles are always fought where our maps are creased [and therefore difficult to read]". All organizational boundaries are, in fact, badly creased. Because organizational effectiveness (efficiency, quality, and facilitating innovation) depends on coordination, managers face a daunting challenge.

HOW THE WORK IS DONE

To complicate matters further, *how* the function is performed is just as critical to coordination as *what* is done. (It may be almost academic to try to distinguish the "what" from the "how," in fact.) Below is an example of one department adjusting the "how" of its work, always for good and sufficient reason, but unintentionally interfering with the work of adjacent departments. Although the changes were essentially trivial elaborations of a function, they had consequential repercussions on the larger system.

A collections department finds that it is sometimes easier to get customers with long-overdue bills to return the merchandise. Their policy is that as long as it is in like-new condition, the merchandise should be accepted for full credit. This leniency is opposed by some sales departments, who argue that no merchandise more than two weeks off the selling floor can be "like new." Gradually, the inventory of like-new but unsalable merchandise has grown, to the dismay of these units.

Collections has given out an 800 number to debtors they have trouble reaching, although this creates congestion on that line, which is shared by other departments. These other groups complain.

Collections now seeks to get additional leads on wayward customers from sales personnel. Sales managers resent the time being taken up by these inquiries and "debriefs."

Collections is resisting pressure from auditing to ignore small debts (under $50) on the premise that limited collection resources should be focused on those people who represent large potential losses. (Collections believes that these smaller accounts represent good training for newer staff members and also, by being easier to collect, a source of reinforcement that encourages staff to keep trying.)

All these are examples of day-to-day routines and habitual ways of doing things that develop in every group in order to make the work easier to perform. These elaborations quickly become embedded as required operating procedures in order to make work life more predictable. It would be extraordinarily stressful to have to decide how to handle every incident, problem, or issue from scratch.

What seems like a comfortable and useful routine to one group, however, can be discomforting to another, and therefore a source of continuing coordination troubles. In the example above, for example, these quite trivial microdecisions about how collections was going to handle various parts of its job created significant work problems in other functions. Also, collections' unwillingness to modify some of those practices was a source of inefficiency from the vantage point of the larger system.

These routines also shape the priorities and trade-offs that groups will make when there are conflicting demands or ambiguous problems to be dealt with. These determine how data will be handled and what will be communicated to whom. As a result, these can be critical to performance.

Priorities and Trade-Offs

If two departments are asking for help with a software glitch, who gets attention first, or who gets the better people (assuming there is a scarcity of programming personnel)? The answer, of course, is the department that is most important. Importance, though, is in the eyes of the beholder. Therefore, some departments with a real crisis on their hands may find themselves waiting while a more favored unit gets preferred treatment.

A similar choice has to be made in technical decisions. For example, how rugged should a motor housing be, or how impermeable should a wrapping be? How strong is "strong"? How safe is "safe"?

> As orders declined, a division fabricating technical components decided to encourage its internal engineering department to look for external customers. Initially, given the high reputation of the firm's products, a number of contracts came in, but gradually the work dried up. In seeking to assess the cause, customers were surveyed. Many said that the engineering work the group did was "too expensive." But what did that mean?
>
> On closer examination, it turned out to mean that these engineers were specifying excessively costly components. Having worked for years on products that had to be maintained for their operating life by their own manufacturing organization (where lifetime maintenance was more costly than the original product), they had grown used to specifying only the most durable and reliable components. Obviously, for many uses this meant that needlessly costly components were specified— that is, the trade-off between cost and durability was unwarranted. For example, the engineers had specified electric cabling with such unique sheathing that it could only be purchased in thousand foot lengths from one U.S. fabricator!

> A bank sought to decrease its bad consumer loans by adopting tighter standards. It developed a formula by which it would reduce the maximum amount it might loan a customer with a given financial profile (payment record, use of short-term advances, overdrafts, and so

forth) on the basis of past bank experience with that loan applicant. The credit group decided that people who used their credit cards to get cash advances (essentially short-term loans) were less creditworthy than those who did not use that option. By not consulting those who were more expert in credit card usage, they managed to antagonize an important group of high-income card holders who used that feature of their credit card and had a near-perfect repayment record.

Again, these are mundane, everyday choices that managers make in the process of deciding how their unit's work gets done. But while mundane to be sure, they have a profound impact on the integration of the work among departments and on costs and the ability to adapt to ever-shifting external market demands.

Multinational companies have very tough trade-offs when they must make a decision regarding the location of a new overseas laboratory or factory. There are a number of legitimately competing criteria that have to be traded off against one another. Country managers and marketing executives will want the new facility in their jurisdiction to build better political relationships. (Most countries, obviously, want the economic and technological benefits that are derived from having such institutions.) Functional heads of R & D or manufacturing see the need for economies of scale that suggest consolidating worldwide operations in a single location. Effective decision making requires some process of both considering and integrating this diversity.

Focus of Attention

Another element of managerial work that influences coordination is each manager's focus of attention. Managers cannot consider (or even know) everything that might have some relationship to decision making. Their jobs become overwhelming if all the personal, technical, organizational, and political factors are considered before a decision is made.[7]

Effective managers learn to distinguish the things that really count from the endless array of data and issues afloat in the world around them. This learning is usually based on their work experiences and the tasks they perform. Thus, a given technology and organization teach the manager what to focus upon and what safely can be ignored or filtered out of their field of vision.[8] (Obviously, not all of this task learning will be correct.)

Another way of saying this is that managers have a number of implicit equations $Y = f(X)$ in their minds specifying functional relationships, where Y is effectiveness and X represents the relevant variables to be considered if Y is to be maximized. What a manager includes in X are the variables considered most relevant to meeting objectives; everything else is excluded.

When some new event or factor comes into play, this filtering can turn out to be costly to managerial effectiveness. The implicit criteria that determine what is watched and what is ignored tend to change more slowly than the situation demands. This culture lag extracts its price in terms of managerial responsiveness unless managers can learn flexibility. Many poor managers rely on so many rules of thumb and automatic reactions that they fail to recognize new challenges and new factors that have introduced change.

A large consumer products company was constantly and successfully introducing improved versions of its household products. When introducing a new version of one of its most important products, the packaging was also changed. Management's attention always focused on the physical attractiveness of the packaging and the ease of holding and pouring the contents.

Only after one new version had been shipped was it discovered that many users couldn't loosen the cap and get the package opened. No attention had been paid to the torque applied on the filling line to tighten the cap, because customers had never complained about difficulty in opening the product. With a reshaped container top, it became important to specify precisely what torque could be used. It took time to understand these previously ignored design factors: the interaction of the threads on the package top (an outside vendor's responsibility), the shape of the cap, and the filling line's procedures.[9]

When a major auto manufacturer sought to utilize a new high-strength, low-alloy steel for the hood of the car (covering the engine compartment), it discovered that the hood "resonated and oscillated" in response to engine vibrations. This made the hood unusable. Prior to that experience, no one had considered the resonance potential of the steel as worthy of assessment; no auto hoods had resonated before.[10]

The jet engine initially appeared to have important and straightforward implications for airframe technology. Established firms in the industry understood that they would need to develop expertise regarding the jet engine but failed to understand the ways in which its introduction would change the interactions between the engine and the rest of the plane in complex and subtle ways.[11]

Peter Goldmark sought to develop a totally new high-fidelity recording process that eventually became the industry standard—the familiar long-playing (LP) record, which supplanted the 78 rpm record. He learned from the industry experts at his company, CBS Records, that the one component in the recording process that did *not* need to be modified for his new technology was the recording microphone; the experts were sure that it was already near-perfect. When almost everything else had been improved and the sound quality was still unacceptable, Goldmark discovered that in fact microphone technology was inadequate (vulnerable to phase distortion). Only after a new microphone was developed did LP technology move forward.

In the words of that careful student of innovation who analyzed the LP record development, "As so often happens, what everyone knows is not worth knowing, and what everyone swears by is often worth swearing at."[12]

Often what appears as a trivial modification of a product can have costly (and ignored or misunderstood) ramifications, but these get missed or filtered out by managers and professionals who are working with this product in one way or another. They get ignored because these elements are not within the normal focus of attention of those responsible, or because they are considered inconsequential. In either case, no serious attention is paid to the change, and profound problems result from this biased or skewed management attention.

The well-known failure of the U.S. auto industry to identify a change in consumer tastes eventually gave the Japanese a dominant share of the market. Small Japanese-made cars, high in quality and economical on fuel, first became popular in the far West. Their obvious success there was dismissed by U.S. auto manufacturers as essentially a fluke because, they told themselves persuasively, Californians were known faddists and counterculture enthusiasts. They were sure that the U.S. heartland wanted the kind of cars Detroit had always made.[13]

FAILURE TO MATCH A COMPETITOR'S INNOVATION: THE EXPLANATION OF THE PAE CASE

The previously described detailed study of the photolithographic alignment equipment industry offers many examples of how success blinds management to what are critically problematic issues. The research discloses why and how competitors who were losing market share failed to focus on the right work issues.

It is worth examining some of the researchers' detailed field data. Below is part of their explanation as to why one firm in their study, Kasper Instruments (formerly a very successful U.S. manufacturer with a cadre of skilled engineers and designers), failed to meet the challenge of a Japanese company, Canon, which had introduced a product that was destroying Kasper's market. Canon introduced a so-called proximity printer (or aligner) that had very real advantages in comparison with Kasper's contact printer. Kasper then developed its own proximity aligner, but it was never successful because it was technically inferior to Canon's. This is what the researchers believe that the data show as to why Kasper's almost complete copy of Canon's machine was never very successful:

> Our analysis of [this] industry's history suggests that a reliance on . . . knowledge derived from experience with the previous generation blinded the incumbent firms to critical aspects of the new technology. . . . [In] a proximity aligner, a quite different set of relationships between components is critical to successful performance. . . . Kasper conceived of the proximity aligner as a modified contact aligner. . . . [It] was managed as a routine extension to the product line. . . . The firm "knew" that its gap setting mechanism was entirely adequate and thus devoted very little time to improving its performance. [This was the critical element in the new technology;

65

it required very delicate coordination of several other components if it was to work effectively.][14]

Know-How. Managers use the term *know-how* to refer to the important but poorly understood (by them) interrelationships among tasks and function that determine quality and effectiveness. These mysterious factors come to haunt the manager when there is some technical or market change.

Often there is a more up-to-date understanding of the changed technology or market in the "data banks" of lower levels of management or among the employees themselves. This know-how (meaning that it is undocumented and must be extracted from knowledgeable, experienced participants) can be a critical resource. For example, organizations that suffer heavy turnover or that purposely urge early retirement often lose an understanding of how things really work that resides no place else.[15] After the individuals' departure, some tasks suffer performance degradation. Some tasks can't be performed at all, because no one is left who knows how to do them.

Culture Lag. Another way of generalizing about what managers focus attention upon is to predict that the organization's culture will emphasize what previously has been critical. For example, IBM has been criticized for continuing to emphasize design values and user services that were relevant to its enormously successful mainframe computers as it shifts some of its emphasis to smaller machines.[16]

Substantial leadership energies are required to shift attention from what was relevant in the past to what is important for the present and the future. Organizational values and conventional wisdom— what everyone "knows" is true—do not change easily.

Access to Information

What managers attend to is a function not only of past experience and bias but also of the information that is readily available. A trite example is that sales or customer service departments are more customer oriented because they see much more of the idiosyncracies of customers than do manufacturing personnel.

In more complex organizations, there are many ambiguities over who gets what information. Because information is a source of prestige (and power), access is by no means available on equal terms to all comers.

Coordination

> P & G's [Procter and Gamble's] initial attempt to build European product management capabilities involved the creation of a European Pampers czar who was responsible for coordinating disposable-diaper strategy across subsidiaries. The experiment failed because . . . [among other things] the appointee had only limited access to the necessary market information.[17]

The restructuring decided upon by P&G top management to improve coordination thus was never properly implemented. The reason was a culture lag in how communications flowed among managers in the decision chain. Top management changed the boxes in the organizational chart, but not the communication flows.

The information that a manager is privy to shapes how the manager conceives of and executes his or her job. Information includes what the executive can observe as emergent trends, as problems requiring intervention, and as the differential performance of individuals and units. Add or subtract any of this and the focus, quality, and timeliness of managers' decision change accordingly.

Contact Patterns

Another important aspect of how the job or function is performed is the supporting pattern of interpersonal contacts that is constructed. These routines also affect the information flow. Thus, managers must both understand and seek to mold these patterns to fit the information requirements of the technical system. Where they are not consistent with how a job or task fits other related functions, incumbents may lack timely information upon which to base decisions. Or the information may get filtered by a previous link in the chain, introducing distortions in the data.

Employees and managers learn over some period of time who they should contact when they get into trouble—those who can be helpful, as well as those who need to be informed because some previous commitment is at risk now. Also, managers learn from whom they must get permission before deviating from a standard or commitment, and who can be ignored or even deceived. An experienced manager described this reality in these terms:

> It is typical in business, as in any other aspect of life, to slip the rules in one fashion or another for the sake of expediency or because the rules appear silly or arbitrary. It is also common to hide these petty

deceptions, just as managers may hide mistakes in performance. However, some associates get told the whole truth, so to speak, others part, and still others none of the truth.

Other important contacts that become part of the job include who gets contacted for permission to proceed before some new activity or changed plan gets implemented. Managers frequently complain that their boss consulted a colleague—but not them—before a major decision that affected their area. Similarly, some units will get alerted or warned about problems (for example, in schedules or quality) that some other department is having, whereas others will learn the news at the last minute or after the fact.

It is important to note that this extensive elaboration of how the work is done does not represent on-the-job socializing or fun and games. These patterned interactions represent critical give-and-take and communications exchanges that are critical to coordination. Managers concerned with getting work completed effectively have to understand and help shape these interaction patterns; they are the heartbeat of the work flow. Some examples may give these "hidden" job dimensions clearer focus.

CASE EXAMPLES OF COMPETING DEPARTMENTS WHO MUST COOPERATE
When Customers Are Also Vendors: The Ames Case

Two departments embroiled in destructive conflict in a technologically oriented corporation (referred to here as the Ames Corporation) were observed over some period of time. Their managers exchanged a variety of accusations and recriminations, and their feud threatened a major new technological thrust of the corporation. Looking closely at the issues, however, one could empathize with both managers, because the coordination issues that aggravated them were difficult and the inconsistencies profound. Their conflicts were not driven by personality differences or the lust for power, but rather by legitimate ambiguities in markets and technology.[18]

> One manager headed a product group (A) that had been very successful in developing and then marketing an innovative high-technology product in a highly competitive industry. The product required continuous

enhancements in both software and hardware to maintain its market position. The other manager headed an even newer product group (B) that had only limited market penetration. It represented a much more complex technological and marketing effort than represented by A; however, the products made by A would be an integral part of most B units. Some of the software development work done for B also would be used by next-generation A units. Thus, A and B were each customers and vendors for one another.

To senior management, B represented the larger future market, although A was much more profitable today and would probably remain so for at least several years. In fact, A produced very significant revenues for the company in spite of formidable competition.

A's major problems with B focused on software development. A felt that his group's needs were being downgraded or misinterpreted by B's subordinate managers and technicians. In their programming, they did not take sufficient account of some of the special requirements of certain A models and A customers. B, not surprisingly, insisted that the software was being designed so it would be optimal for future B systems, but that it was certainly satisfactory for A's use. Because B's manager had responsibility for a product that everyone expected would someday represent an enormous market, she did not feel that she should be constrained too much by the other manager's insistence that he had to have something done in a certain way.

The manager of A felt that many technical decisions on the B product were being made without adequate inputs from him, particularly with respect to those aspects of it that impinged on the functioning of A product. He wanted more debate and also earlier information about what was being considered, so that he could have timely technical input. A typical complaint would be that the B group had changed a specification without giving A adequate notice; in rebuttal, B's manager would say that A had received adequate notice. Furthermore, there really was no objective standard as to who was right. The manager of B was particularly concerned that A would delay decision making by endless wrangling if decisions weren't made that were optimal to A. This could delay the B product's entry to the market.

Not surprisingly, B could cite many instances in which A's technical decisions (to improve A product) were not well suited to the future configuration of group B's product. And because these were high-cost changes (in time and dollars), they delayed the kind of A product changes that B felt she really needed. A and B also disagreed over whether there was an appropriate division of scarce technical resources and whether the priorities each had with respect to what needed immediate attention were being injured by the other's demand for resources.

Because B's was the broader product (and included A's product, among others), there were frequently arguments as to whether a sale contemplated by B was primarily made up of A product and, therefore, ought to be handled by A personnel (and credited to A's revenue) or whether there was enough of the broader product for it to be considered a truly B sale? Again, this was a question that could be argued legitimately to favor either party.

Thus, the issues surrounded both the content and the process for making decisions. Who should be consulted or should "sign off" or control a given decision, and which could be made by one or the other executive autonomously? These were debated endlessly.

Discussion. One of the reasons for presenting this detailed example is to illustrate that coordination conflicts are not solely or even primarily battles over turf or prestige. To be sure, politics complicates the inherent technical problems; however, there is an enormous amount of legitimate inconsistency and uncertainty at the boundary between these two departments that provides a fertile breeding ground for mutual suspicions and animosity.

The interface of A's and B's work is complex and ever changing. Without real leadership on the part of the managers of A and B and their common boss, one or both products will suffer handicaps in the marketplace. And as their relationship deteriorates, so will the coordination between their activities. (In the next chapter, I will consider the leadership skills required for effective coordination.)

U.S. and Canadian Divisions Fail to Collaborate

What follows is another example of the ambiguous coordination issues between departments that are both cooperative and competitive at the same time.

This prestigious international high-tech corporation had two product development groups with somewhat similar skills and responsibilities, one in Canada and the other in the United States. Each focused on the needs of its market; however, the Canadian group handled most of the more complex product development assignments.

The U.S. unit was impatient to get a product modification of a Canadian-designed product that was now popular in the Unites States. As is typical, they felt that their market needs were not getting the right priority, particularly when compared with similar requests the Canadian team handled originating in Canada. The U.S. group then decided to do the product development themselves, because it seemed to be very doable and straightforward in terms of engineering.

After a year of effort and several million dollars in cost, the U.S. group had to abandon the effort. They had discovered that the minor modification required total reengineering of all of the components, a formidable task for which they weren't prepared and that they probably couldn't accomplish.

What is most relevant is that the manager who bridged the two groups had no technical interest in such projects. She had no way of knowing whether the Canadians had fully briefed their U.S. counterparts on the full technical implications of the "minor" product modification they sought. Nor did she know or learn whether the U.S. group had, in fact, heard and understood what the Canadians were saying.

The budget for the U.S. team probably never should have been approved. There clearly needs to be some monitoring of the organizational process by which technical advice and information gets exchanged on programs where there is high interdependence.

Discussion. These are examples of what is often called *tight coupling*. The elements in a system are so closely interrelated that seemingly minor or trivial changes in one get transmitted almost immediately to other units. When the system is large, the results can be unpredictably destructive to systems performance. It is these "tightly coupled work systems that show "unstable equilibrium."[19] The manager is confronted with a world in which small changes in various work stages and organizational units around him or her cannot easily be ignored, absorbed, or deflected. The return to anything like equilibrium—in which the parts are in some kind of harmony with one another—takes a great deal of managerial effort. Without such leadership, work systems first gradually degrade; then they may literally fall apart.

This kind of interactive system is like the early stages of a pool game, when the table is filled with balls (each of which is made of hard, unresilient plastic) that begin striking each other as a result of a single collision. To the viewer, it can look as though everything is in motion.

There is nothing so unusual about these cases in contemporary companies. Contradictions and overlapping responsibility are very common at the margin between groups, and there are no easy answers as to who is right and when. The technology is very complex with many uncertainties, and the managers of both A and B in the Ames case, for example, can mobilize good technical reasons why the other is wrong. Without very careful managing of their interrelationships, the work of either or both will suffer. The executive over the two managers will need a very sophisticated understanding of both the content and process of exchange to know whether groups A and B are handling their jobs in such a way as to further the division's strategies.

RELEVANCE TO ORGANIZATIONAL AND TECHNOLOGICAL CHANGE

It now should be obvious why Henderson and Clark's once-dominant firms in the PAE industry were unsuccessful in adapting to what appeared to be slight improvements introduced by a competitor. Matching (that is, learning to implement the improvement in hardware) required that management know how to introduce consequential changes in the patterning of the work flows. This involved significant organizational transformations that were not comprehended by those who were attempting to follow the new leader. What appeared to be a modest incremental enhancement or "tweaking" of the hardware required considerable managerial inputs that were not forthcoming.

Successfully introducing a competitive product required changing a wide variety of coordination mechanisms—including how managers assigned priorities, made trade-offs, and shaped and used communication patterns, among others. Also, some technical groups would have had to receive greater attention and predominance; others would have had to revert to lesser positions. To adapt to what appeared to be an only slightly changed technology, managers had to become aware of and then modify hundreds of seemingly trivial, often partially hidden aspects of how work was done.

What management considers to be "minor" changes may make obsolete many of the whats and hows of existing tasks and functions. In doing so, they also make obsolete many of what were hard-won mutual accommodations and interaction patterns among work groups and functions, all of which had served to coordinate the previous work system.

What appears to be an easy-to-accommodate technical change often creates a cascade of ramifications. These, in turn, amplify the initial disturbance to where almost every job is affected and requires change. *Employee values, expectations, and loyalties, as well as work patterns, will all need to be modified if the technical modification is to be integrated into a finely functioning work system.*

In today's organizations, managers are under pressure to keep improving their part of the business. As a result, most of the managerial units encompassed by a given work flow system will be in flux. The improvements and modifications in the work that any given manager undertakes, usually independent of any concern for work processes in adjacent and related work flow stages, inevitably affects these other units. Below are two examples I observed of unanticipated costs of continuous improvement.

> One of the product groups in a company selling to a market requiring substantial technical servicing modified one of its products. Although the modification appeared minor, most customers utilizing the improved product would have to talk with a company technician before they

sought to get service through the normal channels (the service scheduling department). This change in procedure never got worked into the training program for service schedulers, however, nor was there any attention to developing a small cadre of technicians who would be skilled in interviewing customers experiencing difficulty. As a result, customers got whipsawed between confused service schedulers and unprepared technicians. They soon began to lose confidence in the company's mission statement, which assured the world that it took service as seriously as it took production.

A systems redesign effort was undertaken in another company to improve the efficiency of a storage and retrieval system for engineering drawings and specifications. Embedded in the new software enhancement, unbeknownst to anyone but one programmer, was a consequential change: the new software automatically erased a previous drawing when a newer version was stored. (This change had probably facilitated some other desirable changes the programmer was seeking to attain.) The programmer had never been told that for certain purposes it was useful for engineers to be able to retrieve these "obsolete" drawings in order to resolve certain classes of problems. The older drawings still existed within the paperwork system, but it took hours to find them.

Increasing Number of Players (Specialists)

Complicating the manager's coordination challenge is the increasing number of players—that is, specialists and specialized functions. The more units that have to interlock or be coordinated—the bigger the "team"—the more difficult the systems issues. Getting eight departments to coalesce is many times more difficult than working with just two. For example, in response to newly identified problems and new fields of technical specializations, there can be staff experts now in ethics, in local area networks (LANs), in environmental issues, and in cross-cultural management. Almost never is the marginal cost of the increased managerial effort required to coordinate with the new specialty taken into account in assessing whether it is worthwhile to add another center of expertise.

Multinational Organizations

There are a host of difficult management issues associated with coordination within multinationals. It is not unusual to have functional specializations geographically dispersed. Thus, there may be several development laboratories (in Japan, Western Europe, and the United States, for example), or a dozen manufacturing facilities in as many countries. On top of these basic functions, there may be a marketing manager for each region or each type of customer, or both. In addition, there will likely be product managers with either global or regional responsibility. And there are often numerous country managers who seek to integrate the business interests of the corporation with the unique political, legal, and cultural dimensions of their jurisdictions.

One can be sure that there will be overlap among these functions and roles that cannot be defined away by job descriptions and organization charts. Also, their pattern of interrelating will need to change in the various stages of a project or product program. Who does what with whom among all of these participants in a planning stage will not be the same as in the development process or in the production or implementation stage. For example, in developing a product whose initial sales will be in one country or region, consider the possible respective inputs and level of influence of the following key players:

- corporate head of product development (who may want to try out certain new product parameters in this as a test market)
- country manager
- corporate product manager
- corporate marketing manager (who is also responsible for long-range planning)
- regional product development manager
- Manufacturing management (local and corporate)

One recent study provides a vivid example of this functional coordination problem.[20] The researchers sought to explain the surprising failure of ITT to achieve a competitive advantage with its digital switch, although that international communications company was then a pioneer in identifying the importance of this technology to the efficient operation of national telephone systems and invested substantial sums. ITT was seeking to retain its position as a world-class player in the world telecommunications market; developing a leading-edge digital switch was an essential step in its strategy.

The data from this research suggests that ITT failed in large part because they were unable to shift the pattern of interaction and interplay among functional specialists. To deal only with a part of the story, ITT had flourished on the basis of strong country managers and strong country-based R & D facilities, because the telephone market was a national market. ITT recognized the growing need for a basic new all-electronic switching technology (for digitalized signals) as a very costly and highly sophisticated basic new central office component for telephone companies. Development was to be enormously expensive, require the best talent available, and ideally would allow the company to sell broadly in many markets. The latter assumed that a core design for the digital switch could be developed that would suit a variety of national phone companies.

Given its long history of autonomous national companies who owed minimal allegiance to the corporation, however, ITT's leadership was not equal to the task of mobilizing these far-flung development resources, particularly the human ones. It was not able to build a strong enough centralized product development thrust, staffed by the best of its people, compared to some of its competitors. It couldn't get these resources because each of its country units wanted to go it alone. As a result, ITT lost the first part of the race to develop a successful digital switch.

Matrix Organizations

In 1991, press accounts of Eastman Kodak's management challenges echoed a similar theme. Apparently Kodak had become concerned that its various product and functional groups were too compartmentalized. Kodak had developed a new technology, "photo CD," by which regular pictures could be converted electronically onto a compact disk. Top management felt that this exciting new technological competency ought to be integrated with a variety of older Kodak products that were dispersed among many managerial units within Kodak. Thus, the senior executive for imaging products announced late in 1991 that this technology could only be exploited effectively if Kodak managers became used to working in a matrix organization. They were to coordinate, in his words, "within units, across units, upward, downwardly, and diagonally."[21]

The essence of matrix organizations differs from that of traditional organizations in the following ways:

1. There is continuous change. Routines don't last, because some other part of the business demands a new response.
2. Many critical decisions are made by lateral negotiations and persuasion, not by the hierarchy.
3. A great number of functions have to be shared, as among user groups.

All of these represent difficult coordination/systems problems, because there is an ever-changing array of participants and objectives confronting any one manager. As the reader will see in later chapters, such new integrations always impose the need for many more managerial interventions and managerial fine-tuning than anyone anticipated.

Joint Ventures

The high risk and high cost associated with many new technologies and the cost of replicating know-how that exists in other organizations all encourage a variety of joint ventures and interorganizational collaborations. These, in turn, can multiply the number of players in a system and, obviously, complicate the problem of mutual adjustment and the development of self-maintaining work systems. The complications arise from both the physical and organizational separation involved.

Innovation is often associated with major scientific or technological breakthroughs, such as DuPont's invention of nylon or the development of the first rigid plastic, bakelite. Such revolutionary products stem from the creativity (and often good luck) of a well-trained scientist. Currently, tight coordination among a number of separate activities (often dispersed among several independent organizations) seems to be just as important a source of significant new technologies. Thus, management becomes as critical as science and engineering (although the management may well be exercised by technically trained professionals). The following is an example of such interorganizational innovation.

More than fifteen years ago, the Japanese revolutionized the machine tool industry, but not by inventing a new type of machine. Rather, Fanuc, a machine tool manufacturer, fused three separate technologies into a new product. As a result, in five years Fanuc became the largest company in its field and pulled Japan from fourth place internationally in that industry to first place.

Fujitsu, a leading supplier of communications equipment at the time, developed a compact little controller based on a cheap but highly accurate stepping motor instead of the usual feedback controller (which was subject to excessive wear.) A bearing manufacturer, Nippon Seiko, perfected a ball screw with friction low enough for the stepping motor to do its job. And a materials company came up with a Teflon-like compound for coating the machine tool's sliding bed, so both controller and bearing could work more smoothly than ever before. Separately, each was merely a modest advance; together they combined to become a powerful innovation.[22]

As one can easily imagine and foresee, the management of these interrelationships, growing out of complex innovations developed independently in different companies, cannot be easy. Inevitably, there will be reticence in sharing information and in compromising (that is, modifying one's own original formulation) or exploring alternative formulations. One can be sure that the controller, the bearing, and the new material in the above example did not neatly fit together! Extraordinary work leadership skills must have been employed to make these combined technical/organizational interfaces effective.[23]

There is little difference, from the point of view of managerial requirements for coordinating around interfaces, between these multicompany innovations and the Japanese way of handling vendors. As many U.S. companies seeking contracts with Japanese companies have discovered, before contracting for any component, the Japanese will require that the vendor be willing to expose its total technology and also be willing to make many modifications in its normal work routines. These changes will be imposed in order to coordinate the vendor's operations more effectively with those of the buyer.[24]

CONCLUSIONS: WHY IT'S SO HARD TO GET THE WORK TO WORK

I have sought to illustrate and explain the complexity of the work system in which managers find themselves embedded. Systems efficiency and quality require that the parts interlock or synchronize; an engineering department has to produce designs that are manufacturable, or the whole exercise is a waste. The integration is made much more difficult than many managers (or the managers of managers) presume, because those parts of each department or work unit's activities that have to interlock—the boundaries or interfaces, where data or work or ideas get transferred—are much more complex than most managers believe.

There can be hundreds of elements of what specific actions are taken, when, with whom, and how that all affect the total system. Further, these elements have a great deal of fluidity, play, or leeway. Managers are always elaborating and modifying the work processes they control in response to problems and opportunities and new insights. This is permitted because, as we have seen, tasks and functions are so ambiguous.

The elements that are most easy for managers to manipulate (and are, in fact, most adjusted by them) relate to how their jobs get done. In the examples and cases above, these are the focus for such elaborations:

- Trade-offs and priorities (what gets attention)
- Routines and "standard operating procedures"
- Interaction and communication patterns (who learns what and when)

Integrating work for high performance is more complex than management theory and practice presumes, for the reasons explored in this chapter. The manager's challenge is to cause to fit together a large number of elements or components, most of which are *not* being developed and produced by a cohesive work group loyally facilitating each other's tasks. Nor are they fixed.

The great difficulty of accomplishing this integration is shown by the frequency with which companies insist that they intend to decentralize. They thus assume that the adjustments and readjustments will be much easier because they will all take place under a common manager. What this appealing solution ignores is that even with decentralization, the struggles between functions and tasks still take place. They don't get eliminated just because there is a common boss several levels up in the hierarchy (although they may be contained). Also, no matter how much top management struggles to decentralize, there will continue to be centralized functions. These are required because of economies of scale, the scarcity of certain professional skills, and the continuing introduction of new specializations designed to audit and appraise managerial activities and to ensure that managers are not tempted to "hurt" internal or external standards (like air quality, safety, or legal requirements for fair trade).[25]

This inherent instability of the work flow explains some of the peripatetic, even chaotic view researchers obtain when they ask, "What do managers actually do on the job; how do they behave?" They don't seem to spend much time planning or decision making; they are out in the trenches trying to facilitate making things work, trying to make the system operate like a system.

The managerial needs to cope with the inherent instability of the work processes themselves are often ignored because managers have been taught, first, that they don't need to know much about the work, and second, that they need to focus on the intractable problems involving people and very tough judgment issues regarding market strategy. The people issues are primarily authority related (loyalty, commitment, and motivation), not work related. The strategy issues are "number" problems (share of market, cost of capital, and so forth) and risk issues (probabilities and one's taste for high-stakes games).

Managers still think (and are taught to think by their management training) in hierarchical terms, not horizontal or work flow terms. They believe that their jobs should essentially involve top-down strategic thinking and selecting and motivating good people. These are surely not unimportant, but left out are the guts of the business: how competitors and customers behave, and how the technology works.

Nobel laureate Herbert Simon, a distinguished student of organizations, psychology, and decision making, is very critical of the widespread view that general management skills transcend any need for specific technical knowledge:

> What does a streetwise—or, more accurately, organization-wise—manager know? The requisite inventory has never been taken, but we can conjecture that management knowledge falls into two main categories: on the one hand, knowledge about human behavior in

organization and about how organizations operate, and, on the other, knowledge about the content of the organization's work—knowledge that may be largely specific to an industry or even to a particular company or plant.

It has sometimes been argued that managerial expertise is a general skill that can be transferred from any organizational environment to any other. I don't think the evidence bears out this claim.[26]

An example that may confirm Simon's judgment is the transformation of a manufacturer of large diesel engines for trucks. Detroit Diesel had performed poorly for some years when it was a division of General Motors. It became a highly competitive, technologically successful firm, however, when it was taken over by Roger Penske. As president, Penske is known for his close involvement with customers and product development and manufacturing. He takes substantial pride in this involvement: "I'm concerned about the details; I get people smarter than me to handle the bigger issues."[27]

Coordination doesn't come easily. The organization's centrifugal forces are always the stronger ones. These cause technical people to continue employing the same cognitive models and trade-off criteria, even though the market has changed. They cause marketing to do those things that make it harder for operations to do "its" thing. They cause the interrelating of units A and B to continue to dominate communications in a company introducing a modified product, even though the innovation requires A and X to develop more intimate and continuing exchanges at the same time that B and Y need to be learning to work harmoniously together.

This is what I mean by negative synergies: the rational continuities that hamper, if not totally block, adaptation and change. Only managers who have come to understand how difficult it is to attain and maintain coordination are likely to refocus their leadership capabilities and energies toward work. That leadership challenge is the subject of the next chapter.

6

The New Leadership

*L*eadership is an imposing term. It suggests the ability to galvanize followers or subordinates with a compelling vision of a goal worthy of their commitment and loyalty. The cases presented in previous chapters argues for a less dramatic view of leadership, one focused on making the organization work and work well. But can that be leadership? Isn't that simply what managing is all about? Is that so remarkable as to be called "leadership"?

Indeed, yes. The case examples and data presented in earlier chapters show organizations not functioning effectively without middle managers who can exercise leadership. Leadership capabilities are required to overcome the organization's inherent contradictions, inconsistencies, bureaucratic fumbling, and centrifugal forces.

In today's competitive, fast-moving world, leadership cannot be an added premium a company hopes to obtain with every X number of management hires. Rather, it is an absolute requirement if individual tasks are to be integrated and also continuously refocused on the ever-changing requirements of both internal and external "customers" and markets. Almost nothing works without a working leader.

To be sure, jobs get done and functions get performed with managers who are not leaders, but they don't add up to organizational effectiveness without leadership. Work leadership is the ability to keep adapting, modifying, adjusting, and rearranging the complex task and function interfaces that keep slipping out of alignment. Where this leadership is lacking, the contradictions become the wasteful battleground for interpersonal and interdepartmental guerilla warfare over who is right and who should be stuck with the responsibility for failure. As should now be obvious, with the uncertainties and contradictions inherent in modern technology and markets, there is an endless supply of raw material for complaints: "Of course, we would have met the schedule [or budget, specification, or customer request]—if only others had done what they should have done, what they were *supposed to do.*"

THREE LEADERSHIP STYLES

Henry Mintzberg, based on his own and others' research, recently suggested that managers differ from one another in their major focus of attention.[1] Some managers devote their energies to handling and manipulating *data* and information. Others appear to have their major interest in *people.* A third category of managers focus their attention on *action.* (Remember, these groupings refer to the managers' primary focus; one cannot be manager and ignore any of these areas entirely.)

Thus, data-oriented (D) managers would be concerned primarily with gathering, analyzing, and reporting numbers, primarily to meet upper management standards. They manage by reports. The people-oriented (P) manager concentrates on maintaining the motivation of his or her coworkers, being responsive to problems they initiate and looking for signs of disaffection. They pride themselves on sensitivity to evidence of stress and their ability to cope with human relations problems.

The action-oriented (A) managers are always seeking to do something, to change something, to make tomorrow different from today. They seek out problems to solve and new opportunities to consider for implementation in their areas. These managers take much more initiative in going to people who don't know they have problems and seeking to get them to consider change. Characteristically, A managers persistently encourage both subordinates and peers to try something different from what they have done previously. In effect, their managerial life is a never-ending series of projects that need completing.

The findings related in this book, of course, suggest that it is the last group who are indispensable. Chapter 5 described the centrifugal forces that gradually cause jobs, tasks, and functions to become less interconnected, less mutually supportive, and less internally consistent.

The major challenge of getting work done, therefore, is not that subordinates are lazy or cranky (although there may well be some of that). Rather, the core of what is problematic for managers is that the elements that are required for work to be *completed* effectively—with quality, and with flexibility to respond to unique and changing market requirements and in a context of changing technology—are almost always tending to fly apart. The reader has seen how complex job and function interfaces are; worse yet, they are in continuous flux. The simple arithmetic odds of marketing interlocking easily and effectively with operations are not particularly high. As new products and processes are added, the odds even get lower. Most sophisticated technologies and work processes have embedded flaws. Without substantial leadership inputs, *all* complex organizations degrade over time. Negative synergy is the rule, not the exception.

Thus, both the D and P managers will tend to be too passive for the needs of the organization. They perform necessary but not sufficient functions for the real leadership role. Whether a manager is too "hard" (number-oriented) or too "soft" (people-oriented) is not such an important question any more. Neither of the ends of that particular continuum will focus on what this research suggests are the most important determinants of organizational effectiveness.

A SYSTEM'S, NOT A SPECIALIST'S, VIEW

At the core of leadership should be the manager's awareness of the importance of systems and their extreme fragility and vulnerability. These, then, become the leader's primary concerns:

- Subordinates' accomplishments are useful only insofar as they interlock with the work of others.
- The "outputs" of the manager's own unit have to be adapted to the work of other parts of the organization (and thus require continuous change, because these interfaces are in flux).
- A substantial amount of managerial energy and astuteness are required to identify those places where coordination is beginning to fail and to find ways of building or rebuilding a self-maintaining system, a system in which the parts mutually reinforce one another.

- How jobs, tasks, and functions interlock is not fixed. Training, rules, procedures, organization charts, and job designs never ensure coordination. There is always substantial play in the system, which both requires and allows the managerial initiatives that are so central to this concept of leadership.

It is easier and more tempting for managers to assume the specialist's vantage point, in which output problems are the result of someone failing to perform who needs to work more diligently. Keep within your unit's boundaries, this view suggests; let others worry about themselves. Most rewards are seen as coming to those who maximize their own performance, even if it is at the expense of the larger system.

The example below illustrates what is distinctive in the leader's approach to the managerial job.

Fari, a product manager for fluid equipment, was distressed to hear from several of his better sales staff that they were not getting repeat business on the company's new small pump. Its innovative design and small number of moving parts promised a major new market. In his talks with sales personnel, Fari learned that several of their major accounts had been shipped pumps that leaked. This information was a place to begin searching out why the projections had proven to be overly optimistic.

Fari visited with quality control and manufacturing supervision and learned that there was an ongoing dispute between manufacturing and engineering over one of the components, a gasket. Manufacturing claimed that its employees had difficulties installing the gasket; it tended to crack under the pressures specified. They wanted a new design from engineering so as to rid themselves of this source of increased labor costs. For its part, engineering said that this was the correct gasket for the job and that employees were being careless in its assembly or were poorly trained or both. Various supervisors assured Fari that this acrimonious dispute was par for the course; there were always intergroup conflicts in new product start-ups.

Fari sought to go beyond the usual explanations of

"poor communications" or "intergroup antagonisms" for endemic problems to see what might be underlying this conflict over gasket specifications. Through good contacts he had in both departments, he was able to put together an analysis.

As far as anyone could determine, the problem began to appear about six months ago. Finance had been putting pressure on both purchasing and manufacturing because product cost in relation to sales price was high. In addition to concerns about productivity, purchasing admitted that the original gasket manufacturer had almost doubled the price from the time that its component had been specified. Purchasing had then searched out a substitute gasket that met all of engineering's specifications, but it apparently was more difficult to assemble. Employees on the line complained that although it appeared identical to the original gasket, it seemed to be very vulnerable to small cracks when pressure was applied. (Apparently, there was some subtle difference in the material in the replacement gasket that was not being measured by the standard tests the company used to qualify the part.)

Fari knew the market for the pump would not absorb a price that reflected the new cost of the original gasket, and getting engineering to redesign the whole product for a less high-tech gasket would be costly in time and dollars. Based on some additional interviews and a very knowledgeable technician in manufacturing engineering (a group that evaluated new methods), Fari learned that the assembly operation would be improved if special robotic tooling could be obtained that would automate the installation of the elements surrounding the gasket.

Manufacturing had no budget for this capital expense and was adamant that it was not their responsibility to make up for engineering's and purchasing's "goofs." Fari and purchasing, however, devised a way of getting around the stalemate. Purchasing found an equipment vendor willing to rent the required automation equipment. Fari negotiated a deal with manufacturing that Fari's group would pay an additional transfer price to manufacturing representing any difference between the improved productivity attributable to the new equipment and its rental cost. This agreement was dependent upon Fari getting approval from both his boss and from accounting; with some additional time and effort, he got those sign-offs.

In this example, Fari had to work through a number of interdependencies to assess what was really happening. He didn't rely on the usual vague and meaningless explanations concerning intergroup jealousies and employee ineptness. His approach wasn't based simply on analyzing data; it required good working relationships with a variety of knowledgeable specialists. He then developed a creative approach to the problem (again, involving working through issues with others and behavioral skill) and assumed the difficult task of selling this to the staff and line personnel whose approval was necessary.

It would have been more tempting to many managers to pressure manufacturing to work harder, or to get engineering to redesign the pump for somewhat lower efficiency. These approaches neatly compartmentalize the manager's responsibilities from those of others and shift the problem to the latter—in classic GAMP fashion, looking for a culprit.

Fari, however, was able to view the complex interdependencies, and he searched out a systems solution. From his point of view, the time and effort was justified because of his strategy to make this new, small pump the first product in a family of pumps that would have superior performance and put the company ahead of its competition. It was important to make the pump a market success *and* to build the technical and organizational infrastructure to support future products in this new line.

It is worth noting that the troubleshooting on the new pump was but one of a number of continuing responsibilities Fari faced and that required time and concentration. Therefore, all of these actions and interactions had to interweave with other pressing affairs. (In the next chapter, a description of several hours in a manager's day will show the dispersed, fragmented, and time-pressured work life that is the result.)

What are the critical leadership challenges?

In part suggested by this example, but also by many of the cases presented earlier, one can see that the primary challenges for systems-oriented managers (like Fari, above, and Kay Cohen in chapter 9) are the following:

- Comprehending the interrelationship of technology and people issues
- Managing upward (convincing bosses to give approval)
- Managing peers (almost-continuous negotiations and accepting the reality that there is always inadequate authority; many problem solutions lie outside the manager's sphere of authority; now called the "teamwork" issue)
- Accepting the reality that the boundary separating the boss's job from the subordinate's job is permeable
- Engaging in continuous trade-offs, in contrast to fixed rules and decision coefficients (including the needs of one's own division in relation to the larger organization)

These five behavioral and analytical skills extend from major change projects to much more everyday efforts to adapt systems to cope with internal and external customer complaints, technical flaws, and improvement ideas. A manager who seeks accomplishment in contrast to avoiding blame (and proving that someone else is at fault) has to be prepared to handle these on an everyday basis.

PEOPLE AND TECHNOLOGY ISSUES ARE ALWAYS ENTANGLED

What is easy to lose sight of is that these efforts devoted to making the system work almost all involve relationships with people. Although the subject is often technical and most of the issues that are debated are impersonal, the process of problem solving is rarely one of isolated analysis and calculation. Management is working with people—the cliché is correct—but primarily it is *working with people in a context of technical, not people issues.*

Regrettably, many managers seek reductionist answers to problems: the source is "poor interpersonal chemistry," "poor communications," "intergroup jealousy," or "poor motivation." Unwilling or unable to dig more deeply, they never understand the dimensions of what is disabling the work process. Of course, there are personnel issues of equity, selection, and outside family or community problems affecting the work world. But most of the problem solving, my research suggests, is over coordination and integration issues, either seeking to improve things or keeping the work process from deteriorating.

People and technology are tightly intertwined. For every technical interface problem (jobs that don't complement each other), there are a whole host of intertwined "people" problems that must be untangled if the technical contradiction is going to be resolved, and vice versa. For many (although surely not all) people problems, there is an underpinning of systems/technology friction or incompatibility. What is usually called a "personality conflict" or "intergroup squabbling" usually has real job coordination and cooperation issues as its base. (Many of the situations described in the previous chapter played themselves out as interpersonal and intergroup conflicts.)

The complexities of work itself, the technology, and the systems need to be a major focus of leadership, because these have become such a problematical part of the manager's job. But focusing on work process does not mean the long-outdated task of holding people to the grindstone of tough-minded work standards (in contrast to only being concerned with their welfare). Rather, the people challenges are grounded in the technology. Careers and responsibilities grow out of the organization's work systems.

Technology and Business Issues Intertwined

Only with the perspective of a manager can technology and business issues become integrated. (Later, the reader will also see that there needs to be an integration with strategy.) By this, I mean that the manager ought to view the whole process by which a number of jobs and functions are coordinated to produce a product (or elements of a product) or a service. Having this understanding of what it takes to get "things out the door" effectively (in terms of efficiency, quality, safety and so forth), it is the line manager who can evaluate whether the technology is working and/or how new technologies can be adapted to serve the interests of the work process.

For the most part, these issues are not confronted directly by many managers. As I have said, there is a long tradition of separating technology from management. Technology gets handled by special departments like data processing and information systems, technology planning, industrial engineering, and outside consultants.

Coordination Problems of Contracting Out

The most frequent result is that great investments are made in attractive, state-of-the-art technology that does little to lower costs or to increase quality or response time to customers.[2] Prepackaged technology can't be tacked on to an ongoing operation. Senior management is often naive when it assumes that when a contractor offers a price that appears to be lower than what some operation costs to perform internally, there will be clear and obvious savings. The case below explains why the savings may never materialize.

Like many other companies in its industry, Company X decided to contract out one of its critical data processing activities in an effort to reduce costs. Because the vendor was handling this work for a large number of similar customers, it claimed its economies of scale would save X a substantial amount.

The manager in charge of the activity that had to coordinate with this about-to-be-contracted-out function was not involved in evaluating the vendor, nor in writing the contract. This manager soon discovered that the contract failed to require the vendor to handle many apparently minor details that were, in fact, critical to the manager's work flow. Further, the vendor (not surprisingly) insisted on handling Company X's work exactly the same way it handled similar work for other firms in that industry. X had pioneered in developing technology that automated a number of its other operations, however, all of which were related to the contracted-out work. Almost none of the standard practices of the vendor were consistent with this new technology. The manager thus faced the choice between abandoning several million dollars of hardware and software (and the internal efficiencies and higher quality service that these provided) or finding some way of negotiating changes in the contracted-for services.

Fortunately the manager, although not a computer professional, was intimately familiar with the technology needs of her unit and persevered in negotiating with the vendor. Eventually she was able to convince the vendor that it had something to gain in accommodating her needs

90

(in being better prepared for other companies who would likely improve their internal technologies in the coming years).

Without the weeks of persuasion and negotiation led by this energetic manager, the clumsy tying together of the vendor's servicing to Company X operations would have cost many times the presumed savings of this new contract. (Regrettably, most U.S. managers would not believe that they had the authority to question the contractor's methods as long as the formal contract terms were being satisfied.)

MANAGING UPWARD: GOING AGAINST THE GRAIN

Managers seeking to exercise leadership devote substantial energies to identifying the consequential defects in existing work routines and methods or the potential for major improvements contingent upon changing well-established usually uniform staff standards and proce-dures. The most pressing items on their personal agendas are these reorganization/change programs. Most, however, will require tacit or formal permission from upper management. Usually these re-quests are not met with enthusiasm; they appear to involve risk and exposure to the approving manager, they may aggravate key staff groups whose standards have to bend, and they require time and effort to evaluate. (As noted in chapter 3, interest in the "bottom line" is more verbal than behavioral.) They are almost certain to challenge well-established practices and threaten some people's sta-tus or turf.

Most consequential efforts to eliminate the sources of productivity and quality problems or to take advantage of some new market or technology window of opportunity require "shaking up" the existing organization, as well as undoing or challenging existing practices. They inevitably release a cascade of new and difficult coordination problems as previously interlocked interfaces become unlocked. To most upper-level managers, these initiations come as an unwelcome surprise, contrary to the conventional wisdom that management em-braces change. In part, they don't expect middle managers to concep-tualize systemic change that goes significantly beyond the initiator's jurisdiction and authority. Moreover, they expect reports and deference, not pressures on themselves for action.

Thus, these leaders have to be prepared to engage in carefully documented and repeated initiations to their bosses, most of which will have career risks and be stressful. The effectiveness of these persuasions depends on the leaders' previous track record for performance and an ability to document their proposals in a way that demonstrates an intimate and complete knowledge of the systems they are managing.[3] Work leaders often have to build strategic alliances with other groups to obtain the critical mass that gets converted into political clout.

NEGOTIATING WITH PEERS: INFLUENCE WITHOUT AUTHORITY

Intrinsic to this style of leadership is a ready acceptance of the responsibility that extends substantially beyond the limits of one's authority. At least in a larger organization, most consequential improvements or elimination of embedded quality, service, or efficiency problems cause one to tread on others' turf.

There is almost no way of achieving accomplishment without obtaining interrelated changes in many other areas over which the manager has no authority to bring to bear. Almost all of the modifications, shifts, and changes that managers undertake to improve work flows, service, and quality require the active collaboration of other units not under their control.

Too many managers shrink from dealing with problems or opportunities that aren't squarely in their own ballpark. In addition, they rarely seek to improve the performance of other parts of the organization. The following brief conversation may seem familiar to many readers.

> *Bill*: Ellen, I don't know why you are proposing to accounting that if they get their software modified, we can start getting completely accurate finished data to them two days earlier. To do what you are talking about will turn this place upside down for weeks until we get those new procedures debugged. And we wouldn't have to do that if you hadn't thought up that so-called improvement that will show up in lowering *their* costs, not ours. Do you just like trouble?

Ellen: But it isn't that hard to do. We'll learn some things from being forced to tie those data flows together better. It's a direction I want to move in, and after all, we are part of the same company. It's a good challenge for us.

Most managers are only comfortable when their authority equals their responsibility, like the old textbooks say. They have adapted well to training and role models that emphasize blinders. They've learned from GAMP to stay within their own compartments. But this strategy makes for a static organization, and it is what is probably responsible for the results described earlier in the PAE industry. The managers in each company playing catch-up did what they were supposed to do. The problems of adaptation, however, were like simultaneous equations; they could only be solved when managers engaged in extended give-and-take and mutual responsiveness over time, as they learned what worked and what didn't work.

Challenging Powerful Staff Groups

Managers have to be prepared to challenge the decisions of powerful staff groups. These usually involve the latter's power and standards that they seek to enforce. Many of the issues that will arise do not allow for everyone to benefit or to feel that they are "winners." Also, it is easy to be intimidated when higher-level staff often have real clout and easier access to top management. The following is an illustrative example from a large service company.

> Betty was a hard-driving manager in charge of a sales phone center. Against the judgment of the company's telecommunications group, she had purchased new automated voice-response equipment to handle night and weekend calls. The equipment she had selected had many advantages over the competition. Unfortunately, when her new unit was shipped, the vendor was in transition to new software, and the unit did not perform up to the guaranteed specifications.
>
> Betty had established good relations with the vendor's regional sales manager and had been assured that it would live up to its agreement. He was planning to bring in an engineer who would seek to modify the new units accordingly. But in the meantime, Telecommunications

had heard of the performance problem. Their manager insisted that his group was responsible for the corporation's technology, and he would "throw the book" at the vendor.

From Betty's point of view, this was a real threat. His involvement was an effort to claim jurisdiction over the equipment selection and servicing. Further, Betty had learned enough about the vendor to know that a major confrontation and threats would simply delay the correction, because it would bring new levels of management into the situation.

Betty spent an anxious several days insisting to her boss and to Telecommunications that her unique requirements justified her contracting for the equipment. Her previous purchases all worked superbly, and this problem was close to solution. But she knew that the head of Telecommunications took this as a very unfriendly act.

Effective Lateral Negotiations

To have new proposals and projects taken seriously by peers, a manager has to gain credibility. Again, substantial technical and interpersonal skills are required. Perhaps the most important is earning the reputation for reliability and integrity. The following characteristics can help in this endeavor:

1. Really knowing the technology of the operation— instead of bluffing or exaggerating, having solid data that backs up the needed change. It helps to be able to demonstrate this knowledge by verbal presentations and written documents.
2. Having a track record of being responsive and accommodative to peers in situations that have some cost to the manager (giving aid to outsiders for which there is no return to the giver). Always fulfilling personal commitments.
3. Being able to develop some easy give-and-take relationship over time that allows peers to know (and, it is hoped, come to respect) one's basic honesty, sincerity, and decency—in short, one's character. To do this, managers have to take the time to develop some reasonable frequency of interaction with peers. This means taking time to see them when there is *no* problem or urgent necessity.
4. Standing up to criticism and threats and intimidation.

DELEGATION AND THE SEPARATION OF LEVELS

Nonleader managers have a straightforward and logically simple—but misguided—view of hierarchy. For them, there is a clear-cut line separating levels (bosses' work versus subordinates' work), just as there is a nice, neat line separating the work of two departments or two specialists. Unfortunately, delegation cannot be a simple binary decision answering the question, "Who does it, the superior or the subordinate?" (Of course, trade unions may still insist on this for supervisors, but this book is addressed to managers.)

Delegation is not a *decision* about who does what; rather, it is a *process.* The dividing line between boss and subordinate needs to be a highly penetrable boundary. There are (and should be) many ambiguities as to when and where the manager should intervene, and part of the continuing responsibility of the manager is knowing when and how to intervene.

Managers need skill in being involved, in being hands-on managers in ways that preserve the motivation and sense of responsibility of their subordinates. This means that their broader access and credibility to outsiders, and sometimes their greater experience and their knowledge of the larger strategy, can facilitate their subordinates' accomplishing the tasks for which they have responsibility.

Thus, the working leader (or action-oriented manager) does *not* second-guess the subordinate nor require approval of decisions before they are implemented. Rather, manager and subordinate become partners in solving the more intractable problems blocking effective performance, particularly those that require influencing a wider network of participants. Such managers invest heavily in training, helping subordinates see the web of interdependencies that influence their performance. As a subordinate demonstrates increased capability and understanding of the technology and the systems and can both be responsive to peers and get them to adapt to their job needs, the frequency of the manager's involvement diminishes.

Working leaders, however, do not allow their relationships to be limited largely to reviewing performance results. The great quantity of unwritten, finely nuanced, and ambiguous information that managers collect and absorb almost randomly every day gives them a large and critical body of data, opinions, and guesstimates that often are very relevant to a particular subordinate work problem or challenge. Because this information is such a rich stew of real data and judgment, it can't easily be communicated in training for greater delegation of responsibility.

If this isn't to be wasted, the manager needs to provide many inputs to her subordinates in addition to charging them with duties and responsibilities and giving them direction. It is one of the critical elements of being a leader to introduce this knowledge, insight, and judgment in ways that neither belittle nor disenfranchise subordinates.

> A manufacturing supervisor discovered that one particular specification led to unanticipated fabrication problems during the start-up phase of a new product. She sought to get engineering design to reconsider and then to do some redesigning. When her manager heard about this, he intervened, realizing that the issue was more complex than the supervisor knew. The particular specification represented a new thrust by engineering and was not likely to be modified; however, there were other elements of the component's design that, if changed, would make the fabrication of the troublesome element easier. And the manager knew that the way to get those other changes considered in the best possible light was to go to a new group that had just been formed in engineering to handle interfunctional problems.

There are a great many problems facing managers for which they need hands-on experience. This usually does not mean doing operating tasks themselves, but it does mean having direct contact with the supervisors who are close to the work.

Using Participation and Empowerment

Of course, good managers structure work so that many coordination problems are handled by subordinates. Managers who don't delegate and design organizations so that important trade-offs can be made by those closest to the work (or within the head of one individual) are setting themselves up for failure. No manager can possibly deal with all or most of the coordination issues that occur daily, because interfaces are not clear-cut. The manager must depend on subordinates engaging in ongoing trade-offs to facilitate coordination.

Much current management training emphasizes the values to be obtained by tapping employee knowledge and initiative. Managers are encouraged to accept some diminution in their own power as subordinates make more decisions for themselves. Human resource departments often bolster these efforts by helping to train employees to take more initiative and even to assume some leadership roles, for example, in quality and safety programs.

But all of these formal and informal programs neglect the dynamic role that working leaders can play. For them, subordinate involvement is an *interactive, ongoing process*. It is not a special program. These bits and pieces of superior-subordinate dialogue suggest the nature of that process:

> *(To a subordinate)* Jerry, we're getting lots of these returned unopened and damaged. What can be done to cut our losses here?

> *(To a subordinate)* That idea you came up with last week, Helen, is proving to be a godsend. I think we've already cut the time it takes us to get out those reports by three days. What we still don't know how to do is to handle the special requests that come from marketing; those seem to throw lots of other things off while we're trying to get data together. Whenever you've got some free time, I would appreciate your ideas on how to approach that painful situation. Maybe there isn't any more we can do, but I want your best judgment on this.

> *(To a subordinate)* I like what you've done on getting those new standard letters into our files, but I think several have the same problem. Some of the terminology comes across as too abstract and forbidding. Can you make them sound more personal and friendly?

> *(To a manager)* Glad I ran into you. I have been looking at that new design we got in from the development people. Unless we find some way to simplify it, it's going to be a life's work for all of us. If we could get them to modify the requirement that every unit we sell has to be able to use this module, limiting it to the "super" line, the whole thing becomes manageable. What do you think? Can you push them to do that?

Components of an Interactive Delegation

Implicit in these "sound bites" of conversation are these critical leadership elements:

1. The manager has technical knowledge and judgment to contribute to the problem's solution.

2. "Answers" involve an admixture of manager and subordinate ideas and knowledge, formed in an interactive process. The synthesis is superior to what either could accomplish alone. Participation is not viewed primarily as a motivational technique but rather as an essential channel by which more senior managers learn about the realities and the operating details of the work situation.

3. The manager's broader purview and contacts provide essential inputs to problem solving. At the same time, the manager encourages subordinate initiative and creative solutions to problems. This praise is always more meaningful when it is given by a knowledgeable superior who knows the system and the technology. Praise by naive supervisors is discounted frequently as blatant manipulation.

4. Many times the interaction will be spontaneous; no scheduled meetings may be involved. A chance contact or close proximity gives the opportunity to start talking about an obvious and persisting technical problem. Alternately, seeing a problem at about the same time one sees a trusted subordinate (or boss) may encourage the exploration.

5. The interaction serves to diminish the status gap or barrier that normally separates boss and subordinate. In these situations, they are discussing technical problems on roughly equal grounds. Both bring some expertise to the table; each needs the other to complement what they know or can do. Insofar as the interaction involves the boss praising the subordinate, it is in the context of one technical expert admiring the contribution of another technical expert. Such relatively power-free interactions serve to improve the relationship.

6. Most interactions are a composite of several managerial actions. First, the manager is seeking to tap the technical knowledge and insight of the subordinate. The contact also can provide an opportunity for the subordinate to "control" his manager, in contrast to the more typical managerial initiation and control. Moreover, the underlying quality of the give-and-take provides alert managers with some control information: the subordinate's morale, difficulties he is experiencing, and his understanding of the manager's strategy. (Only by dealing with these objectives simultaneously can a busy manager do all of the things required to get through the day.)

Facilitating Empowerment. The manager's most important contribution to participation and empowerment is the adroit use of influence. Many of the ideas, proposals, and problems that subordinates come up with require others to change. The others may be more senior managers who have enunciated a policy, or a peer group with a fixed way of doing things. To be most workable, many of the initiatives of subordinates need complementary changes on the part of others, and the manager often can be useful in obtaining these.

One of the most important contributions of the manager to subordinate empowerment can be in negotiating change with outsiders. Managers who are willing to accept the career risks and time and energy demands of doing this gain esteem from their subordinates. Contrariwise, those who play it safe lose respect because of their unwillingness to represent and fight for their people. Good leaders build *partnerships* with subordinates in which they combine their knowledge and their respective needs, given their differing vantage points.

Interactive Delegation Is Not Micromanagement. It is important to distinguish this process-oriented, dynamic view of delegation from what is sometimes called "micromanaging." There are managers who are fearful of subordinate decision making, who insist on being consulted on every decision and also usually prohibit their subordinates from having direct contact with outsiders. Everything is centralized in that manager's office, to the total detriment of the subordinates' development and effectiveness.

ONGOING TRADE-OFFS RATHER THAN STATIC ANSWERS

The management required by the turbulent managerial context described in the preceding chapters is one of continuous balancing and making trade-offs. This is far different from the search of the GAMP-trained manager for enduring rules or formula-based answers ("just tell me what it means for the bottom line").

Inconsistencies. The managers in the Ames Company (chapter 5) needed to recognize that they would have a continuing series of tough trade-offs to balance the legitimate, but conflicting needs of the two interdependent products. Decision making is going to be highly interactive, time-consuming, and painful, because most choices will involve sacrifices for one or the other manager. There can be no good formula-based answers, nor answers based on the relative status or power of the managers.

Broad, Not Narrow Systems. It is tempting for managers to compartmentalize problems and responsibilities. After all, specialization and neatly divided job jurisdictions are at the heart of GAMP and management training. But as was illustrated by the competitive revolving door in the PAE industry, most work problems or opportunities are not neatly bounded. What appears to be a simple matter of adding a new Y-type component to the Z activator, for example, requires almost every manager to reconfigure in some way what they are doing. Marketing issues affect operations; product development affects manufacturing; and sales affect customer service. It is obviously tempting (and easier) to segment neatly and correlate problem X with department X, but it is totally inconsistent with the inherent interdependencies of real work systems.

Mine and Theirs. The more obvious reward systems and management practices, unfortunately, encourage managers to identify primarily with their part of the business. At that point, there is a comfortable association of personal career interests and task clarity. Assuming leadership, however, requires managers to keep rebalancing the legitimate needs of their own areas with the needs of the larger system.

Successful working leaders will struggle with their own senior managers, as well as with peers, to obtain and maintain the resources and policies they need to be effective at what their people are supposed to do. Such struggles are necessary and require leadership, because priorities in resource allocations and decisions about which manager is "right" can't be made by a scientific calculus.

> The centralized systems group was insisting that the department purchase automatic call directors (to route incoming phone calls) that were manufactured by Company X, because it was convinced these were the most cost-efficient. A manager with one of the largest incoming-call volumes had surveyed alternative vendors and found a manufacturer, less famous than the one

favored by the centralized support group, that was
selling equipment with many features that were more
relevant to his needs than the X brand. It took five
months of careful presentations and many statistical
studies to get approval to deviate from the central staff's
recommendation, but the result was an increase of
productivity of 65 percent. This was close to double
what could have been attained had the more favored
company's product been chosen, but the manager had to
be willing to wage a time-consuming battle that seemed
endless at the time.

At other times, however, leadership requires that managers concede
to initiatives from outside that will make their own jobs more difficult and their goal attainment more problematic. These are instances
where there clear benefits to the larger system that outweigh paro-
chial concerns. Obviously, many such assessments represent subjec-
tive calculations rather than objective facts, but highly motivated
managers seek to maintain some sensible balance between what is
needed for unit integrity and the needs of the larger organization. A
hallmark of leadership is the ability to make these continuing trade-
offs in a way that reflects the reality of the situation, the needs of
the smaller system for which one is responsible (to maintain internal
integrity), and the needs of larger and/or adjacent systems to which
one also owes a commitment.

Poor leaders always opt for one or the other: either they consistently suboptimize (making themselves look good or saving themselves effort), or they always opt for what their boss or a powerful
peer wants (avoiding any possibility of being considered disloyal or
insubordinate). Maintaining a leadership position requires the manager to accept the inherent contradictions that will occur between
the requirements for internal integrity and the legitimate demands of
adjacent departments and the larger organization.

FLEXIBILITY

The opposite of a bureaucratic style, obviously, is an adaptive, flexible style. But what does that mean in practice? There are limits to
the amount of flexibility a manager can demonstrate. Understanding

these limitations is useful in answering the question of what it means to become "more flexible."

Without reasonable routinization, predictability, and continuity, a manager couldn't cope with the normal day, which is filled with demands, incidents, and problems (and opportunities). There is usually just too much going on in a dynamic organization for the manager to respond to every stimulus in a creative fashion meticulously tailored to the uniqueness of the situation.

Thus, managers have to rely on some standardized responses. They have learned which ones work for them, given their personalities, their style of management, and the culture of their organization. Situations that threaten substantial punishment (cost, disappointment, embarrassment) or gain deserve attention and the application of flexibility. Similarly, observed anomalies ought to be addressed with flexibility; these are situations in which the manager's predictions or expectations (usually based on past experience) are not fulfilled. This ought to alert the manager that some unknown, new, and potentially threatening (or rewarding) situational factor is present.

Many managers do not easily shift from routine to flexible responses when anomalies appear or high risk/reward factors are present. Too many continue with their well-programmed and rigid behavior.

In 1987, the Food and Drug Administration summarily dashed the hopes of Genentech that TPA, its genetically engineered drug to dissolve blood clots, would be approved for sale in the United States.[4]

Several years before, the firm had been advised to submit TPA to the FDA Office of Biologics for approval, rather than to the Office of Drugs. The former had handled earlier blood clot dissolvers; it would be their task to evaluate the manufacturing methods and help the company plan tests of safety and effectiveness. The Biologics office led Genentech to believe that it would not need to undertake arduous, long-term studies of the effect of TPA on patient mortality. Genentech only would be required to provide medical evidence of the effectiveness of TPA.

By 1986, there were already indications that the Office of Drugs was not happy at being excluded from the approval process for genetically engineered drugs. (It was by far the larger and more influential unit within the agency.) In short order, it presented Genentech with a very long list of questions challenging the clinical methods and results of previous tests and was very critical of the fact that there was little evidence that the drug's use significantly altered mortality rates.

According to the Wall Street Journal's researchers, Genentech felt that these questions were either a rehash of questions they had already answered for the Office of Biologics or ones they didn't have to answer at that point. Another drug firm executive felt that this was a naive response: "[We] constantly ask the FDA people if the studies we're doing are enough or correctly designed. They change their minds a lot, and every company with experience knows that." Genentech's determination to continue along its path didn't falter, and this may have led to its initial failure to get FDA approval for general distribution of TPA.

Rigid managers often have an "illusion of control." In almost a religious fashion, these managers can be reassured by the aggregated data they receive in their periodic reports; perhaps more so now that these are often computer generated.

In one large company, a senior manager, Gomez with a good deal of technical sophistication was reviewing the performance of a critical operating unit with its manager. The manager, Jones, described the unit's performance as excellent, and for evidence he pointed to one key statistic in the monthly report. Gomez was dismayed when he noted that the critical statistic represented an invariant proportion of another number, and when he pointed this out the subordinate scoffed at the "coincidence."

In tracing it down with the help of programmers who examined the underlying software, Gomez discovered that the number that gave so much reassurance was absolutely meaningless. When the report format had been designed and then programmed, the designers had not been able to find a way to automate the collection of data that would produce that particular statistic, so they essentially created a dummy variable. They had that number appear as a fixed percentage of another number (which was real). The manager, with such faith in his computer printouts, never noticed its predictable variation.

More flexible managers constantly search for new, fresh methods to probe the functioning of the systems for which they are responsible. They ask different kinds of questions; they take every opportunity to query people who have something to do with the system (customers, vendors, and employees, among others). They are continuously alert to the possibility that some new, unpredicted factor will threaten performance or improve performance. They want to identify such unintended change early enough to do something about it.

> A marketing manager with one of the major railroads rejected the request of a company that wanted the line to build a spur line to its plant. The rejection was based on the railroad's formula for such decisions, which required that the construction cost pay for itself within a relatively short period by increased freight loadings. The manager was overruled by a superior, who felt sure that this particular company was expanding so rapidly in the railroad's territory that substantial increased business would be generated by the goodwill created. It might take some years, but the company was certain to be a good customer of the line.

Flexible managers are superb at ingesting large quantities—and, more importantly, diverse quantities—of information, data, insights, and suggestions. They probe multiple sources and are able to interrelate technical, political, personal, and economic data in ways that are focused on their own business needs. The following example depicts a flexible manager in a company making components for portable computers:

> I recently read that liquid-crystal display (LCD) demand is going up more rapidly than most companies had anticipated. Since most of our major customers require these, I can imagine some of these companies having component supply problems in the months to come. I am going to check whether we have adequate measures of our customers' vulnerability to supply shortages and how quickly their pro-

duction could be interrupted and, in turn, cause cancellation of our components. I have learned in the past that orders on the books don't mean much when customers' businesses run into trouble, and therefore you have to do more than simply look at what the numbers say.

This is a very simple example of a manager seeking to integrate diverse kinds of data and to do some extrapolations to identify possible future problems requiring an intervention.

Leadership Trade-Offs: Dynamic Balancing

There is no way to provide static job responsibilities or technology specifications in most contemporary dynamic organizations. There need to be nimble real-time accommodations. For example, in the Ames case (chapter 5), in which two organizationally adjacent units each produced outputs necessary for the other manager to complete his or her work, each manager has to carefully rebalance short- and long-run considerations with some frequency. When are the longer-run needs of product B (for investment dollars, for software specifications, or for using scarce engineering talent) excessively interfering with the short- run needs of product A? And when does A's long-run needs for new models (with their attendant engineering investments) interfere with B's short-run needs to fix an apparent systems defect?

This balancing of short and long term, and one's own needs versus those of an interrelated other organizational unit, all require a leader's continuous judgment. It is far easier (and tempting) to assume that one can make a fixed decision, for example, that A will get these resources and work to this fixed plan and B will get those other resources and meet appropriate specifications. Not only will the managers of A and B find this easier (and more likely to reduce stress), but their common boss will also be tempted to measure them solely by such criteria. A short definition of leadership could be someone who refuses to get locked into formula answers.

Phil Perez was a middle manager working in film manufacturing. Because he was working late, he overheard a supervisor telling a coating crew that they were to dump a batch of newly produced emulsion. In response to Perez's shock at the waste, the supervisor pointed out that he had no choice. There was absolutely

no approved paper stock available to coat with the fresh
emulsion, and company rules prescribed that only
quality-tested stock could be coated. Quickly calculating
that there would be little additional cost to wasting
emulsion-coated stock that did not meet quality standards
than in throwing away the emulsion itself, Perez sought
a way of obtaining untested stock.

In a brief time, he discovered that there was no way to
get the stock released from its manufacturing area
without a signed approval form, and that all the forms
were locked in the office of the manager for production
control. Perez had the supervisor get a watchman with a
key to that office. As luck would have it, the forms were
locked in the manager's desk. Perez forced the desk lock
himself, however, and left a note. He got the appropriate
approval form that the paper stock area would accept. He
took full responsibility for violating a number of rules.

In contrast, the GAMP manager presumes that careful planning, explicitly defining all the parameters in advance, establishing goals,
and waiting to judge results is all that leaders do!

Creativity

These balancing and judgment decisions can be considered creative
because the manager is using improvisation, freshness, and often
quite original reconceptualizations of the problem to find answers
that are relevant to broadly understood issues. Managers need to
integrate information from diverse sources, including a knowledge
of people, of technology, of organizational culture, and of current
strategies. Rather than using tried and true solutions, simplistic max-
imizations, or well-honed and comfortable decision rules, creative
managers adopt and adapt methods of analysis suited to the unique
features of the problem. Knowing that there is no right answer or,
in most cases, even an answer that will endure, they seek to integrate
a variety of interests with their particular goals and strategies. (The
strategic issues are discussed in chapter 8.)

Managers are being highly creative when they are able to see significant patterns in diffuse, tangled data and information. As many
have noted, the skill of problem *finding* is perhaps more important
than that of problem solving. And problem finding depends upon

uncovering trends, patterns, and interrelationships when they are not readily apparent to others. Often, noting new anomalies in the functioning of systems (both inside and outside) and following up on surprises (where things are not as the manager predicted) are primary sources of creative insight.

Coping with Ambiguity

Handling the inherent uncertainties and trade-offs in managing systems involves the manager in coping with ambiguity. Decision making is discomforting when it is not based on simple data crunching. Ambiguities are always stressful, and the ones managers face also provide substantial career risks. As nature abhors vacuums, most managers abhor ambiguity.

But ambiguity is inevitable in modern, diversified organizations, where change continuously upsets the desired coordination among the specialized parts. It is therefore discouraging to read research findings concluding that many managers either fail to recognize these uncertainties or become incapacitated in the face of ambiguity.[5]

LEADERSHIP LEGITIMACY AND TECHNICAL COMPETENCE

Most of the cases in this and the preceding chapters deal with effectiveness. But leaders also need recognition and credibility to survive and flourish. Working leaders have to challenge conventional wisdom and the hierarchy and often go against the grain of accepted norms, rocking boats that don't like being rocked. They frequently must go up against powerful staff groups (who have standardized policies and procedures) and functional peers.

Their energy, assertiveness and initiative can easily be misperceived as pushiness, arrogance, or unwillingness to be a "team player." Persistence can be transmuted by peers into the belief their colleague is just stubborn. Bosses often see these managers as difficult or troublesome. Women and other minorities probably are most vulnerable to this kind of misperception and to attributions of excessive aggressiveness or other negative characteristics.[6]

What inhibits these misperception is technical competence. Managers with in-depth knowledge of their operations and the capacity to document the issues (and the potential solutions) verbally and in writing earn respect from peers, even though it may be grudgingly given. And intelligent senior management bestows legitimacy on managers who are truly well informed and can document well their requests for change and resources.[7]

CONCLUSION

Naive managers or those seeking to exchange comforting simplicity for reality perceive jobs and tasks as neatly fitting together "if everyone does what they are supposed to do." More sophisticated managers see a wealth of fluid complexity. Efforts to interlink tasks into effective systems are complicated by a wide range of communication linkages and patterns of give-and-take, by conventional and unconventional rules and norms, and by an intricately patterned set of mutual expectations. Even slight changes in work processes, technology, or even people can have profound implications for work flows and the boundary between jobs.

Managers need to seek an understanding of what is required for effective coordination and for systems maintenance. Without this knowledge, a whole range of quality, productivity, and implementation of change problems are undiagnosable. The leadership component, again, is a balancing act—balancing the need for some intimate detail with the need to back away from a level of involvement that would interfere with other managerial responsibilities.

Teamwork Versus Standing Alone

Although consensus- and team-building skills are critical for managers, at times one will be left standing alone. The systems one is coordinating and maintaining will be threatened by a staff group's ill-advised rule or standard or by another department's new initiative. Working leaders have to take on the burdensome responsibility of tough negotiations and persistent demands that the other party modify its decision. Obviously not all of these will be won, and some efforts will be ill-advised, but managers who are serious about making things work are going to have to balance their role as a good team player with their role as an advocate of effectiveness.

This conflict can often be observed in departments that are best able to view the needs of the customer. Many departments will seek to change product standards or designs for what are logical reasons, but the result will degrade the company's product or service from the vantage point of the customer. Customer advocates, even in companies that are serious about customer satisfaction as being the primary goal, have their work cut out for them if they are going to maintain the integrity of the system that delivers that satisfaction.

It is both ironic and destructive that managers, for the most part, have not been trained to assume responsibility for the effectiveness of work systems. As the reader has seen, contemporary organizations are much more vulnerable to coordination failure than were more traditional, more routinized businesses. Although the failure may not be as apparent as in the PAE industry or telephone-company examples described in earlier chapters, organizational miscoordinations are still consequential for efficiency, quality, successful innovation, and failures in customer responsiveness and service.

Most Quick Fixes Fail

Most companies keep looking for "magic bullets" in new and restructured forms of organization and new, consultant-based programs. Managers, however, ought to be the first line of attack, not the last. They are best able to see the interrelationships of tasks, functions, and controls. Most externally imposed "fixes" are clumsy and ill-fitting to the real work that needs to be accomplished and even destructive of effectiveness. Good managers should know their internal needs, their external customers, and how to resolve the continuing work dilemmas and inconsistencies.

United States management has neglected to enfranchise its managers as working leaders. Yet U.S. culture encourages personal initiative, the challenging of conventional wisdom, and the development of creative solutions to the inevitable conflicts and contradictions that bedevil competitively pressured, change-oriented modern technology.

The kind of leadership described here, however, also takes personal courage. Being realistic, business organizations (for the most part) do not welcome the lower-level initiatives that require rethinking standards, procedures, and established ways of working. Both powerful staff groups and other functional peers are likely to resent leaders' pressures upon them to modify their routines or organization-wide standards. These managers know that theirs is a high-risk sense of responsibility.

There is little recognition of how crucial (and rare) are those action-oriented leaders who place their own career interests second and who do not limit there concerns and energies to their own organizational units. More typical are conventional blinders that limit the manager's purview to what is straight ahead and inside the chart box; this is the best way of maximizing personal scores on whatever accounts are being kept. Astute managers without the leadership strengths described here find irresistible the temptation to shift problems as well as costs to adjacent departments. (The analysis of the role of senior management in chapter 11 deals with its contribution to encouraging or discouraging work leadership.)

7

High Performance as a Source of Motivation

Most leadership models presume that high motivation causes high performance. It seems almost obvious that if the manager can find well-motivated (high inner drive) subordinates and then bring the best out in them, the result will be excellent performance.

But it may well be that this seemingly logical model has cause and effect reversed. Employees involved in high-performance settings are more likely to be motivated than those working in average or mediocre organizations. *Being part of an effective work organization is motivating.*[1]

In many of the cases cited in this book, it is apparent that employees who see that their manager can create a high-performance environment gain enthusiasm and commitment. This, in turn, causes performance to ratchet up still further: "[It] may be that high performance creates a cohesive and enthusiastic culture as much as the other way around."[2]

WHY PERFORMANCE CREATES MOTIVATION

This "other way around" should not be surprising. Successful organizations are less likely to have managers looking for culprits and nagging for improvements in output. With high performance comes less need for unpleasant manager-subordinate confrontations over work issues. In departments and work units that meet their performance

111

goals, employees are less likely to feel "put upon" or "left holding the bag" for poor output or quality. And, on the positive side, they are more likely to derive satisfaction from being part of a "winning team." And this can be very satisfying.

Absent, meanwhile, is the kind of cynicism that flourishes when managers tolerate poor quality or service or performance.

> As one employee told me many years ago in an auto plant: Why should I bust my [rear] when I see the company letting cars go through with broken parts or even no parts? They don't want good work; they just want work, my sweat. Even if I give some of it, it all gets lost in the mess created by their stupidities. How can you respect bosses like that?

Fatalism Versus Active Responsibility

Working in an organization in which work problems aren't solved can produce a sense of "learned helplessness." Social psychologists have long emphasized the distinction between individuals' sense of inner control and their belief that the critical events in their life are out of their control. Not surprisingly, individuals who believe they are masters of their own fate, that they can influence outcomes, are much more likely to take responsibility than those who believe they have little or no control over what occurs.[3]

Employees who feel that their work situation is helpless—that the productivity and quality for which they can be held responsible are out of their control—may quickly lose any motivation they may have had. After telling management that performance is being injured by this or that defect in the work process and seeing that nothing happens, employees become disillusioned. Under such circumstances, management calls for higher performance are almost laughable.

Subordinates with even minimal identification with the organization resent a management that persistently ignores poor performance. Although there is little systematic evidence, it is likely that some companies may not be very energetic in dealing with marginal professionals and managers who can influence the work environment and the work systems. Often, in contrast, clerical and production workers are watched closely and disciplined when performance is subpar.

"GM is a classic example of the consequences of extended managerial in-breeding. Between 1977 and 1983, fewer than 100 salaried workers—out of well over 100,000—were dismissed annually for poor performance. If someone fails to produce results, he is usually reassigned to another location."[4] If accurate, this very low number is quite revealing, particularly given the problems that GM faced with performance during the past decade and the fact that it was not committed to long tenure for its hourly work force. Discharge is not motivating, but organizations that fail to confront serious performance problems *demotivate* employees who are committed to performance.

Empowerment

Managers who take the initiative to clear up work problems are also those who are more likely to have the personal courage to represent and defend subordinates who have been treated unfairly or who need redress that is controlled by upper management or a human resources department. It is probably naive to speak about empowering subordinates whose managers are unwilling or unable to deal with organizational impediments to high performance. Only working leaders who have the energy and the organizational skills to initiate corrective actions when there are coordination and work flow problems can expect to empower their subordinates to take more responsibility.

> *Programmer in a service organization*: My work load is enormous, and I have been given a good deal of autonomy as to how I do my work. But I just don't have any will to tackle these tough problems any longer. My management knows that the new equipment we purchased was the wrong choice, but no one has the guts to say the emperor has no clothes. As long as we're trying to program this equipment, we're never going to get anyplace.

Thus, giving employees more autonomy, authority, and encouragement—empowering them to make many decisions on their own and to assume responsibility for results—can be a hoax and appear like hypocrisy to them when managers don't assume an important role in solving work problems that involve "outsiders" (that is, bosses and peers).

Moderate Stress as a Motivator

Effective organizations are likely to have change as a constant; therefore, it is expected and not feared. Systems and technology that aren't working get replaced, and management is always looking for new ways of doing things. It is likely that the moderate stress produced by the need to keep adjusting work methods to these change is motivating.

Repetitiveness and the absence of challenge dull the senses; creative energies get focused on "fun and games" and petty coercive comparisons (about perks, work load, and personal space). The need to cope with new problems and new job requirements, in moderation, can be a stimulus to overall performance.

An Italian executive was asked, "Why has Italian business flourished in recent years in spite of the cumbersomeness of doing business in Italy, with its chaotic politics and communist trade unions?" His answer:

> Many of those obstacles encourage the businessman to be spontaneous and creative in finding ways to work around the government, even its tax policies. . . . We have all learned to be ingenious. . . . Every day comes a new challenge. And that flexibility, and alertness carries over to everything we do.

> *American executive with experience in Brazil*: "Brazil was one of our best-performing foreign subsidiaries. Given its inflation, managers every day had to rethink pricing and inventories and, of course, salaries. No one relaxed; it was a hothouse of decision making, and I think that really helped overall performance."

The ideal motivational climate is likely to be some balance between regularity, security, and predictability on the one hand and challenge, a stretch, and some uncertainty on the other.

Ambiguity versus Clarity

In the same fashion, leaders balance providing coherence and clarity with allowing a reasonable amount of ambiguity and inconsistency. Successful managers absorb (and do not transmit) most of the frustrating contradictions and provide their subordinates with a sense of reasonably clear goals and guidelines as to how to reach them. At the same time, particularly for more responsible subordinates in more complex environments, the manager needs to provide employees with the realistic context in which they have to make dynamic trade-offs and cannot rely on simple decision rules. For example:

To a sales manager: We want to hold the line on prices; otherwise we are going to get our competitors cutting prices and we will be no further ahead, even behind. You have to use your judgment on when an important customer can only be retained with some price concession. If you use this too frequently, however, I'll be unhappy.

To summarize, this table may be helpful:

Motivation Depends on Balancing

Security	*Insecurity*
Comfortable work targets	Work targets requiring stretch
Clarity in goals and decision criteria	Ambiguity; need for trade-offs

CREDIBILITY

In my earlier fieldwork in industrial plants, it was always quite evident that most employees lost confidence in managers who tolerated bad work or were not able to "fix" things so that work flows operated smoothly.[5] Subordinates become very cynical about managerial protestations of the importance of performance when nothing is done to correct poor work and poor workers. Organization researchers are never surprised that bureaucratic organizations shift blame downward (at the same time that managers seek to shift credit up the line.) Though performance is often a function of managerial/technical problems, such organizations find it easier to ignore these tough problems and seek to adjust for inherent work problems by increasing the effort expended by workers.

Supervisor in a large services company: You won't believe this. Management has been having trouble installing a new software system, and we rely on that system to access accounts and data on a minute-to-minute basis. Well, the system may have as much as two or three hours downtime in a day. You can imagine what that does to our performance. But the head of the division has been blaming low output on poor employee productivity and poor attitudes. Everyone is mad as hell.

Managers who are "out to lunch" in terms of their ability to facilitate effective performance have almost no credibility as leaders. Employees grow frustrated when their efforts to provide quality output or service are blocked by systems defects. In contrast, managers who truly understand what subordinate managers are facing and where facilitation can be useful gain enormous credibility. A recent study has sought to explain why Anders Scharp, the new CEO of Electrolux (the Swedish appliance giant), has been so successful in integrating a diverse group of European and American manufacturing groups:

> On a personal level, Scharp's keenness to get involved in strategy discussions with most of the units beneath him is legendary within Electrolux. So is his ability to judge the effectiveness of a factory layout or product design just by wandering around the plant and asking the right questions. The respect which this creates is one of the factors which has eased the integration into the group of major non-Swedish household appliance companies.[6]

An interviewee recounted a similar compliment.

> *Supervisor to a new boss*: I can't tell you how happy we all are. We've never had a manager before who took our technical problems seriously, immediately started making phone calls to other groups, and fought with upper management or those staff technical people when things were going wrong. All the managers we've had just took what they were given, even when it wasn't workable. They never wanted to stand up for us, but maybe they didn't understand the work the way you do.

This situation is quite understandable. With a boss who doesn't understand what makes things work, or how they should work and when things aren't working, subordinates get left holding the bag. They can become overwhelmed with a sense of helplessness as a result of being held responsible for performance problems but not being in a position to make a real difference.

With poor or mediocre management (at least in the United States), when profits decline or profit goals are not being met, an almost knee-jerk reaction is to blame workers and to push for higher output and lower labor costs. Employees are often blamed unfairly for low output or quality when work is badly organized, systems are breaking down, and management is inept.

A financial services company installed, with the help of consultants, a very costly new automated system for handling customer accounts. The consultants had done a poor job studying the work flow requirements of the operations involved. Further, the technology had many inherent flaws that created excessive equipment downtime. Both problems handicapped employee performance. When productivity was unsatisfactory and the projected labor cost savings not realized senior management immediately blamed employees for "not working hard enough."

Vicious Spirals

Even worse from a motivational point of view are spirals of declining effectiveness. The following is a typical example of such a self-feeding managerial debacle:

The Hanover Insurance Company would often experience an unexpected large influx of new clients from their policyholders. When these backed up, causing a rise in the "pending ratio" (and embarrassing managers who were evaluated on this number), department managers would put great pressure on their claims adjustors. Under these pressures, there were often resignations, which reduced the number of people who could work to settle claims. These, in turn, led to more pressures on the staff. Another frequent result was less careful evaluation of claims and increased claim losses that still further increased upper management's discontent. These probably would also add pressure on adjustors, further reducing their effectiveness.[7]

Nothing is more destructive of motivation than managers who fail to comprehend the system's source of work flow problems and who simply apply additional pressure downward instead of restructuring the work after identifying the source of the problem. In the insurance case above, claims adjustors needed better training. Ironically, organizations that have allowed costs to escalate and performance to decline through management ineptness are most likely to lash out against workers under new competitive pressures. This, in turn, can initiate a spiral of declining motivation, further injured performance, and further increased management pressure. Moreover, subordinates who view their bosses as being almost solely interested in how the current job will propel them to a higher level in as brief a time as possible know they will not be getting much help on performance problems.

Influence of Knowledgeable Managers

In contrast, a manager who is knowledgeable on work and technology subjects is much more likely to be able to perform a critical leadership function: facilitating the work effectiveness of subordinates, enabling them to act in what will be a rewarding fashion.[8] Such managers are much more likely to be adept at buffering their people from other staff or line departments who are making unrealistic demands. Although managerial gumption and initiative help to accomplish this, more important is the ability to mount a well-documented case as to why the outsider's request or behavior is inconsistent with technical needs or requirements.

> This is the first manager I've ever had who knew when my "plate" was full. In my experience, when your boss gets pressed on something, he pushes it down for you to do the necessary grunt work, with no thought to what you are involved in. On my last job, we were in the midst of a major technological conversion when my manager wanted some backup data for a speech she was going to give at a trade association. It took a day and a half to get that ready when we were fighting for our lives to get the system up and running.

Similarly, subordinates admire a proactive boss who gets them needed resources and is able to modify what comes into the department in ways that makes their work more doable. Often such efforts, because they have short-run political costs and take substantial managerial effort, are contrary to the immediate self-interest of the manager. But putting aside self-interest in favor of follower interests earns significant credibility points as these managers prove they can "take the heat." In addition, managers who earn a reputation for really knowing what they are talking about and for being able to explain the specifics of how an outsider may affect inside operations is more likely to win concessions when seeking to buffer or represent his or her department.

REACHING DOWN: EMPOWERMENT THROUGH INTERACTION

When the manager is interested in and knowledgeable about the technology of the operations, this facilitates day-to-day relationships with her subordinates. First, the best of such managers seek to improve their knowledge constantly by interviewing subordinates about what is actually taking place. Such discussions have many obvious relationship-building advantages over discussions of why output isn't higher, or about who messed up. Most employees savor being able to tell their boss why and how things work and what the problems are, as well as to demonstrate their own competence and commitment.

Such intimate knowledge about the realities of the work process and the technology also allow positive reinforcements to be more meaningful. It is substantially more reinforcing for a subordinate manager to be complimented in response to a significant work coup that may have involved tough negotiations with peers and/or staff experts (and retraining of subordinates) than to be congratulated on simply meeting a standard.

The continuously learning boss, in reaching down to "keep up," also allows the subordinate to play the position of instructor or expert, reversing roles by teaching the boss something. This narrows the status gap that separates the two and is very satisfying to the subordinate. Here is one manager's description:

> I now worked for a division manager who had a reputation for chewing up managers. I had been warned to avoid him. Most thought of him as someone you never spoke to unless asked a specific question, and if possible, you avoided anything controversial or negative. After I had been there about a week, he contacted me about some minor matter, and I took that as an opportunity to fill him in on some of the plans I had for overcoming some technical problems. Much to my surprise, I discovered that he was reasonably well informed on our technologies, and we had an extended exchange about what was happening currently in the department. As

long as we were discussing solely technical questions, he was a pleasure to talk to.

Only managers who have learned that the work is not perfectly preprogrammed, and that they can have control over structure and technology, can communicate sincerely to subordinates that they want to hear about problems or new solutions. Naive managers don't get told much, and their performance suffers as a result. Worse yet, when a manager makes it clear that everything has to be right because he or she planned it right, few subordinates have the temerity to bring up bad news. Many organizations have succumbed to the naive belief that things were going well because bad news was bottled up at lower levels.

In discussing technical problems on a technical level, the usual power/political/psychological barriers to full communication get lowered. It is on these technical issues that managers find it easier to have a frank one-on-one discussion.[9] Real empowerment may only occur when subordinates can openly challenge or criticize what they feel is a technically wrong decision on the part of their boss. And such empowerment is likely to occur only when both boss and subordinate can speak on comparable technical terms. Joint problem solving in which each party interacts freely, not conscious of power and status differences, builds solidarity.

Operationally, within work organizations, to be empathetic as a boss means the capacity to understand and *share* the real work frustrations of the subordinate. Managers who seek to give the impression of being empathetic (perhaps because they have been taught that is a useful supervisory tool) but who do not have an adequate technical understanding of the issues can be perceived as manipulative and insincere.

It is rare to find an employee who is not pleased when the boss or the boss's boss wants to learn how things work. They take pride in explaining what they do and why and how. Obviously, though, this pleasure is dissipated when the real reason for the inquiry is control rather than education. Only the manager who is able to build a trusting relationship with subordinates who see him or her as really facilitating their work can expect to be alerted to quality, efficiency, or service problems that threaten the integrity of the system. As one middle manager told me:

> I stayed late and began talking with one of the people who reported to my night manager. After we got done exchanging pleasantries,

she told me why her job had become much more difficult since the process had been changed. I knew immediately that there had been a mistake, since that systems change should have made her job easier. And when I tracked it down, indeed, there was a flaw in the system.

Employees who don't have confidence in their management don't volunteer such information. In my fieldwork notes, there are countless cases of situations where employees saw things going wrong—and even knew a good solution—and failed to tell anyone. Partially, this reflected pure resentment ("Why should I go out of my way to help that kind of management?"). But it also reflects the employee's conclusion, based on past experience, that no one really cares much, which is the saddest commentary of all on how some American businesses have been run. By "no one cares," of course, they mean that managers don't show any energetic pursuit of improvement, of tracking down problems. They give orders, collect numerical data and deal with personnel grievances in those situations; they don't exercise working leadership.

After the manager has acquired some proficiency, many of his or her discussions with subordinates will be in the context of two technically knowledgeable people engaging in problem solving, again leading to a sense of equality. But this kind of discussion can't occur unless the manager wants technical insight, and it also often requires that the manager start with some foundation of knowledge as a jumping-off place.

Compliments provide the greatest reinforcement when they come from technically knowledgeable superiors. Then the manager can provide detailed feedback on what was so good about the performance (and, perhaps, so challenging about the situation). Without this insightful context, the encouraging message often is perceived as manipulation from the point of view of a sophisticated subordinate.

CHALLENGING THE PROCESS

Managers gain esteem from subordinates as being real leaders when they don't take the methods, systems, technology, and even goals that have come down the hierarchy as fixed.[10] They actively search for opportunities to show growth or improvement. They are willing to challenge their bosses and key staff heads; they experiment and take risks. Here is an abbreviated interview with one such manager:

> When I got into the job, our function was defined simply as providing a narrow range of services with a fixed technology, most of which was controlled by outside departments. [The work involved limited skill and no technical knowledge, and the managers reflected this.] I saw that there were a number of things we could do that would not only improve the quality of those services but also add other services that would have high value to the corporation. I didn't want us to be at the mercy of an outside group telling us how we should operate in order to fit their convenience.
>
> I began training some specialists so, for example, we could do a lot of our own programming and even our own training, tailoring both to our unique needs and saving a bundle in the process. When it came to purchasing some new technology, my boss wanted me to go with the same manufacturer who dominated all our systems. But I made it my business to learn what was available and how the field was developing and lobbied for equipment that was being produced by a relative newcomer. It has turned out magnificently, and now other parts of the business are buying the same thing—and we are also beginning to service some other groups as we have learned how to push this new equipment to its limits and do new things with it. The manufacturer sends potential customers to see how much we have been able to do by really getting to learn the technology.[11]

This manager's subordinates are enthusiastic; she inspires confidence. Here is a manager who has a mission, who is willing to take risks in negotiating with more powerful people, and is aggressively building a dynamic department that changes almost daily. She has a clear, partially self-defined agenda that is more demanding of her and her people than the goals defined by the management plan. But it is those very demands and the spirit they produce ("We are all part of an elite team") that drives the whole unit to perform superbly. (In twelve months, its productivity doubled, and quality improved by 50 percent.)

Note also that the manager has sought to design the work process so that she can directly handle most coordination issues and be responsive when employees have problems. Her employees are not helpless; they know they have a manager who is prepared to intervene. Therefore, they are indeed motivated.

MONITORING: GOOD GETS BETTER, BAD GETS WORSE

If organizations enhance motivation by having people work in high-performance settings, the maintenance of that effectiveness is obviously of great importance. From what has been described earlier, there is a positive spiral that rebounds to the benefit of the manager and the organization:

High performance increases employee motivation (and confidence in the manager); also, the superior-subordinate relationship is enhanced. Both combine to further enhance performance, and this, in turn, still further increases motivation.

Of course, there is also the destructive reverse spiral:

Low performance diminishes motivation and increases destructive superior-subordinate conflicts, further injuring motivation and performance and accelerating the downward spiral.

Earlier chapters have described the vulnerability of work systems and coordination. Thus, managers must be effective at monitoring those systems.

Limitations of Scorekeeping

What managers appraise (for rewards, promotions, and the like) obviously has a profound effect on what their subordinates focus upon. In the classic example, when a manager only counts how much gets done, quality, cooperation, and everything else suffers. Just as important, if a manager can't spot systems problems, there is no way that effective coordination is going to be maintained over time. (In chapter 3, I described how work systems degrade without significant managerial inputs.)

> In a number of companies using job classification systems like the Hay System, many managers believed that a major inducement operating for their colleagues was to obtain an *increase* in the number of subordinates. More

people under you could mean a higher salary bracket. As is obvious, however, such incentives usually militate against efficiency.

Traditionally, managers use monitoring as though they were score-keepers. These traditional managers see themselves as setting "hurdle" rates, the same way they set minimal rates of return to assess a capital investment. If the subordinate fails to make the hurdle, there is some kind of managerial intervention. But these results tell the manager little about the underlying sources of problems needing attention (or sources of effectiveness needing reinforcement), nor do they aid the manager in predicting when and where performance problems will occur—perhaps the most critical type of monitoring.

These practices represent the GAMP-based "deceit of the bottom line," the conviction that those accounting figures are, in fact, valid measures of effectiveness. Managers intending to take charge of their areas need to monitor *people, tasks, and technology* and their inter-relationships. How does this translate into day-to-day appraisals?

Anomalies and Discontinuities

Effective managers maintain high systems performance by seeking explanations for every performance problem (in contrast to simply assigning blame or inducing people to "work harder"). They keep asking why, again and again. Anomalies are one of the best indicators that the system of coordination is not functioning effectively. "The manager's basic job is a contingency one: knowing where work is *not* progressing satisfactorily and where compensating adjustments are necessary."[12]

A major customer called to complain that the product she received lacked the appropriate documentation. When a senior manager finally learned about this (accidentally, during a social event), he discovered that the customer had then been sent the correct materials, but no supervisor had investigated the source of the lapse. When it was researched, a minor but critical systems failure was revealed. Documents were being made ready for shipment by an employee who liked shortcuts. She had memorized the product numbers of the current equipment line, and she essentially undertook a superficial visual inspection in order to pick the correct material to enclose. She didn't bother to find the specific model number, which could require some manual manipulation of the equipment or a perusal of some documents. The mistake occurred because the company was now shipping a second generation of one of its products that looked almost the same as the first generation; not tracking down the source was an invitation to further quality problems.

A credit card issuer changed its standards for giving cash advances, and in some cases the new limits were 80% lower than the previous ones (depending on credit history). When two customers called in disbelief that they were being held to such a tight limit after having had perfect credit histories, the supervisor thought it important enough to bring it to the attention of his manager. On researching those two cases, it was discovered that the system that was being used to adjust the credit availability limit was flawed: anyone whose card had been replaced during the two months preceding the implementation of the new credit policy was considered by the automated evaluation to be a "new cardholder," and new cardholders were allotted only the minimum credit for their first year.) Although fifteen hundred cardholders had been similarly misclassified, only two had complained. It took substantial managerial initiative to probe a situation that appeared to be a random mistake.[13]

If American companies are to compete on quality and service, anomalies can't be discounted as flukes or careless errors; there needs to be a careful search to be sure that there is not a *systemic* cause that will cause additional problems. Anomalies provide the best early warning of coordination malfunctioning.

A customer of a major financial institution had taken out a special kind of customer loan that was to be repaid by automatic monthly deductions from the customer's checking account. At about the time the loan was to be repaid, the customer received a strongly worded letter about an overdue payment and a steep penalty for missing a payment date. Because these payments were supposed to be automatically debited, he called the branch to find out why he was considered late. It turned out that the software system only allowed for a fixed monthly repayment. The last payment of most loans would be for a slightly different amount, and therefore it could not automatically be deducted.

Until this complaint, that system flaw had not been detected or in other cases complaining customers had just been given credit. This branch manager investigated and insisted that the bank make some changes in the process so that good customers would not be angered by a systems failure. A small issue, to be sure, but these are the kinds of interconnections that injure quality and an image of good customer service.

When a new product or process or service is coming "on stream" is the best time to identify coordination problems. If they are not uncovered at this point, they often get covered over by employees or managers who compensate for the defect. Once this takes place, the miscoordination is disguised by redundant work stages, people, or technology.

Two departments insisted on maintaining work procedures that were incompatible when paper or data flowed from one to the other. Over the years, however, each had added extra personnel and extra data processing capacity to compensate for this misalignment. Several management audits that sought to eliminate organizational fat failed to identify these unnecessary procedures. Over time, both managers had grown so used to the compensatory activity that they probably would have been hard-pressed to operate without these. Only when an astute new division manager took over and began to examine the work flow was the discrepancy uncovered.

There are similar sources to many of the excessive hierarchical layers one finds in many organizations: organizations get steeper when coordination problems don't get solved. When department D is complaining that department E is doing work that is not consistent with D's needs, and E insists that D keeps changing specifications faster than it can change procedures, a great deal of intervention is required of their common manager.

When there are lots of such stalemates and disagreements flowing up the line in order to be resolved by a higher management level, that level gradually gets overburdened. At some point, additional managerial resources are required to handle the need for intervention and conflict resolution. Such managers in turn require their own managers, and over time, the hierarchy itself will grow taller. The layering decreases efficiency profoundly.

The creation of extra organizational levels, and perhaps extra staff "watchers," to cope with unresolved coordination issues often sets off a downward performance spiral. The superfluous levels and people complicate and slow decision making and adaptation. This, in turn, makes the organization function more poorly and may be the motivation for top management to employ more watchers and expediters, further complicating the organization.

> Ever since a critical product development project was delayed, we now have an extra layer of management watching us, plus a staff group by whom every change (of specification) request must be approved. This slows our ability to make rapid decisions and, I think, increases the time it takes to get a new product out the door.

Understandably, subordinates become demotivated in sluggish, layered organizations in which change is difficult because so many permissions are required and their own manager is constrained by excessive controls. Their sense that the system has become top-heavy and bureaucratized destroys any motivation they may have had to do more than the job minimum requires.

Modeling Systems Skills for Subordinates

Managers who are motivating because of their influence and status in the larger organization usually cast broad nets both within and outside the organization in order to keep learning about the technology of the marketplace, as well as that of the workplace. They learn to ask artful questions and to listen carefully particularly for unexpected responses. They devote substantial energy to learning about and working with peers who control needed resources, authorizations and priorities. They earn credibility with peers as with subordinates: by demonstrating technical competence, knowing their operations.

> I knew that the legal department was important to us. Therefore, I was delighted when I got the opportunity to propose contract language for some innovative technology we were purchasing from a new vendor. I could have gotten legal to write much of the contract, as they did for many other departments, but there were a number of things that I wanted that were not orthodox. For example, the performance guarantee (how well the equipment would perform) had to be related to our complex work environment and to a variety of operating conditions. It couldn't be a simple formula about running at such and such a speed and not breaking down for X period of time.
>
> So I spent a couple of weeks with my people coming up with several pages of carefully worked-through performance objectives, as well as the actions we would expect when performance fell below those levels (number of service people on call, hours to fix, availability of substitute and supplementary equipment when speed and quantity objectives were not being met). By then I was also in a position to defend each of these with the vendor's representative, who challenged many of them. By the time we had finished, legal said that this was the most thoughtful and protective (of the company) contract they had ever seen. Since then, they have been enormously cooperative.

Thus, by being energetically proactive and believing in continuous learning as well as continuous change, such managers, in their own behavior, model the attitudes and behavior they hope to encourage in the best of their subordinates. In turn, the subordinates come to respect the influence and effectiveness of their leader in shaping the work setting.

Creating a Microculture

Standard management dogma holds that managers are captive to the culture created by top management. To be sure, its influence is powerfully pervasive. Often overlooked, however, is the more local influence of energetic and skillful leaders within middle management. By means of the behavior they model and their willingness to take personal career risks to challenge and sometime change the external constraints operating on their work systems and subordinates, they can create a unique and highly motivating subculture within a larger organization.

CONCLUSION

Real empowerment and a motivating environment can best be provided, at least for more professional and technically sophisticated supervisors and employees, by managers who are technically proficient and involved. They provide two essential leadership ingredients. First, they create exciting work settings that are progressive, have momentum, and are oriented toward change and problem solving.

In contrast, nonleaders hold tight to existing routines and procedures, waiting for staff executives or more senior executives to introduce consequential change. Their work settings are bland at best, rife with unsolved, festering problems at worst. Their subordinates learn quickly that neither they nor their managers have much control over the factors that really determine performance. The latter learn helplessness and cynicism and to blame outsiders—other departments, upper management, or fate. Attempting to achieve high subordinate motivation appears as naive as tilting at windmills.

Secondly, working leaders engage in meaningful technical give-and-take with their subordinates. This reduces the status gap between them and acts to empower subordinates. The latter learn that their knowledge and advice are taken seriously, that they can have a consequential impact on management decision making. In addition, they gain a sense of self-efficacy in being encouraged by a knowledgeable boss.

8

Strategy from Below

S trategy making, of course, is usually considered a top management function, given its responsibility for long-range planning. But there is also a consequential strategy-making process that originates from below, from managers and professionals who are at middle levels of the organization. Products, services, or competencies frequently get developed that were not (nor were they likely to have been) foreseen by top management.

This obviously requires consequential leadership capabilities: to get resources, to change the routines of others, and to gain top management acquiescence. At times, well-designed and -executed strategic thrusts can even contradict existing top management strategies or result in their modification. They have the advantage of being based on a manager's intimate familiarity with the realities of technology and markets. Because leadership in implementation will be spearheaded by the strategy's originator, there is very high motivation and commitment to making it a success. And that enthusiasm and commitment can reach working levels of the organization more directly.

AUTONOMOUS STRATEGIC INITIATIVES

Robert Burgelman has called these "autonomous strategic initiatives." He provides us with a powerful example of what can be accomplished by a knowledgeable, persevering, and persuasive professional who is also a manager.[1]

Intel Corporation, one of America's foremost designers and manufacturers of semiconductors, had decided to focus its development efforts on microprocessors that were part of its complex instruction-set computing (CISC) X86 product family. Its 286 and 386 chips had been enormously successful, and most PC's were built around them.

Some years ago Intel had decided not to enter the reduced instruction-set computing (RISC) processor business. Innovative chips cost many millions to develop, and the company sought to focus on what it thought were its competitive advantages and where the market was headed. But one of Intel's bright technologists, Les Kohn, disagreed with this strategic decision. He was a RISC enthusiast and devoted great energy to getting Intel to change its mind. For some time, his persuasive powers led to no change in Intel planning.

He eventually decided that if a RISC product could be designed as a coprocessor to work in conjunction with a new Intel microprocessor in its X86 family, he might be able to get the substantial budget resources approved that he needed for the development effort. Presumably, he also decided that if a competitively advantaged RISC chip could be designed and create a market, its potential profitability would cause top management to reconsider its strategic decision to stay away from RISC technology.

With astute product championing, Kohn did get the needed budget, developed a first-rate RISC chip, and then went out and sold it to a number of customers as a stand-alone processor, *not* a chip that was a coprocessor. It was a success in attracting substantial new business to Intel, and seven years after he had begun his campaign to have Intel develop a RISC chip, top management formally modified its product strategy to include Kohn's chip.[2]

Top management sometimes adopts new strategies that have minimal impact. Nothing changes; the new words are perceived by line managers as justifying what they have always been doing. It takes leadership to both give operational meaning to a strategy statement and to change deeply entrenched ways of doing things. The next case deals with a middle manager who took literally top management pronouncements that his old-line commodity paper company should become more customer oriented, produce more differentiated products, and thereby become more profitable.

Inducing a Paper Company to Become More Customer Oriented

Eliot Felix worked as a middle manager in a very large paper company. Given his technical training, he recognized the profit potential in some new technology coming out of the labs; he had been involved in some of the development work that proved its feasibility. The new techniques that it created would allow the company to produce significantly more attractive, colorful, and customized advertising on the shipping corrugated cartons they manufactured. In turn, the cartons would have other uses besides serving as packaging, and they would command a premium price from customers for whom they had been specially designed.

Senior management had already committed itself to shifting the company's focus from that of a commodity manufacturer to one that was more customer oriented. Operationalizing this concept, to Felix, meant that the customer had to have more control of the product. He also realized that this would require a virtual revolution in the mind-set of many functional heads. They saw themselves as manufacturing what the company had decided was a good product, which would then be sold by a sales staff. The customer was on the receiving side, not the initiating side. (Of course, this concept also made their jobs easier, more predictable, and more routinizable.)

Felix saw this new graphics capability as being a major vehicle for shifting the culture of the organization to one that was customer focused and customer responsive. It was this vision that Felix sold to upper management, but he also sold it by convincing his own boss (who might not have understood all the nuances of the technology) that whatever happened, the new program would not and could not cause him embarrassment. Felix believed that was a critically important first step.

To get the support of senior management, Felix had to adopt a very new role: to move from being someone who took instructions to one who initiated new activities. Such a move represents a major shift in behavior and in the picture a manager has of his or her own functioning, Felix; in particular, felt the magnitude of the change in his level of responsibility.[3] During a later interview, Felix commented on how stressful it had been to sense how many millions of dollars he eventually became responsible for using effectively. But he also had learned the following:

> If you have a good case that you are willing to present forcefully—putting yourself out on a limb—and for which you have good supporting data, and you do it often enough, they begin to hear you. Eventually, they are probably going to give you enough rope to see whether or not you are going to hang yourself or make it work. In my case, I sought to emphasize how what I sought to do would put us ahead of the competition and how fast the markets we would serve were growing.

Obviously, senior management's concurrence was necessary for Felix to get the consequential funding he needed (some millions of dollars for new facilities and equipment). It was also needed to signal to other managers that they should be cooperative. But their approving the project and resource allocation wasn't enough to encourage such redirection on the part of lower-level managers.

> The managers who could make or break my program had to believe that top management really internalized this new strategy and they weren't simply mouthing words. The key senior manager, therefore, had to begin doing other things that were consistent with my strategy and also explaining to others in ways that showed he understood and approved of all the implications. And whatever was said about my new program had to be said unambiguously and enthusiastically, or some people would presume they were picking up some mixed message.

Felix then moved to put a team together comprising the functions he would need to implement this strategic thrust.

> I had to have team members who were not "stakeholders," that is, they were not simply *representatives* of their functions [who merely give and get information]. I needed people who would make personal and functional sacrifices for the good of the program. This was not simply a problem of selecting the right people; it was also a challenge of finding incentives that would encourage them to be real team players—for the most part, these related to convincing them of the attractiveness of the program and what they would lose by way of influence and career impetus by being left out.
> I also wanted them to see how complex our problems were, so I

took them overseas with me to view our international business. This trip had another advantage: working as an American in a foreign culture that is new to you, you feel somewhat helpless, and I think in that state you are willing to absorb really new ideas that might appear more radical in a more conventional setting.

Felix got some of the line managers who would have some painful adaptations to make to go along by showing them that the additional funding that would be forthcoming could help them complete some of their own long-sought improvement programs. But with respect to other key functional groups who would be affected by the program, Felix took the position that it was important not to let others make decisions for him based on their perspectives and standards. After all, these had been shaped by the previous culture. (For example, he pushed hard to get the human resources staff to change its views of what would be appropriate compensation arrangements for the staff of this new program.)

In any new initiative, it is necessary to maintain the confidence of top management, particularly because no innovative program progresses smoothly in a straight, upward-sloping trajectory. Felix also knew that he would require certain additional authorizations from key senior managers. According to Felix, this required

recognizing that these are busy people with crowded agendas. Therefore, I knew I had literally to force my way onto their schedules. Sometimes it's hard to be that pushy. And during each meeting, I made sure they agreed on setting dates for my next two or three meetings with them.

These meetings were part of my self-discipline program. By knowing I was going to meet the first of next month with VP Mr. X, I knew I would have to have a certain level of progress and completion for those "etched in stone" deadlines.

I also learned in maintaining these contacts and holding these meetings with my superiors not to ask permission to undertake the future steps that I thought were necessary. After all, that is the more typical posture you find yourself in: can I or can't I do this? And this leaves you open, very obviously, to being told, "No"—and, in fact, that is the usual response. Instead, I would always take the position that I was going to try X for Y period of time, and I will be back at Z time to report on how it worked out.

Finally, Felix learned that he needed to build an external network of informants. But this didn't come free:

Most people aren't going to talk with you unless they are going to get something in return and unless they feel you are really worth talking to. For example, I had learned you get second-rate information about customer needs by talking to their purchasing departments. You need to deal with the real user, and in my case that was marketing heads. But they won't see you unless it looks as though it is going to be worthwhile from their point of view.

I also needed to see technology people in other organizations. I even made special trips abroad to see people whose work I respected. But I always gave as good as I got by way of technical exchanges.

Thus, autonomous initiatives aid the firm in developing new strategies that had not been conceived by or had been rejected by top management. The result can be new organizational competencies, new products, and new methods of doing business. There is a good analogy to the federalist principle of the United States, under which states have the opportunity to experiment with initiatives that, if successful, can be adopted by the central government. One of the most successful computer companies of the decade, Sun Microsystems (who, in a few years, grew to become a multibillion-dollar world leader in workstations), has been described as fostering these initiatives: "[At Sun,] product strategy percolated up from independent divisions rather than being imposed from the top."[4] These cases above, and similar ones in the literature, usually focus on the personal motivations of the initiator or product champion. Not surprisingly, these are goals like career advancement (a vehicle by which one can gain visibility and new responsibilities) and the opportunity to get additional job satisfaction (by using unemployed personal skills). But this research suggests another goal that is perhaps even more useful to the firm: a source of implementable initiatives.

PROBLEM-BASED STRATEGIC INITIATIVES

Earlier chapters describe the critical leadership role that needs to be filled, particularly by middle managers, to facilitate the coordination, work completion, and systems requirements of the organization. When handled skillfully, these leaders serve to make work systems effective, high in quality, and responsive to the customer. In contrast to the autonomous strategic initiatives, these leaders often introduce more inner-directed change.

Many times, the problems with which they are coping are not soluble within the confines of existing top management strategies or directives. A major change is required, which can become a strategic initiative. An example should assist in clarifying the distinction between these problem-based initiatives and the strategy change illustrated in Intel's move (described above) into the development of RISC chips.

Evolving a New Technology Strategy to Solve Old Work Flow Problems

Mary Coel headed one important unit within the accounting group of the First Corporation, a large financial services firm. Her unit handled customer accounting and handled large volumes of both paper and telephone calls. In 1988, the company was adding substantial accounts, and Coel's unit was swamped with work. She knew that there was little likelihood she could hire enough people to work the backlog down to a reasonable size. For example, the company wanted customer complaints to be resolved within two or three days; given her current work methods and staffing, the required time was closer to fifteen days, a continuing source of embarrassment in discussions with her boss.

Related to the problem in Coel's eyes, was her unit's dependence on a centralized computer services division and its mainframe technology. That system not only lacked the flexibility to adapt to some of the ingenious work changes Coel had dreamed up, but was also dependent on a pool of centralized programmers who were either too busy or too rigid to be helpful in responding to many of her requests.

At that time, Coel had been reading about the advances being made in imaging technology that could store and provide ready access to vast quantities of correspondence and records. She found one vendor who was developing software that was consistent with her own conceptions of work flow—equipment that would not simply store and retrieve but facilitate the movement of work from one employee and one stage to another.

Senior technology people and upper management had shown no interest in supplementing the current hardware by investing in imaging technology and supporting PCs. But Coel saw this emerging technology as the only way she could get off the treadmill. She now was on one in which her people were constantly fighting to catch up with and stay ahead of the ever-increasing work load. Coel undertook a number of detailed analyses and eventually was able to demonstrate that the equipment would pay for itself in less than two years. She was willing to take the career risk of committing to a 50 percent labor savings in her area if she could get approval for the investment.

If developed properly, this technology initiative could also be designed to solve several other problems. Coel was determined to get out from under her great dependence on a sluggish, centralized computer service group and an inflexible mainframe computer system. She needed to be able to attract and retain within her own department creative people who could help develop new work flow systems as well as program them. (The versatility and flexibility of the new PCs that would be an integral part of the imaging technology made this partial autonomy a realistic objective.)

It would also be possible with this new equipment, Coel reasoned, to add other functions to her department that were now performed by other units but were closely related to her functional responsibilities. The capacity and flexibility of the equipment she had chosen could easily handle these functions and thereby eliminate a certain number of interunit coordination issues.

Thus, the new technology could simultaneously cope with a variety of problems Coel faced, both organizational and technical. It was her means of getting off a treadmill produced by increasing work loads and an inability to add staff or get suitable changes in existing technology. New technology was also a key that opened other possibilities for Coel's department. Required for implementation, however, was an extended process of educating her boss (and boss's boss) and learning how to "massage" the capital allocation process.

In addition, Coel had to work her way around the experts in the data systems group, who normally had a major voice in equipment acquisitions of this type. Not only were they unfamiliar with the specific technology she wanted, but they also had some reason to be unenthusiastic about (1) equipment ideas coming from "laymen" and (2) equipment that would increase the technological autonomy of a key line department. Over some period of time, Cole was able to find technological specialists within the firm who would endorse her selection, and she also showed the central data systems people that this equipment could and would interface for a number of functions with their mainframes.

It took about eight months to work through the management decision process, and of course, Coel had to fit those efforts into an
already full day of dealing with the immediate, short-run problem of
keeping existing systems running. But she realized that it was only
through this kind of major change that she could move from always
being behind to being ahead of her work problems.

Several years later, First Corporation began adopting imaging technology and greater use of distributive (that is, decentralized) data
processing throughout the organization. Coel's operation is still considered the most advanced application, and potential users come
from various other countries as well as around the United States to
view her now well-established strategic initiative.

An Innovative ATM

Harvard professor John Kotter describes an NCR general manager's
strategic initiative that bears some similarity to the efforts of Eliot
Felix and Mary Coel.[5] In 1980 NCR hired Jim Adamson as general
manager for its Dundee, Scotland, plant that, among other products,
manufactured bank automated-teller machines (ATMs). Adamson
took over a demoralized operation that had been producing a trouble-
ridden, low-quality product. Its current customers were so dissatisfied that they were refusing to accept additional units that they had
previously ordered.

After engaging in extensive conversations with current dissatisfied
customers and getting to know the plant and its work force, Adamson evolved a strategy that would transform the operation. Previously, the plant had simply modified an ATM design that had come
from the parent company's facilities in Ohio. Adamson conceived of
a product that would meet the customer needs he learned during his
intensive exploration of the British market: very high reliability (at
least double current performance), low-cost maintenance, simple
connections to the emerging bank electronic-transfer networks, and
moderate total cost. If successful, it would be a world-class product.

But the plant, its engineers, and its skilled employees would only
be able to develop this product if Adamson could get NCR top management to allow Dundee to discontinue its manufacturing of mini-
computers and if he could get control of software development,
which was now also being handled at NCR's central offices. Adamson had learned how critical these structural changes were by close
observation of the work processes at Dundee and discussions with

his managers. He also recognized that supervisors and employees would also have to learn how to work to high standards of quality, something that they had not accomplished in the past.

Kotter's own description of how Adamson handled the functional, Ohio-based groups that he was seeking to displace are revealing and are similar to the behavior of Coel:

> Sometimes he backed away from an argument and quietly did what he wanted anyway. Sometimes he directly confronted people, using market data as a shield or spear: "What customer did you get your idea from? Mine comes from talking to these fifty customers." Sometimes he appealed directly to Charles Exley, the CEO [of NCR].[6]

Obviously, substantial leadership skill was necessary to pressure successfully for the organizational changes that allowed Adamson's "vision" to be realized, but the result was a product that secured a world leadership position.

MAKING STRATEGIC DECISIONS FROM BELOW

Strategic initiatives from below are heavily inductive, in contrast to the more deductive strategies of senior management and their formal planning processes and staff planners. It is worth assessing and summarizing this approach to strategy-making:

1. Such initiatives grow out of an in-depth understanding of work-level or operating problems. These could involve customers or vendors or the internal processing of work or technology and product development issues. Often the problems focus on major inconsistencies between what is being demanded of the manager and the resources he or she has to employ to satisfy these demands. The initiative, at least in part, is designed to solve real problems that hinder the organization (or its products or services) from attaining high effectiveness or to cure the ailments responsible for organizational degrading. They are *not* the result of blue-sky thinking or career ambitions, although there may well be career consequences.

2. When successful, these initiatives usually involve solving a number of problems with a single blow, so to speak. (There are usually positive second- and third-order effects, as policy strategists would say it.) For example, if Coel is able to add a sophisticated and chal-

lenging new technology, she can attract more technically trained staff
and provide challenging jobs for them including developing new innovative services.

Some have as their primary thrust the elimination of a consequential "managerial effort sink": a problem or set of problems that keep
eating up valuable managerial time. In effect, the initiatives look
backward and forward—backward in the sense that they seek to
overcome past problems, and forward in the sense that they anticipate new benefits, some of which are unrelated to the old problems.

3. The strategy initiatives observed are often creative solutions to
these problems; they don't represent simple extrapolations of existing trends or techniques. They often require a synthesis of a number
of trends and elements that were not heretofore interrelated. They
demonstrate that the manager is able to tease out patterns from diffuse, tangled issues and in situations where others may only see discrete, unrelated events and topics.

> The marketing manager of a medium-sized metalworking
> plant in Kentucky was aware of the continuing decline
> of the company's traditional market as a result of changes
> in the auto industry. The company had always
> manufactured a small range of parts for the auto industry.
> He decided to go on the road to meet with a variety of
> manufacturers to find small metal parts they were
> currently buying that his plant might be able to produce,
> given the equipment it had and the skills of its employees.
> He had read in several business publications that
> companies were having trouble obtaining reasonable
> prices on certain small-volume orders of nonstandard
> metal parts. When he found a possible "fit" and the
> customer named a price that would likely get the plant
> new orders, he went back and worked with
> manufacturing engineers to get some idea of the material
> costs involved. He then met with union leaders in the
> plant (who knew that additional layoffs were pending
> because of a falloff in the plant's traditional lines). He was
> able to convince them to work with experienced
> machinists to come up with a productivity target they felt
> they were willing to try to meet.
>
> In a number of instances, the manager was able to bring
> new business into the plant, get it produced profitably,

and retain about 90% of the work force intact. Essentially, he developed a technique that allowed plant employees to "bid" on new work. Obviously, their bids were too high in some cases, but because they really participated in the process, their bids in other cases were right on the money. It is also interesting to note in this case, that the marketing manager who introduced this organizational innovation did not have to understand the new work methods and adaptive shortcuts the newly empowered employees were going to use to hit the targets they had agreed to.

4. The manager has to take into account current strategies and policies of top management. In the cases of Mary Coel and Eliot Felix, they knew that top management had made some commitment to investing in new technologies for the future and in becoming more customer oriented.

5. The strategy, in turn, becomes a stimulus to subordinates and peers who sense a new momentum: the energy of management, and the stretch required to implement the initiative. For example, although Adamson's engineers were at first skeptical about their ability to produce a product twice as reliable as competitors, they eventually upped his target by another 50 percent![8] Often, those managers who are most successful are able to verbalize the new change in a way that dramatizes its significance, as well as its value for subordinates (for example, in creating better or more secure jobs).

6. Inevitably there will be resistance from these same peers and subordinates, who have real investments in existing ways of working. Introducing autonomous strategic initiatives is very different from undertaking a so-called green-field operation or working in a skunk works, where the manager can work like a small business entrepreneur. The consequential strategy moves described here require the ability and the patience to "work the organization," to influence and persuade others it is worth their while to accept changes in their standard ways of working or in their turf or jurisdiction. This is a far more difficult challenge than starting afresh or working in isolation from the organization.

7. The manager is willing to incur additional work, even some chaos, that will be a handicap in terms of performance (and internal costs) in the short run. The investment is made because he or she can calculate the long-run benefits.[7]

8. The manager, in addition to being persuasive, patient, and creative, also has to be willing to assume substantial risks. Many of these initiatives require new resource allocations and commitments based on *projected* savings and improvements. The manager's reputation is on the line until those benefits have been achieved. In the short run, there can be career decrements.

9. Successful new-strategy initiators recognize that most support for the above is conditional. Its continuation depends on continued progress and on the manager's ability to verbalize and demonstrate that progress.

IMPLEMENTATION TRADE-OFFS

Of course, the manager does more than conceive of strategic solutions; they have to be implemented. What may sound like a simple, straightforward change in direction may have manifold repercussions at the operating level. And, of course, the failure to integrate effectively the great numbers of modifications of current practice will spell failure for the new strategy.

It may be instructive to look closely at the impact of a strategic change as it played itself out deep in the organization. What follows is a relatively simple example.

> Exxon had been involved in three oil spills in the waters surrounding New York harbor during the 1990s. Given the economic and public relations cost of the Valdez tanker disaster in Alaska and the outcries from city officials, Exxon committed itself to improving its practices for unloading and loading oil. Essentially, it shifted its strategic emphasis from cost-effectiveness to safety (that is, eliminating the likelihood of an oil spill almost regardless of cost).
>
> A company study disclosed that changes such as these had to be made in day-to-day operating procedures:
>
> • Ships in poor condition are not allowed to dock at their terminal (a procedure was established to check out the ship's condition while it was approaching).

- Mooring lines are checked more frequently, because "snapped lines" can cause a spill.

- Hoses through which petroleum products are transferred must be less than three years old.

- Hoses that will carry hot asphalt cannot be in use for longer than six months.

- Incoming ships have to give seventy-two hours notice before they dock, so that the compatibility of their unloading equipment and the terminal's equipment can be assured.

- Whenever petroleum is being transferred, one member of the crew must be assigned to activate a warning alarm every twenty-five seconds. The shrill sound helps keep crew members alert and therefore more likely to spot the beginning of any spill.

- Three tugs (on either side and astern) "guard" the tanker, and a tug is assigned to guide each tanker through the channels leading to the Exxon terminal. Another always stands by in case the tanker has trouble docking. (Apparently, in the past, it was not unusual to have tankers bumping into each other and into other obstructions that could cause the hull to spring a leak.)

- Various vessels now carry containment booms, so that spilled oil will not spread.[9]

All this minutiae and detail helps emphasize how something like improved safety (or quality or service) ramifies through a work system. Almost every work step needs modification, and many parts of the organization, as well as outside organizations, also have to be brought into alignment. Many functions will have to contribute to assessing what needs to be done. A large number of changed practices have to be designed and imposed. In many instances, this will require consensus building in addition to direct orders.

One can make explicit the leadership skills required of a middle-level manager who sought to initiate this kind of strategic change, and deal with the large number, cost, and dispersion of the required changes. Such changes are not easy, but without such leadership, the strategic shift is likely to mean very little in the way of changed performance.

BUREAUCRATIC VERSUS SYSTEMS CHANGE

Carefully orchestrated, detailed change in work processes and roles and tasks contrasts sharply with the way change is introduced in bureaucratic organizations. In these, the manager has no involvement in work systems; the manager's job is making policy decisions and setting standards. Thus, one can imagine a traditional manager responsible for the same oil loading and unloading operations described in the Exxon case above coping with that series of costly and embarrassing spills by "decisive" actions like the following:

1. Announcing a new policy of environmental protection having high priority. Thus a new position will be created (titled "Spill Avoidance Officer") whose responsibility will be to reduce the incidence of spills. This officer will prepare regular program-improvement recommendations and design a related training program.
2. Requiring that as part of their annual appraisals, managers in the terminal function will be evaluated on the number of barrels of oil spilled in their geographic areas.
3. Making it clear that starting with the current year, each terminal manager will be expected to reduce the quantity of oil spilled by 20 percent from the previous year's spill level. When the annual spillage exceeds that amount, a report shall be prepared for the vice president for terminals explaining the deviation, with copies sent to the senior vice president for oil products distribution.

HOW COMPANIES NEGLECT THEIR OWN INNOVATIONS

There are two major reasons why significant inventions, technical breakthroughs, and major innovations developed within companies may not result in profitable products. One is that there can be extraordinary technical impediments in seeking to commercialize a laboratory development. The other reason is the managerial one: there is no effective leadership. A consequential technical advance usually requires the consummate skill of a product champion to overcome the organizational barriers that will block its emergence as a regular product line of the company.

No matter how much potential innovations have, they will not be realized without astute, skillful, and energetic managers dedicating themselves to overcoming the inevitable technical and organizational impediments that will arise. Without such sponsorship, given the cost and frustration that are almost always associated with something that is truly pathbreaking, the odds are very good that an innovation will fall through the cracks and its initial economic advantage dissipate.

Contrary to myth, new technologies do not usually have a momentum of their own that carries everyone along. Few members of top management are likely to recognize their future potential. Their development will shift resources away from other needy programs, and their success will require that many comfortable routines and jurisdictional lines be modified substantially. Without a champion, very little is likely to occur beyond some admiration within a small band of technicians who understand and savor the breakthrough.

Xerox and the PC. One of the most famous of these failures was that of the Xerox Corporation, whose PARC laboratories in the 1970s developed the concept and the software and hardware for the first personal computer (PC). (The software was so user friendly that it was adapted by Apple and became a vital component of their extraordinarily successful Macintosh.) But the PC got lost when managers at Xerox were unable to develop an organization to sell it effectively to their internal top management or to external customers in a world that had not heard of PCs.[10]

Bendix and Fuel Injection. In a parallel case, the Bendix Corporation developed fuel injection in 1951. In 1967 they eventually licensed it to a German competitor, Bosch, who sold several million units before Bendix finally began selling its own fuel injection devices. This occurred almost twenty-five years after the invention had been made!

It was only after a group-level manager took charge of the strategic management of Bendix's fuel injection that Bendix sold units to a major customer (the Cadillac division of General Motors) and developed the production capability to manufacture this innovative product. And to think that Bendix, in terms of its corporate strategy, always saw itself as one of the world's major innovators and manufacturers of engine and brake components for the automotive industry![11] One manager's industriousness, not top management strategy, created the first American fuel injection capability.

IBM and RISC-Based Computers. In 1975, IBM developed what came to be known as reduced instruction-set computing (RISC). This innovation in microprocessor technology formed the basis for the extraordinary growth of workstations that revolutionized how engineering would be performed. But that technology was exploited by other companies at IBM's expense, and it was not until 1990—fifteen years after the innovation was perfected—that IBM introduced its first commercially successful RISC computer.[12]

These corporate failures to exploit their own technological advances are not the result of stupidity or an inability to foresee the future. These were all large companies, and there were many competing ideas and innovations, and the future is always uncertain. For example, one of the reasons IBM did not take advantage of its RISC breakthrough is that this technology would have competed directly with its highly profitable mainframe business.[13]

Thus, it is not surprising that most innovations do not get implemented and developed into salable products and services without a midlevel manager (a "product champion") who both fully understands the technology and has leadership skills.[14] Such critical managers build a team to further the development of the product. Simultaneously, they seek to win the attention and support of top management, who must at some point supply the resources and counter the resistance of those feeling threatened by an innovation that could injure their routines or their support.[15] But a CEO can help:

> A former CEO of the Mead Corporation, James
> McSwiney, pushed Mead into pouring vast sums of
> money into LEXIS, a software-based information service
> that was a major departure from Mead's paper-making
> business. LEXIS eventually became highly profitable and
> the most widely used data bank for lawyers and judges
> in researching prior cases and judicial decisions.[16]

WHEN TOP MANAGEMENT STRATEGY IGNORES WORK-LEVEL REALITIES

Most strategy is made by top management with a good deal of attention to external market, technology, and financial considerations and an effort to predict future trends. The internal factors considered always include things like organizational competencies and comparative advantages. But in reality, it may not be that easy to assess what the organization does well (or poorly). For example, accounting reports, including P & L statements, are often deceptive. Senior management can make serious strategic errors by not having some thorough grounding in the realities of operations.

A Costly Merger

The Eclipse Company decided to merge with Ajax, another large company in the same industry, primarily to get economies of scale and to eliminate a good deal of redundancy in their two sets of similar operations. Eclipse had to decide in advance which senior managers in the two organizations would get the major line positions. Both were in three lines of business that were somewhat related but still distinct. Eclipse sought to put the very best people from the combined organization into these top slots.

One of the businesses that was a major source of profit was selling a product that here will be called B (in order to disguise the industry and the true names of the organizations). Eclipse top management believed that picking an executive to head the B business was a "no-brainer." Ajax was much more profitable in Bs than Eclipse and had more than double the latter's sales. Ajax's current head of B was appointed head of the combined business, and not surprisingly, he chose to retain most of his senior managers in their current positions. This left Eclipse managers to be folded into the more junior positions.

What Eclipse senior management hadn't assessed was the source of those apparently greater profits. For the preceding five years, Ajax had been investing heavily in B, whereas Eclipse top management had steadfastly refused to give its B management any additional resources to expand. When the merger actually took place, Eclipse B management was shocked to discover that Ajax was extraordinarily inefficient and badly organized. Even taking into account the difference in volume, Ajax had two and sometimes three employees for every task that Eclipse had one. Its margins were actually very poor, but it had been highly profitable because the past five years had been a seller's market in Bs.

Worse yet, Eclipse had spent those years fine-tuning its operations, even though it had to make do on a shoestring. Its managers had implemented what was probably one of the industry's most efficient and adaptable work processes, all on the basis of the kind of autonomous strategic initiatives discussed above. Eclipse's B technology and methods were so flexible that with modest incremental cost, they could have handled the entire work load represented by the Ajax acquisition. But their managers never had the opportunity. The Ajax B team refused to even look at the technology or the numbers; for them, this was a political decision. They had no intention of acknowledging that they were "second class." They insisted that the technology and techniques that Eclipse's B management had perfected be abandoned.

The result was a combined operation that probably had costs that were 50 to 80 percent greater than they would have been. To add insult to injury, the Ajax team also implemented a costly capital investment program that had been put on the books just before the consummation of the merger. The many millions this would cost would create a new computer based information system that would not match the one that had been created in Eclipse.

One of the many impediments that Ajax worked with was their failure to employ talented middle-level managers. They paid poor salaries at this level, and had people with little ability to deal with technology and systems issues; they were all just "high class" first-line supervisors. (This could have been the result of being top-heavy with highly paid senior managers in that division.) As a result, Ajax had to use consultants for every technical improvement, and the consultants never learned the details of the business well enough to duplicate the kind of fine-tuning that the systems-oriented Eclipse managers had achieved.

STRATEGIC MERGERS, COMPANY CULTURES, AND SYNERGIES

The example above may be a microcosm of the issues that confront merged companies. Typically, the failure to achieve the synergies that had been anticipated in a carefully orchestrated strategic combination of companies is attributed to the difficulty of merging very different corporate cultures. There is no denying that companies do have distinct cultures, and blending them in a newly combined organization has to be troublesome.[17]

Such broad explanations as "clashes of culture," may however, disguise more than they reveal in terms of the problems of realizing the synergies in mergers. In the Eclipse case at least, the problems are more narrowly focused. The implementation of the painfully worked-out merger (the companies had been negotiating for two years) did not reflect the realities of the work systems of the two companies. The key decision makers used bookkeeping profits to assess the relative effectiveness of Eclipse and Ajax management. Given the limitations of profits as a measure of managerial ability, one would not expect that they would be a reliable guide.

Worse yet, the actual implementation, following those broad decisions concerning whose managers would get key positions, were made in the traditional way—corporate politics as usual. But as long as senior management has no other criteria than overall measures of short run profitability, it is predictable that political considerations will win out. Obviously, for a number of "rational" political reasons, Ajax wanted its systems to predominate in the merged enterprise: it was more comfortable, there was less need to adapt, it "saved face", it didn't require facing up to having tolerated lagging technology and inefficiency, and it was just business as usual.

The major advantage of having sound technical information available on the operations of work systems is the possibility that the decision making context can be shifted from who is bigger, stronger, or more powerful to what is better. Expected synergies turn out to be ephemeral in mergers, and cultures persist in clashing just because political considerations predominate. And politics inevitably fills the vacuum left by a shortage of valid information and by the absence of managers experienced and knowledgeable enough to negotiate in technical terms. After all, if these don't exist, what else is there to base decisions on?

CONCLUSION

An in-depth understanding of how things work (or don't work) to accomplish the basic purpose of the enterprise needs to be added to the strategy-making process. Operating realities can become embedded in strategy in two ways.

The first is encouraging (in other words, training and rewarding) middle managers to behave strategically and to generate strategic initiatives. This requires that managers learn that they can shape organization structure and technology directly by implementing creative, ambitious, self-generated plans. They do not have to rely on staff experts or consultants or top management to initiate these.

The second is to have senior managers who are making strategy become knowledgeable about operations. At present, there is an enormous gap between plans and implementation. The usual excuses that "plans were too ambitious" or that "the culture blocked change" grow out of the failure of top management to have any interest in how things work.

There is substantial evidence that the traditional GAMP view of strategy making is a very limited one. Mintzberg's research is most persuasive in supporting the conclusion that successful strategy making requires extended, intimate involvement with technology, customers, and markets, much more so than analytical skills:

> Strategies grow like weeds in a garden. They take root in all kinds of places, wherever people have the capacity to learn (because they are in touch with the situation) and the resources to support that capacity. . . . Of course, this view is overstated. But it is no less extreme than the conventional view of strategic management.[18]

Mintzberg refers to "emergent strategy," in which individual business units undertake many strategic initiatives. Some will succeed; other fail. Among the successful, a small number will have generalizability for the larger organization, and astute top management will embody these in its newer strategies.[19]

Yet the view that successful strategy is associated with the omniscience of far sighted top executives, relying on tightly reasoned economic quantitative analyses far removed from operations, is strongly entrenched. It even leads to rewriting history.

> After the Boston Consulting Group, on an assignment for the British government, analyzed Honda's great success in the motorcycle market, business case writers at the Harvard Business School developed a Honda (U.S.) motorcycle case study for MBA students based on its research. The case stressed the careful analysis and planning Honda executives had done to enter and gain ascendancy in the U.S. as well as British markets. The reality apparently was far different, according to a well-known management researcher.
>
> When Honda first entered the U.S. market, it had

intended to sell large motorcycles to a traditional
motorcycle consumer: the leather-jacketed, confirmed
biker. But their models turned out to be unsuited to the
extended, arduous usage of avid American cyclists. They
frequently broke down. More or less inadvertently,
Honda discovered an untapped market, the casual
around-town user who was attracted to a simple,
inexpensive, lightweight bike. Meanwhile, Honda had
designed its so-called Supercub 50cc model for the
Japanese market and was sure it was unsuited to the U.S.
biker consumer, who wanted large, powerful, relatively
costly equipment. It had imported a small number of
these, many of which were used by Honda managers for
their own commuting, and it was truly surprised when
consumers wanted them. Only after a substantial
demand surfaced did Honda evolve this reactive
strategy.[20]

Not all strategies, as Mintzberg's balanced overview notes, origi-
nate with the initiative of well-informed middle- level managers. The
Honda case, however, illustrates the importance of relatively senior
managers having an in-depth knowledge of operating-level issues and
the capacity to be flexible, to shift when performance begins to deviate from what their strategy has anticipated.

A very large financial services company suffered a
consequential loss of profits because of its inability to be
flexible and its ignorance of operating-level realities. The
company had two major products for the retail market,
managed by groups A and B. Top management
anticipated that the product A would be the more
successful for at least several years and allocated resources
accordingly in their formal planning. What they had not
looked at, however, were the differences in operating
effectiveness of the two product groups. As resources
poured into A (and its volume of business increased), the
ineptness of its operations became more apparent.
Regular customers abandoned the product when they lost
patience with A's inefficiencies. In fact, the delays in
paper processing caused A's product to fall behind the

performance it had been able to generate before receiving all these additional resources.

By way of contrast, B's processing and operations were becoming increasingly efficient because of excellent middle management, driving down its costs and improving its level of service. B's profits soared. Sadly, top management did not shift resources in response to these results. B had ample capacity to handle much higher volumes with no additional cost had the company provided resources to invest in more marketing and new business acquisition.

The company sacrificed substantial profit potential by not taking advantage of B's management skills. It is not clear that top management ever recognized that management effectiveness, as opposed to astute senior management thinking, had any relevance to strategy making.

Creative Leadership and Strategic Initiatives

Most discussions (and checklists) to aid managers in developing strategic initiatives emphasize an economic perspective:

• Careful assessment of competitive advantage based on market and competitor analyses.
• A vision of what the organization can become.

The cases above suggest a rather different view of this leadership skill. The managers described in these cases had built up substantial intellectual capital concerning how things worked based on continuing, intimate experience with the work, the technology, and the people doing the operations. Pairing this with a comparable knowledge of internal markets or external customers' needs, they were able to come up with new or improved products or services. But these were innovations that were grounded soundly in the indigenous competencies of their people and their systems.

This might be called *creative integration* of internal capabilities and external needs. It is a leadership function because it requires knowledge that synthesizes a variety of tasks, systems, and external requirements in ways that go beyond the purview of the typical supervisor or skilled professional. These initiatives require more than sound and original thinking to be successful; they require gaining authorizations, selling their potential for new resources, and gaining the cooperation of many outside groups.

Most importantly, such integration is a creative process because it is not a computerlike function of matching up lists (say, of internal skills and external market demands). Rather, the really successful strategies represented ideas and directions that were truly imaginative and based on conceptual thinking.

The concepts underlying the new initiatives, however, were arrived at *inductively*. They grew out of well-grounded experiences in which *all* the managers had literally or figuratively gotten their hands dirty by immersing themselves in the real phenomenon that they were managing: customers, technology, people. They knew their part of the business from the ground up, and it was only because of this thorough knowledge that they could come up with realistic and promising forwardthinking new strategies.

Senior Management's Contribution

If strategic thinking is to benefit from knowledge derived from middle management at operational levels, senior management has to be willing to accept initiatives from below, recognizing it is not omniscient. Many new strategies will evolve by successive approximations, by learning how they "fly" when implemented. These senior managers also should themselves be knowledgeable about operations.

In traditional, bureaucratic organizations, the kind that flourished with simple, highly routinized, stable technologies, top management could make decisions in its executive cocoons. In a dynamic world, executives have to be immersed in the realities of the customer, of technology, and of service and product delivery. Then they must be prepared to admit mistaken judgments and to zig and zag with the realities that appear at working levels of the organization. There is growing recognition that many company strategic options grow out of the organization's "core competencies"—critical capabilities and technologies it has learned to do better than most of its competitors. These competencies, upon which successful strategies can be built, are created by working leaders. Such management is necessary to truly perfect complex systems. The relationship of core competencies to the managerial skills we have been describing is detailed in chapter 11.

9

Managing Stability and Managing Change

There are several current and popular myths in management. They are consistent with traditional management principles that most managers have been taught. They sound reasonable and logical, even commonsensical (and many academics have "proven" them), but the data presented in this book suggest that they are nonetheless myths. Even so, they have a consequential influence on management decision making.

Myth #1. There are, and ought to be, significant distinctions between managers who manage what appears to be stable systems and those who can cope effectively with change. (In fact, conventional management wisdom reserves the term *leader* for those who are able to introduce consequential change into their organizations.)

Myth #2. Only line managers with product responsibilities can assume general manager-like responsibilities—that is, manage the interrelationships among functions, balancing and trading off among various activities with a "bottom line" result that measures their effectiveness.

Myth #3. So-called self-managing (autonomous) groups or teams require little external leadership.

STABILITY AND CHANGE:
POINTS ON A CONTINUUM

It is traditional to distinguish three kinds of managerial interventions: (1) systems maintenance (maintaining work flow routines), (2) adaptation, and (3) consequential change. But all, in fact, involve very similar coordination and change challenges. All involve understanding the fragility of work systems and being able to improve their functioning *by continuously introducing change.*

Systems Maintenance

Robust organizations that are able to maintain effective coordination represent a major managerial achievement, given all the inherent centrifugal forces of disintegration. Good managers spend a significant part of their time identifying causes of systems malfunctioning, which may be problems of quality, efficiency, service, or even safety. They are forever on the prowl for ways of making the system function better as a system, that is, as an integrated whole.

Such malfunctions may be present if certain customers are complaining repeatedly of late delivery, changes in tooling take too long, new employees make too many errors, or quality defects keep occurring. Active, involved managers treat these as potential symptoms that the work system may need to be rethought, reconfigured, or retrofitted. They look first for structural causes when a problem is recurring, rather than presuming that some individual is at fault. (Motivation or training or communication may turn out to be a problem, of course.) Listen to one manager describe her philosophy of systems maintenance:

> Although our work involves some very sophisticated technology (by way of computers and software), we have installed most of it ourselves and insisted that it be designed so our own people can maintain it. Obviously, we buy technology from outside vendors, and internally, we depend on some centralized data services [and mainframes], but all the interfaces have been fine-tuned to our needs and are understood and modifiable by our own people.
>
> We are continuously collecting real-time data from our operations which tell our managers not only *how* well

we are doing, but also tell them *where* retraining or staff development is required. So training is almost a continuous activity in response to our regular controls. It consists of everything from working with one manager who doesn't understand how to apply controls to a group of employees who are badly handling one aspect of their job. And that is one of the additional reasons why we insist on tailoring all our technology to our unique needs: it is only in that way that we can build in the kind of control our managers can use to assess efficiency, quality, and service on a continuous basis.

Since we insist on close involvement with whatever technology is placed in our area, we are also more likely to be able to improve it. My managers are constantly picking up ideas for making these automated systems work better. For example, the screens that get displayed on the terminals often lack some critical piece of information; the operator has to take extra minutes to go to a different data bank. Or we discover that one terminal operator could complete some piece of work herself if she could key in certain parameters which would allow the computer to produce a finished report. All those things are not that hard to do when you understand the basic software and have someone in your area who can develop the "fix."

A small amount of additional code then allows us to save thousands of dollars over a year in labor cost. And no one is working harder; in fact, their jobs are both easier and more interesting when you can build them up this way, on the basis of incremental improvements based on observing imperfections or opportunities.

One would hardly describe this manager as settling for stability and routine and forgoing real leadership. She is, however, engaged in seeking to build a self-maintaining system—a work system that operates with minimal managerial intervention. When managerial intervention is required, it is directed toward rebuilding the system to move it toward greater regularity. But building that system, in a dynamic organization, requires an almost never-ending series of creative interventions, as well as negotiations with insiders and out-siders to allow these to proceed.

In contrast, less effective managers are passive until some plan or budget deviation forces them to take action. Of course, by this time the real results often can be very bad. Worse, such managers are content to "meet the plan"; their operations don't get better. The status quo is easier to maintain than a constantly improving operation.

It is easy to observe operations in which poor coordination has been covered over by adding extra people, extra work steps, and redundant supplies. Because of these extra (and costly) resources, these operations continue to function with what appears to be reasonable efficiency. Only managers who are truly close to those operations can spot these "pasteovers," which are hiding unresolved coordination glitches. The imposition of just-in-time methods helps spot the redundancies created by managers who have been ineffective in eliminating coordination problems. The requirement that work move nonstop between stages will quickly pinpoint places where this smooth interlocking of tasks and functions is lacking.

Everyday maintenance is not a frozen-in-time-and-space status quo. It is continuous fine-tuning, adjusting, improving, and retrofitting of people and technology. As we sought to describe in chapter 5, the interfaces separating jobs have such complexity and volatility that it is impossible for these jobs to interconnect properly without managers undertaking substantial and continuous change efforts. *Nothing stays coordinated for very long without managerial efforts designed to facilitate that coordination.*

Change is required to get stability, but this change is not a one-time thing. Good managers will be finding ways in which their systems have subpar performance, or can improve performance, with regularity. It is unlikely that a manager can exhaust the possibilities and requirements for change in maintaining high performance in a short period. Middle managers with tenure less than several years cannot learn all the things that are interfering with effectiveness, nor try out an adequate number of new initiatives that could improve systems performance.

Thus, the view that two kinds of managers, leaders and administrators, should coexist is patently false. All managers need to be change agents. (Although not all will, of course.) And, usually, as luck and Murphy's Law would have it, just about the time a manager has managed to fine-tune her operations, an adjacent work flow stage or external vendor or customer makes a change or demand that throws the system out of kilter. The response required is *adaptation.*

Adaptation

Managers are not an island to themselves. Many, of course, have fantasies of being one and thus not having to cope with being "tossed around" by the ill-timed or ill-chosen (from their point of view) decisions of others. Other internal departments and external customers and vendors keep buffeting the organization with their changes. An earlier work flow stage can no longer deliver needed data early on Thursday; a trusted vendor changes the composition of a critical component; or a support group modifies its technology so that a whole new series of problems are created in getting it to be responsive to "normal" requests. As described in chapter 1, the frequency of such changes will keep increasing in fast-paced, competition- and technology-driven contemporary business.

If quality and performance and service are to remain at high levels, such external changes require internal adaptations, and they are very similar in terms of leadership energy and skill as what is required by maintenance.

Major Changes

The only real difference between a major change and an adaptation is the amount of change. The following is an example from our research files.[1]

A Line Manager's Struggle to Introduce a New Technology

Kay Cohen was anxious to improve the performance of her department. She had felt there was some ambiguity in corporate strategies. There was a good deal of emphasis being placed on cost reduction (that is, becoming the lowest-cost producer); at the same time, though, there was a strategic thrust based on getting closer to the customers. For a long time it had not been clear what the implication of these apparently contradictory strategies were for her unit. Hers was a relatively self-contained unit that produced a variety of custom glues and adhesives for other manufacturers. She was relatively new on the job, and she knew that some of her fellow managers questioned whether a woman could "make it" on the manufacturing side of the business.

As she sought to put together her plans and budgets for the 1991 fiscal year, Kay realized that there was not much she could do to improve performance. Her sales revenues depended on the division's marketing department, and most of her raw materials were purchased in small quantities from large chemical companies. That gave her little room to maneuver on price. Her employees worked as an effective team; morale was high and quality excellent.

Kay then realized that there was one significant area for improvement. She depended on an internal source for unique solvents that were used to make about one-half of her custom glues. But even here, she was a small customer (albeit "in the family") compared to the big external customers of the division, Process Chemicals (PC). As a small customer, she frequently had to wait days for a delivery from PC (because the company had a strict policy limiting inventories). Understandably, PC was reluctant to let a small order from her interfere with the preparation of a large batch going to an important customer. But this delay hurt her ability to give fast turnaround time to her own good customers. Further, she often had to accept a less than optimal solvent if she was really pressed, just because that was the type closest to what PC was processing that day or that week.

Kay had read some weeks earlier in one of the chemical engineering publications she regularly perused that a small Oregon company, Dill Chemicals, had come out with some new equipment that could produce relatively small quantities of the raw materials she used. She then undertook an extensive investigation to find who sold and serviced the equipment in Chicago (where she worked) and what customers Dill could identity for her to interview.

About fifteen phone calls later, Kay had satisfied herself that Dill was no fly-by-night operation. They had actually been in business nine years, and this particular piece of equipment had been sold for other purposes for five years. There had been only one customer for the solvent version, and Kay decided to fly to New Orleans to talk to that company right after her scheduled meeting with a manufacturer's representative in Chicago. By then she had drawn up a list of about 25 questions she wanted answers to with respect to the efficiency, reliability, and operating characteristics of the Dill units.

It took about a month to get this data in hand. After using some spreadsheets and a lot of analysis, Kay felt she could justify a capital investment of $450,000 (the full cost of the equipment, training, and maintenance). The return on the investment (ROI) would come in close to 20 percent.

Kay then had a preliminary discussion with her boss, Mike Graflin. She had hesitated to go earlier because she knew his reluctance to support new capital projects during this period, when all budgets were being cut to the bone. Her informal presentation emphasized that the new business that could be attracted by fast turnaround time on custom orders, plus the savings generated by lower material costs, would help her build the business. She felt that her numbers were conservative, because she would be buying some additional flexibilities that would allow her to expand the range of her product offerings. Mike said he would think about it, but he warned her that PC would fight it "tooth and nail." He also suggested that she consult Jim Travis, an engineer in the corporate staff technology group, "before going any further on this Dill equipment question."

Kay had forgotten the company even had a staff technology group, but after meeting with Jim she arranged an appointment with Travis. She was really beginning to get excited about the project when Travis called back to say that he had to go to the West Coast for ten days on a rush project, and he would call when he got back to reschedule the appointment. Before Kay had a chance to digest that bit of bad news, Graflin called to say he had gotten her a fifteen-minute slot at the next month's division steering committee meeting. This required a real spit-and-polish presentation, with carefully prepared overheads and a lot of number crunching.

Now Kay began to worry. Final budgets were due in four weeks; she still had a lot of data to collect and get analyzed on her existing activities. And, of course, she still had her days filled with the normal human and technical problems of running a relatively complex, diverse batch operation with upward of one hundred products and eighty employees.

Kay needed to see Travis in order to even have a chance of getting her boss's support. She also needed time to talk with the marketing people to get them behind her, and to sound out an old friend in the finance area as to what details she needed to watch in her formal equipment purchase proposal (EPP). (She had never before gone through the long, painful exercise of filling out one of these torturous EPP forms designed by the finance department to discourage the weak of heart.) In addition, there was the need to get some measure of the opposition that PC would mount to her proposal; she had some lingering hopes that they would be delighted to be rid of this pesky internal customer. In her spare time, she worked up her steering committee presentation.

Questions of what to do first and how to get enough time to do it all began to intrude, and Kay had her first sense of panic. Why was she doing all this? Her unit, though not great, certainly had been doing all right, and her boss was simply pressuring for the usual 5 to 10 percent improvements for the next year. She probably could have gotten some or most of that by introducing a couple of new products one of her chemists had cooked up that marketing thought it could do something with. But although she would do that, it was not a major challenge, nor would it result in the kind of major improvement that this project could provide. Further, the Dill equipment would finally give her some long-run autonomy and end the time-consuming (and demeaning) pleading and bickering with PC.

She decided it was worth the effort to take her best shot at getting this through. But she now realized that she had to see Travis first, both to avoid antagonizing her boss and to legitimate her interest in this new technology (because she was not an engineer—which, of course, might be one of the first issues the steering committee would probe). Kay called him and discovered that he would have an evening free when he was in Los Angeles. She booked a flight that would allow her to put in a half day at her office, see Travis for dinner, and take a red-eye back to Chicago. She also prepared a compact summary version of all of her work, which Travis promised to take with him and read on the flight before their meeting.

On the plane Kay was apprehensive, but Travis thought she had done a good job researching Dill. That was the good news, but he also said it would be wasteful to use the Dill equipment for the more mundane solvents she used; she should continue to "buy" those from PC. Being truly anxious to be rid of the PC connection, Kay's first instinct was to fight that part of it. She had only a limited amount of time, however, to get Travis to in effect "sign off" on her proposal. She could see this was not a casual suggestion of his; he felt strongly about it.

Kay agreed to start out for the first six months splitting the sourcing, but she said that if the Dill equipment was as efficient as her research suggested, she could cover all her needs without using PC. Travis thought that a reasonable period to experiment with this made good sense. Then he added just one more complication: "You ought to see Phyliss Cyzak in our office; she's really expert on maintenance and turnaround times for that kind of equipment. Have her send me a copy of what she gives to you." Still another bridge to cross!

Back in Chicago, Kay had her meeting with her contact in finance, who proposed that she "go back to the drawing board" to be sure that she could justify an ROI of 25 percent, with the corporation charging its units 15 percent as the cost of new funds. To do that, Kay realized that her unit had to count on really substantial new sales to be generated by fast turnaround time from customer order to loading dock.

As soon as she got back, Kay got on her boss's schedule. When they met and she reported on Travis's support, he agreed to support her proposal. But he warned, "Remember, you've got your neck out on this one. When everyone's budgets are being squeezed, if you do get fresh capital it better really pay off, or both of us are in trouble." She managed to corner Phyliss Cyzak, who ironically was a lot less flexible than her boss and less willing to make time. But persistence and patience (and not saying what she was tempted to say) finally paid off: the data were forthcoming, and though they were less optimistic than Kay might have liked, they still justified most of her assumptions. Thus, Kay had lots to negotiate with marketing's Juan Colon, who was the second key lever (Travis had been the first).

Juan turned out to be very helpful. He was not disinterested in her proposal to have about a dozen product types that a customer could get within seventy-two hours of placing an order, but he was reluctant to put numbers on that enthusiasm. She asked if he would be willing to call one or two of the customers most likely to be interested, get their reactions, and to meet with her again in a couple days. Juan agreed, and at the next meeting he was pleased to report that there had been substantial interest, more than he had expected. Customers had wanted as close to zero inventory as possible. Over the next several days, Kay and Juan exchanged sales estimates for the coming year that could be "defended in court." These would be a critical part of her EPP.

Kay had not been looking forward to discussing all this with Chris Doppi of PC, who was part of the old guard of tough, macho managers. She was not prepared, however, for how really angry he got. Essentially, he accused her of trying to injure his costs to get back at PC because "they don't jump every time you say boo." He pointed out that although her orders were only 5 percent of the total output, because they used available people and equipment, the corporation basically had a close to zero cost for those material she used. What he didn't say, but Kay now realized, was that this also gave him a nice cushion to cover any inefficiencies he had.

Because Chris seemed intractable at this point, Kay asked if they could have lunch together the next day. She hoped to review her orders for the past year and show that by continuing to use his simpler solvents, only 30 to 40 percent of the solvent volume would be lost. She decided not to mention that this might disappear as well if all worked according to her plan. She wondered if this was deception on her part. Chris was still unmoved and said he could not support a proposal that would injure the corporation by making one of its key units less efficient.

At this point Kay had Mike, her boss, on her side—sort of. Travis in corporate technology would support the proposal, as would Juan Colon in marketing. She had at least sounded out finance to get the lay of the land. Only one obvious land mine, PC's Chris Doppi, had not been cleared. She decided that she would have to take a chance and proceed without his blessing.

Mike's voice would be a critical one when the EPP was assessed, and Kay sought to strengthen his resolve should there be an internal conflict between Chris and Mike's divisions. Based on the relationship she had built with Juan, she was able to get marketing to prepare some projections for 1992, assuming these fast turnarounds, that would show a potential improvement of more than 30 percent in unit profitability. With a lot of confident talk on her part and those numbers, she felt that Mike had switched from being a reluctant cosigner to an enthusiast. Such results would help put his division in a much better light when budget time rolled around in 1992.

Just when things were beginning to look more hopeful, Kay learned that Chris had been circulating some materials suggesting that the Dill company had financial problems. He knew, as did she, that the company was very reluctant to buy equipment from startups and from companies unlikely to be in business for the like of the equipment. She got another friend with connections in the brokerage community to get some data sheets together on Dill's finances, including a Dun and Bradstreet evaluation. This, Kay felt, would strengthen her boss's hand at any meeting in which this came up. She avoided, however, the temptation to also give Mike an analysis of how much her business allowed Chris to be sloppy with production scheduling: her solvents could be slipped in to fill unused machine time or taken out of production when a "real" customer had needs.

At this point, Kay had some thoughts about whether the game was really worth the candle. She had been knocking herself out on this, and yet she knew that there was a good deal of uncertainty in top management on whether her division was worth keeping, given its overall competitive position in the markets it served. Wouldn't it be something to go through all this and then have the division sold?

The final approval that came down a few weeks later seemed almost anticlimactic; but it was not the time to rest on laurels. Kay immediately put together a task force to work out problems of implementation for the Dill machines. It included an engineer with a lot of technical experience who Travis could free up from his staff, her most experienced production supervisor, a member of the division's maintenance group who knew a good deal about equipment start-up issues, and an experienced operator. Kay would sometimes act as chair for the group; otherwise, it would rotate. Their assignment was to provide a time line of issues that would need resolving and actions that needed to be taken in order to expedite the installation and use of the Dill equipment. For example, they needed to see whether Dill could provide an adequate training manual for their operators and what modifications or additions would be necessary to suit their needs. There were at least a hundred such issues.

The value of the task force was that people developed a loyalty and commitment to making this project work and to each other (which meant that it would have some priority in their busy schedules). They were more likely to be helpful and "walk the extra mile" for a group to which they were tied. Also, because they represented many of the major interests involved, they could quickly exchange ideas and work through problems from a multifunctional point of view. For example, the maintenance representative wanted a week to work out any bugs, but the production supervisor argued that the cost of that would just be too high. The man from corporate technology answered the issue by saying that other parts of the company would bring in new pieces of equipment on a weekend: "It is worth the overtime for a couple technicians to have the free floor space and the uninterrupted time." The group decided that they could safely schedule one regular workday and the preceding weekend. Many trade-offs and flexible exchanges went this way. During the period this was taking place, Kay scheduled a meeting with a member of the corporate legal staff, who would be responsible for drawing up the contract with Dill. He had already spent some time with Dill's representative for the Midwest and knew in detail the technical claims the company made for these machines and their standard maintenance contract. Kay didn't want a standard agreement; she wanted the contract to guarantee certain performance specifications and also guarantee that in case of breakdown Dill would have the equipment functioning within seventy-two hours, even if that meant flying in replacements. There would be penalties attached to these requirements, of course.

Shortly after that meeting, Mike, Kay's boss called her in on a different subject. In the course of the conversation, though, he indicated that he thought she was too aggressive in some of her lateral relations. As an example he used her initiative to the legal staff: "Kay, they thought you were trying to tell them how to do their job, and I think you were! They are the experts in contracts, not you." Kay's efforts to explain why she wanted something more than standard language didn't seem to move him. She began to think that he might be critical about a lot of the pressureful contacts she had been involved in over this equipment.

In about three and a half months after her first discussions with Mike, Kay had the new equipment. The installation had gone well; the test results were excellent. In less than a week, as per schedule, they were producing needed raw materials for Kay's unit.

Then a series of problems emerged. The first was that the production runs produced liquids that could not immediately be used in production, and these were being stored in drums adjacent to the Dill machines. A division safety inspector spotted this almost at once, and he indicated that the department had to get approved, explosion-proof storage vessels, double lined and shock proof. The solvents needed to be in secure storage within twenty-four hours. When Kay learned that the cost for new vessels would be in four figures and that she might have to wait a week or two, she undertook a telephone surveillance of the entire division. Sure enough, there were two such containers, old but serviceable, in a warehouse facility. They were quickly moved to where they would be useful.

The second problem was more serious. Several employees complained they were getting headaches and even nausea from fumes coming from the Dill equipment. Maintenance quickly identified a ventilation problem—in particular, a flue that seemed to be inadequate. Although there was some indication that there was a product design fault, Kay decided it just wasn't worth her time to get into this one and took the cost of building a replacement flue into her budget. (She assumed that there would be an appropriate time to request reimbursement during some future discussions with the Dill representative).

There were also some unanticipated issues involving job classification, as the two employees assigned to the Dills felt that the additional responsibility involved in operating these expensive, complex machines should be reflected in a higher wage rate. There was a battle with plant maintenance over getting more air flow into the area: There was more heat generated than expected, and the first reaction of maintenance had been there was nothing they could do about it. A few more meetings and a lot more phone calls and persuasion later, both of these situations were resolved. (Kay had gotten maintenance together with human resources and told them that she hoped they could agree on the requirements for circulation, but if they didn't or couldn't within a couple of days, she would make the decision. If they didn't like it, they could tell her boss.)

Shortly after this, Kay was working until about 8 P.M. (as she frequently did), and she thought she would take a walk through the production area. She spotted Artie O'Brien, a second-shift worker she hadn't seen in about a year. Even though it was late—and she had been working now for more than twelve hours—Kay stopped to inquire how he was doing and shoot the breeze for a few minutes. As she thought the conversation was ending, Artie said, "Kay, as you may know, we do much of the cleanup work on the second shift. Now the first shift has been told by their supervisor to turn off the heaters in the Dills at the end of the shift to save electricity. But that means that when we come to clean them out, it takes two or three times as long as it should because everything is congealed. If they had a rheostat or something and could just leave them on half power or something, our productivity would go up enormously." This was a new one to Kay. When she approached the supervisor the next day, Artie's analysis was correct: the supervisor, feeling that he was following an earlier directive of Kay to do everything possible to cut costs, had insisted that his shift have all machines turned off before they left.

The really significant surprise to Kay, however, was the bankruptcy of a major customer for her specialty glues. The previous year, the customer had represented 19 percent of her volume; the resulting drop in sales made a shambles of all the projections Kay had used in the EPP and with Mike. For some months, the performance of Kay's unit was substantially below her projections, and she sweated blood. Her boss had a number of pressureful things to say about how bad this would look on their records. Gradually, though, the improved product mix and customer service began paying off. By the end of the fiscal year Kay's unit had more than made up for the loss, and she had exceeded her budget—by only 2 percent, but it was still a great comeback after the bankruptcy.

Looking back, was it worth it? Kay thought so. To be sure, more time, effort, blood, sweat, and tears had been involved than she had originally intended. But the upcoming year was looking great, and she was anticipating a number of new products that she would now have the flexibility and resources to produce. Several customers took the initiative to call her directly to express their appreciation for the extremely good delivery times and indicated that would make her company their vendor of choice for all their glue needs.

Discussion

The behavioral detail included in this case illustrates the enormous managerial effort, skill, and persistence in "working the organization" required of a manager who seeks to introduce change. And this wasn't that consequential a change; a naive manager might have thought the implementation would be child's play. But note the number of managers who had to be involved, each with distinctive personalities, causing the technical issues to be obscured by communications and political considerations. Small technical details often made a critical difference (for example, the problems created when the first shift turned off the heaters causing congealing on the second shift).

The most significant aspect of change from a managerial point of view is that many of the comfortable routines get lost; the hundreds of massaged interfaces now have rough edges. Over time, existing technologies have had their coordination problems solved by many undocumented adaptations that involved negotiations and compromises. Change opens a Pandora's box of problems, many trivial, but each threatening performance. In essence, problems ricochet, as efforts to deal with one create miscoordinations at another point of the interconnected system. All of this must be dealt with in attempting to reinterlock the uncounted interdependencies that arise from the multiple interfaces of each function. One has to wonder: how many contemporary managers, modeling and pleasing their current bosses and seeking to climb the career ladder quickly, would devote the unflagging energy demonstrated by Kay? It is knowing the reality of what is involved in demonstrating leadership in introducing change that will cause organizations to select and reward managers capable of accomplishing this quite remarkable tour de force. As long as introducing change appears primarily to be a problem of getting people to sit around a table and come to an agreement, however, these kind of leadership skills will not be developed.[2]

Kay's problems did not result from workers fearing the unknown, but from peers (other managers) resisting the known. And throughout, interpersonal managerial problems were inseparably intertwined with technology issues. No manager could deal with one without understanding the other.

Managers who are working leaders don't seek to insert ready-made, store-bought (that is, textbook or consultant) solutions. They recognize that in order to work well, any "fix" must be fully integrated into the routines of the organization. Therefore, every new input has to be finely tailored into the unique jobs and work configuration for which peers and subordinates are responsible.

GENERAL MANAGERS VERSUS FUNCTIONAL MANAGERS: IS THE LEADERSHIP DIFFERENT?

A reasonably accepted definition of a general manager is a manager who has direct control of most of the functions necessary for completed output. Ideally, this is an output that allows that unit to be a profit center. General managers thus have to develop those leadership skills associated with balancing and trading off or optimizing the contributions of each of the key functions necessary for completed work. From the point of view of management development, it has been assumed without question that functional managers are not in the same league with general or product managers. To get real management experience, one has had to move from heading up a function to the more diverse and broad level of responsibility.

Although functional managers usually aren't profit centers (they are more likely cost centers), however, and although they obviously don't control a wide range of other functions, some of their managerial challenges can be quite similar to general managers. Within most functional units, there are a diversity of tasks that have to be coordinated. The difficulty of integrating these tasks, eliminating errors, improving efficiency, and finding technology to expedite the process depends in part on how big, how dispersed, and how complicated these units are. But almost regardless of size, in some measure the same managerial-change challenges exist as in a general manager's job. (It is worth noting that some of the detailed cases and quotes in earlier sections of this chapter are from functional departments and functional managers.)

Unfortunately, as long as managerial challenges are viewed in traditional GAMP terms, those boundary or interface problems and the potential for continuous improvement and innovation are not perceived in functional departments. Only "product" type organizations have real managerial challenges built into them. Like any such prophecy, this one is also self-confirming and, many functional managers do not show much work leadership.

> The Vice President for manufacturing was impressed with the need to turn around his operation. He introduced a number of organizational changes that enabled his people to provide a very different level of product service. With a major reduction in retooling and turnaround time, manufacturing could produce a wider range of product at highly competitive prices. Just-in-time methods further lowered costs. The vice president had expected that this new manufacturing competency and cost structure would enable the marketing division to mount a new, more aggressive strategy in relation to existing customers and new customers. Instead, he found that marketing was indifferent to this new potential in manufacturing and had no interest in thinking through or implementing a new strategy that would reflect any of these accomplishments.

It was not its functional (in contrast to product) structure that caused marketing to be sluggish and nonadaptive to manufacturing. The situation called for leadership ability; the head of marketing lacked it, and perhaps so did their common boss (who was a product manager). Thus, senior managements may fail to have realistic improvement expectations for their functional managers. And functional managers may respond by not being dynamic and innovative on organizational issues.

It is often asserted that functional managers cannot be "real" leaders, because they don't have profit performance measures. But as noted in chapter 3, profits are hardly foolproof measures. There are many measures available to assess how well a functional manager contributes to corporate strategy. Service, quality, cost saving, innovativeness—all can be measured, and all can be as useful as measures of contribution as unit profit. Nonfinancial measures can perform the same control function as financial measures. They can tell the line manager (in this case a functional manager) what he or she needs to do to support the corporate strategy (for example, to reduce the time taken to develop a new high-speed film from six to two years.) And it can tell senior management how well its strategy is working (for example, on reducing time to market for new products) and where intervention is required.

DO SELF-MANAGING GROUPS NEED MANAGING?

Organizations keep rediscovering the advantages of having highly interdependent functions encapsulated within an organizational unit (in a department, team, or work group). This way the countless everyday communications, exchanges, and trade-offs can take place easily and informally. Professionals and managers working for a common boss are going to be more willing to compromise to facilitate and complement the work of a colleague than they would be for someone from another department. This obvious advantage of organizing on the basis of interdependence rather than functional specialty could only be missed by a GAMP-trained manager who still believed that all communications must flow through the common boss.

No real-life manager, of course, could absorb, think through, and reroute all these requests and ideas. The manager has to depend on teamwork to accomplish the coordination. And teamwork means the almost effortless compromises and reciprocities that should take place among colleagues seeking to get a job done, not to stake out territory or assert status.

In recent years, this concept of intertask exchange and reciprocity has been extended to handling some of the support activity that normally takes place outside the unit. So, in a socalled self-managing team, the group itself may handle materials requisitions, negotiations with human resources and quality control departments, and even selection of new employees. But this does not eliminate their need for management and a manager with leadership skills. Just as computers did not create paperless offices, self-managing groups do not create managerless organizations. By eliminating lower-level supervisory tasks, they emphasize the importance of the middle manager's real leadership role.

Managers in place over autonomous groups have critical roles in negotiating with external groups whose routines contradict or inter-fere with the work of their units. And they must also negotiate for resources, new technology, and approvals with higher management. Most importantly, they need to have a strategy for the future that gives direction to their units. They have to shape the trade-offs that employees make in deciding how to deal with daily inconsistencies or contradictions (such as which internal or external customer deserves priority).

Going back to the earlier discussion of maintenance, adaptation, and change, the greater the self-managing capability of the work group, the more the manager's focus shifts to the latter two elements. But these require the most demanding of human relations skills.

CONCLUSION

There is no rest for the weary. Management in modern change-oriented and competition-pressured organizations requires very simi-lar leadership skills to routinize, to adapt, and to introduce change. And functional managers and managers of autonomous groups don't get an exemption. If their units are to be successful in maintaining their internal and external interconnections—in making the systems work—they have to be energetically and technically involved.

In our view, management and leadership are synonymous in the contemporary world. Managers who are not leaders can only be fail-ures.

10

The Decision Process and Management Teams

Making decisions also involves a work process; it is not usually an isolated, individual calculation. To be sure, some decisions are not orchestrated; they are made in the manager's head. One of the major advantages organizations derive from having involved managers with knowledge of work-level operations is they have the wherewithal to make some decisions themselves.

> Many Japanese automobile plants traditionally had college-educated supervisors directly in charge of manufacturing operations, particularly in the early stages of a new model year. These managers had the training, as well as the knowledge, to make modifications in the plans that had come down from the engineering departments that had created the new model's manufacturing methods (often in consultation with employee groups, of course).

In many of the cases presented in preceding chapters, it appears as though many American managers don't have the involvement in their operations to make sensible technical decisions. In practice, many rely on staff technical people who may or may not have the same breadth of perspective and strategic point of view the manager would have. Where managers don't have this confidence and/or must rely on combinations of staff departments and even less well-informed senior managers, decision making is much delayed. It can also be less pertinent to the problems being addressed.

DECISIONS REQUIRING TEAMWORK

But most decisions require teamwork, inputs and debate among many managers, line peers as well as staff. When critical knowledge and the points of view of key managers are excluded from the decision process, the resulting choices are usually deficient.

Two similar businesses merged. To senior management in the surviving organization, it looked as though the management information system in the acquired company was superior to its own (given some superficial comparisons). As a result, the order went down the line that this new software was to be installed. Two well-informed and relevant managers had not been consulted, and they knew that the "superiority" was based on carefully massaged data. In fact, the acquired company's program was substantially inferior. The decision stuck, however, and substantial costs were incurred to install the deficient system and to find alternative ways of handling problems that had been dispatched routinely by the previous system.

Two organizations competing in the same market handled their decision making quite differently. The first was very functionalized; marketing and operations were isolated from one another. Their performance was distinctly inferior to their competitor, who allowed operations managers to have an input into marketing decision making.

Managers inevitably have limitations regarding how broadly they can conceive a problem. Their own training, their experience, and the goals of their current departments all will constrain or bias their interpretation of the "facts."[1]

Some anonymous sources assert that AT & T may have had some setbacks in selling certain new telephone services because their competitors gave greater weight to the importance of customer billing software. AT & T may have been too technologically oriented, considering billing technology unworthy of so much emphasis.

NASA had more difficulty in launching some of its hardware in the early years because the specialists in launch procedures had almost no voice in design decisions.[2]

Allowing inputs—that is, orchestrating a process by which various specialists and interested groups get a chance to influence decisions in which they have a stake and/or to which they can contribute expertise—does not mean that these decisions are made by consensus, or that a group responsible for some function or activity can't handle its own affairs. It does mean that the responsible managers have to listen to and come up with responses to those with different points of view.

The Leader's Role in Rebalancing Decision Weights

In a contemporary world filled with multiple goals and contradictions, good managers have to make trade-offs. Decision making is not simply adding up facts (and probabilities) and deciding the optimal course to move most expeditiously toward *the* goal. Goals change and elaborate depending on the strategies of the manager and the organization. As they change, the weights given to various interests, the data, and the decision criteria will change. Then the strategic rebalancing of the weight to be placed on various considerations also needs to be transmitted to subordinates, and that is a leadership responsibility.

Product managers were expected to weigh heavily the market potential for any new product in deciding whether to launch it. Other factors included the value of having a full range of products for certain markets and preempting certain potential product initiatives by competitors. In this case, the development labs had come up with a product that would give the company a toehold in a new market. But the product did not seem to offer enough advantages to threaten the commanding lead (in market share) of the dominant firm in that industry. The

product manager decided she could not justify additional
expenditures, because it was unlikely that the product
would ever become a real winner. Senior management
then had a series of meetings that strengthened the
weight placed on having some product in this new market.

Thus, most decision making represents an orchestration of inputs
and viewpoints of those with relevant information and influence; it
is not the product of one person reflecting in solitary splendor.[3]

Orchestrating Who Gets Involved When

The weight that various factors play in coming to a decision can also
be modified or adjusted by changing who gets involved and when.
An astute leader makes sure, for example, that an experienced marketing manager gets involved in a discussion of product redesign relatively early rather than relatively late. A very technical organization,
all of whose managers are very quantitative and linear in their thinking, may need to have more imaginative, creative, and spontaneous
specialists brought into their decision processes if a customer and
marketing viewpoint is important. GAMP-trained managers can't
think in these terms. To them, decision making is done by the person
or unit with the proper authority.

A customer service manager complained that a contract
was being drawn up with a vendor that would cause
grievous problems with customers, and that his group
needed to have some input to the terms of the contract.
The department with functional responsibility related to
buying these items refused. They simply stated that the
service group had the responsibility to handle the
merchandise *after* it was acquired.

A Blow Against Groupthink

Functional diversity (and other kinds of diversity as well) can help
shatter "groupthink", the propensity of managers who work closely
together with common experiences and group ties to evolve an unrealistic consensus.[4] Creative leaders have to work to counter the tendency of some subordinates to cope with high-risk decisions by evolving a quick, safe consensus. This is the source of that traditional

wisdom that speaks of throwing an outsider or a very different kind of person into a managerial group that is too cozy.

A careful study of corporations who lost their leading edge, who became less successful over time, suggests that their senior managers failed in this leadership function of rebalancing decision weights. The study concludes that a major source of market failure is the tendency for functional groups who were responsible for corporate success under one set of external circumstances to continue to dominate key decisions even when their assumptions and norms are less relevant. Thus, organizations that became successful because of their product innovation abilities (superb R & D, usually) find it difficult to shift some control to manufacturing or marketing. In the same way, organizations that learned to market superbly and achieved fine financial returns from that specialization found it difficult to give greater emphasis to manufacturing or R & D when circumstances changed.[5]

This unfavorable biasing of critical decisions can persist, of course, because most such decisions are filled with ambiguity and uncertainty. It is not obvious, except to an astute leader, that decision weights are misallocated or that the decision "chorus" needs a rebalancing of voices.

> Some significant portion of the multibillion real estate losses of the banking industry reflects this failure in executive decision making. During the go-go days of ever-rising real estate prices in the 1980s, many banks went all out to put more real estate loans on the books. Under pressure and inducements from their bosses, loan officers were accepting extravagant property assessments, encouraging–and sometime forging—exaggerated borrower assets and income, and hiding other borrower debts and even other mortgages on the property.[6]

Managers who are not leaders find it tempting to look only at a single goal (just as many bank managers in the 1980s looked only at the size of their real estate loan portfolio). Simply to maximize and further such goals allows one the confort of having easy numerical measures of success. But good decisions are almost always balanced decisions, because there are usually multiple goals involved.

How Top Management Orchestrates
Decision-Making Participation

A recent study of multinationals concludes that Ericsson, a Swedish-based corporation that has been successful in advanced telecommunications, owes some of its technological and market effectiveness to its sophistaced understanding of what leaders need to do to orchestrate the major decisions that shape the business.

> Ericsson's organization has never allowed one organizational perspective to dominate and others to atrophy. . . . [Rather] than search for an idealized, static concept of organizational fit, Ericsson has pragmatically accepted that ambiguity, overlap, and change in management responsibilities are inevitable.[7]

The authors give a number of vivid examples of Ericsson's dynamic balancing of influence and decision-making power among specialists.

- Historically, Ericsson, like other telephone equipment manufacturers, established country-based subsidiaries to sell its equipment. Over time, these units became excessively autonomous and ignored advantages that could be secured by utilizing more common technologies and accepting more centralized sources for these. Product managers therefore were given more influence over these decisions.
- When a new and not fully understood technology was evolving, management diminished the autonomy of product groups and encouraged centralized engineering groups to exercise more control of the technical functions that were embedded in these product groups.
- When these product design uncertainties were resolved and the more pressing questions involved negotiating with individual governments, rebalancing was required. Many countries demanded technology transfer and local manufacturing in exchange for buying telephone exchange equipment. Ericsson then gave a good deal of decision-making power to the management of country-based subsidiaries.
- The advent of still newer electronic technology and new technological uncertainties caused Ericsson to again increase the power of the centralized R & D function.[8]

MIDDLE MANAGERS AS DECISION TEAM LEADERS

Middle managers can exercise the same leadership initiatives once they recognize, as Ericsson did, the following:

- The most important business decisions almost always involve substantial ambiguities and uncertainties. Being rational and well motivated does not guarantee good decisions.
- Also, these decisions depend on the interplay and interaction of specialized viewpoints (product managers, country managers, centralized and decentralized R & D staff, marketing managers, and so forth). They are not usually made by one manager working in isolation.
- Thus, the leader can only get optimal decisions that reflect the current situation and the leader's strategies by frequent rebalancing of the relative influence of the specialized executives who must be involved in the process.

The last involves changing the organization structure, communication patterns (who gets access to what information and when) and resource allocations. Note that these are the neglected leadership actions that appeared to make it impossible for companies in the PAE industry to be successful in duplicating technology changes introduced by dominant competitors.[9]

Rebalancing Influence Patterns

Leaders also need to be sensitive to personal differences in ability to be articulate spokespersons and/or to dominate meetings. Dominant and articulate representatives of less important functions or points of view can sway a group meeting to ignore the points of view of other, more relevant functional representatives. For example, when a newly critical specialty is headed by a self-effacing executive with limited initiative or assertiveness, extra managerial efforts will be required to cause his or her views to be taken into account at the right stage of the decision process.

A skillful, very senior executive brought out the special technical knowledge and unique viewpoint of a modest scientist who was the most knowledgable person in the room on how a particular research area was developing worldwide. His voice was being lost in the competition for "air time" to more dominant and self-assured managers. The information he contributed saved the organization from making a major commitment to a technology that was soon to be obsolete.

Usually the intermixing of relevant viewpoints and specialties is more complicated, because decisions get made over a period of time and in a variety of meetings and geographical settings. Under these circumstances, the manager has to assess the dynamics of these meetings—who was there and what role they played. (Regrettably, in large organizations there is a strong tendency for upper management to hear only a single voice, a consensus viewpoint in which all disagreements and alternatives have been erased from the record.) The observations of an experienced manager reflect these decision conundrums: "When I was a kid, I thought that most decisions were matters of choosing right over wrong. . . . I'm still looking to make a decision like that. It seems that all my decisions are between two goods or two bads."[10]

Thus, good decisions depend on carefully balanced weights (for the factors being considered) and balanced inputs from specialists who have ideas, information, and preferences to contribute. The manager has to orchestrate the participation of key people who represent critical specialities. Most of all, managers who are leaders are very sensitive to the dangers of groupthink and to the temptations of a focus on maximizing simple, single aggregates (like the size of a bank's real estate loan portfolio).

LEADING CROSS-FUNCTIONAL TEAMS: MONITORING THEIR DECISION MAKING

Business has discovered the value of pulling together functional specialists whose outputs need coordination into a common work group or team. Thus, development, manufacturing, and marketing specialists might work together on a new product team. These teams approximate the advantages of matrix organizations, in which technical people have a project "home" and a specialist "home." Membership in a relatively small project team builds loyalty to the project and encourages the specialists to take into account in their decision making the needs of other specialists who would normally be at earlier or later stages of the work flow. Because they continue to work for functional departments (such as manufacturing), their training and other commitments cause them to represent and demand those decisions from the project team that will be essential to meet the technical standards of their home function.

These teams are a way of using a structural innovation to give a large organization some of the advantages of the team spirit of cooperation bred in small groups. But there are leadership issues surrounding the decision process of these groups.

Cross-Functional Decisions

The objective of these teams is to integrate the diverse and potentially conflicting requirements of several functions whose work is interdependent. Thus, development specialists could specify a technically correct design (consistent with current trends in technology) that would create horrendous manufacturing problems or that would have marketplace disadvantages. Such development decisions have to accommodate manufacturing and marketing needs.

This is a simple statement of what cross-functional teams are supposed to accomplish, but the reality is more complicated. In particular, the decision process needs to be inclusive of a number of technical trade-offs for team effectiveness. Further, there needs to be a continuing series of decisions as the project evolves. And, managers responsible for such teams need to assure themselves that his process actually works. Dissecting the dynamics of decision making in these teams provides guidelines for their management.

Interface Negotiations

This is what cross-functional teamwork means in practice: making interfunctional trade-offs to facilitate coordination and the integrity of the total system. It is a demanding decision process, and the requirements go beyond simply putting people together who will like each other. They go to the heart of the concept of teamwork.

As described earlier, the interfaces between functions (as between jobs or tasks) usually are complex and ambiguous. These interfaces represent the boundary conditions that determine how one function needs to interlock or synchronize with other functions. The interface for operations, development, or any other function includes a number of microdecisions about the proposed changes. To simplify, there are two kinds of microdecisions:

- *What will be done* (the actions that will be taken)
- *How it will be done* (the criteria for internal decisions, trade-offs, what gets high versus low priority, who gets what information and when and in what sequence, what will be the control signals that alert people that something is wrong or needs modification, what tasks will get more experienced personnel, and so forth).

Thus, in a planning or project group representing diverse functions (or regions or products), the manager responsible for the team's performance will expect that each member will have a unique constellation of "microdecisions." These have evolved as that individual has done earlier work and anticipates what he wants as an outcome from the new project.

But each of these will be more or less negotiable depending on how important it is to the participant's work patterns and values and how much flexibility there is in the system (to allow for change). The dynamics of the group consist largely of exploring one another's needs and expectations and then engaging in a trade-off process by which these all become mutually consistent.

The trade-offs are typified by exchanges like the following.

- "You are making design decisions that presuppose that there will be a turnaround time of twenty-four hours. That is just too long for the requirements that are being imposed on us by our users; fifteen to eighteen hours is the maximum we can consider. What can be made less complicated or less time-consuming to speed the processing?"
- "If I specified a stronger shell for that rear element, which will be somewhat bulkier, can you reduce the amount of space you need for the generator?
- If we promise a new customer that he or she will receive a certificate of ownership within seventy-two hours of the time we receive their first payment, can you meet that deadline? And will finance allow us to do this before the customer's check has cleared if we can keep the outstandings below $50,000?

Leadership Monitoring

The leader will want to know how the team is functioning as a team in order to provide critical input if team effectiveness wanes. But what is team effectiveness? Below is an outline of how one manager measures effectiveness by observing the team in action.

1. All team members are responsive to requests from other team members to consider modifying their plans to take into account the consequences for other functions.

   A type of trade-off that needs leadership understanding and encouragement is one like this: at present, A's department's work contributes $2 per unit to the total cost of a finished item, and the activity undertaken in B's department costs $8 per unit. If A will modify how its work is done it will increase A's cost by $1 per unit, but decrease B's cost by $3 per unit. Clearly A will suffer on its cost "report card," but if the leader has created the right management appraisal and rewards, A will accept that change for the overall system improvement generated.

2. In real crises, team members are willing to seek out alternative ways of accomplishing their objectives. On occasion, a previously unknown and creative alternative will maintain the integrity of the function and also provide a different interface element more suited to other functions that have to be coordinated.

3. Team members are candid about their requirements; there is no tendency to inflate the importance of a boundary element because it is easier to do the job that way or because that is the comfortable, routine way of doing it. Individual team members have the skill to articulate verbally and/or in writing why they need certain boundary elements from functions controlled by other team members.

4. Team members provide each other with as much advance notice as possible regarding how they are progressing on their own assignments and where they are likely to have trouble meeting time, cost, or performance specifications they have agreed to. (In ineffective teams there is a great deal of with-

holding. Managers assume or hope that their deficiencies will never have to be revealed because other team members will get into trouble, thus providing them with more time to work through their problems.)

5. When discussions and negotiations are taking place, team members provide full and open information to others. They avoid the common practice of providing such narrow responses to inquiries that other managers have to play the equivalent of "twenty questions" to tease out all the relevant facts and ramifications of what is being discussed.
6. Team members avoid inflating their requirements or exaggerating their demands in order to give the appearance of compromising when these get deflated to what are their real positions.
7. No team member seeks to win an argument or gain a concession to assert primacy over others.

Thus, involved leaders can observe how effective the team is at making decisions based on continuous trade-offs between the real needs of individual functions (if the integrity of the function is to be preserved) and the needs of a well-coordinated system. They can observe who the good and poor team players are, as well as the capacity of the team to arrive at creative solutions to what at first appear to be legitimate impasses (that is, where the absolute needs of one function are totally unacceptable to another function). They can also spot whether or not their subordinate managers who make up the team are able to gain trust and credibility from their other team members. They know that team members have to be perceived as credible and trustworthy for fruitful trade-offs to take place.

A good manager knows how such reputations get constructed and can therefore coach and assist subordinates on how to attain credibility with peers. Trusting other people (believing that they will do what they say and that they need what they say) and attaching credibility to their decisions is a product of team members who excel at the following:

- fulfilling commitments (delivering on their promises)
- demonstrating thorough technical knowledge and competency within their function (knowing the real needs of their function and the nuances of how things work, and not having to rely on rote recall of subordinate briefings; also, knowing the

strengths and weaknesses of subordinates who will be implementing decisions)

- showing flexibility (the capacity to improvise in departing from comfortable routines and traditional ways of doing things, and the willingness to help out others in ways that may make their own work more difficult)
- providing full disclosure (being candid and forthcoming, and giving as much advance information as possible)

Although some of these may sound trite or obvious, they are the criteria that team members use in assessing each other. The leader has to be able to intervene when team members are not able or willing to perform these "good team member" behaviors. Otherwise, the cross-cultural team will not realize its potential for making the kind of decisions that assure rapid and high-quality implementation of innovations.

The leader has to be involved enough, close enough, to the group's interchanges to make these judgments. However, there is also another reason to be a "working leader" to facilitate team effectiveness. The leader has to handle some critical external coordinations. A seemingly rigid requirement can often be changed if some staff or company policy can be modified, an exception can be granted, or some external (to the group) procedure or process can be changed. The manager over the cross-functional team needs to be technically adept and energetic enough to negotiate for these changes with higher management or other staff groups.

Is a Team a Small Group

For obvious reasons, most managers seek to have all their interdependent subordinates under their direct control and identifying with a small group (in other words, decentralization). In most larger organizations, and given the realities of modern technology, this is often unrealistic. Key functions will be outside, and that desirable strong small group commitment won't evolve. Effective leaders, however, can still demand the same kind of effective trade-off process by continuous monitoring and intervention.

Negotiation is the lifeblood of the Japanese multinational. Although all the ones I have studied have formal profit-center structures, few of the divisions are fully self-contained. Manufacturing and sales are deliberately kept separate, so that they must negotiate with each other over prices and volume targets. In addition, there is negotiation between the products divisions, which buy and sell from each other.[11]

JANUS-FACED DECISION MAKING

Being two-faced smacks of hypocricy. But leaders often must meld contradictory requirements and balance contradictory requirements. To expect consistency (that things "add up") is to be naive. It is more realistic to expect that when the manager dutifully seeks to be correct in meeting requirement A, this choice may well injure requirement B.

Consider what previous chapters have illustrated about the necessary contradictions of being a working leader.

- Delegation, of course, is a highly useful basic management tool, but there are many times when the manager must not only look over a subordinate's shoulder but be involved in the work.
- In the same fashion, managers obviously need to be able to see the "big picture" with all its interrelationships and implications, but for many problems they need a great deal of exquisite detail before making a decision.
- American management has been accused—correctly—of expending too much time and energy on analysis and of being indecisive, but for some problems it is wise to wait for more data, for the situation to develop, and for time to "test the waters."
- Although bosses expect respect for the chain of command and it is useful for many purposes, there are times when bypassing or ignoring the formal hierarchy will be appropriate. Similarly, a manager's decisions usually must be consistent with the organization's rules and policies, but at times they will diverge.
- Managers need to be time driven for the most part, communicating a sense of urgency to peers and subordinates, but there also will be the occasional need to slow the pace of decision-making, to be more contemplative. (This is surely the case in

many overseas settings, where the inappropriateness of U.S. managers' impatience is legendary.)
- They will need to confront, stand firm, "tough it out," or insist on some decisions while compromising on some and backing off completely on others.

Managers need to respond consistently and loyally to most of their boss's directives and strategies, but there will be times when these need to be challenged openly. The same applies to subordinates: Managers must courageously represent employee interests and needs frequently, but at other times their decision will be to deny.[12]

CONCLUSIONS

Leaders need to be adept at orchestrating decisions. Many decisions require contributions from widely dispersed specialists, as well as by group heads whose work is interdependent. The Japanese have a deserved reputation for spending extended periods of time assuring themselves that all relevant parties have thoroughly explored the ramifications of some change or innovation before allowing a firm decision to be made. The time and effort required to incorporate all of those views, and to evolve consensus on what is desirable and workable, gets repaid fully by the more successful implementation that can then take place. As U.S. business is being pushed to innovate more rapidly, to introduce new products in two years rather than six (or, in the computer industry, often in less than a year), the ability to integrate diverse specialists' knowledge becomes even more important.

Leaders have to be close enough to the decision processes of subordinates to assess their effectiveness in building mutually responsive decision groups and management teams. These require that the members be fully forthcoming and candid with their own technical requirements, as well as responsive to the needs of others for modifying those requirements. In most development groups, these requirements keep changing and evolving as work progresses, making continuing coordination an absolute requirement.

These negotiations get spoiled if status, power, and personality skills become the more relevant factors that determine outcomes. Involved managers can spot these "spoilers," which inhibit open exposure and open confrontation. When there are consequential power differences, for example, the less powerful have everything to gain by being secretive and understating their disagreements. The more powerful are tempted to assume that others feel as free to confront as they do, and that "there are obviously no secrets among us." Only leaders who accept the importance of broad participation in the decision process (because they understand the system's technical interdependencies) are likely to seek to observe and test the extent to which *all* relevant voices are heard and understood.

Just as important, leaders need to reassure themselves that sensible trade-offs are being made among the contradictory requirements to assure the systems integrity. There is absolutely no doubt that real contradictions will occur in every new development, where A's preferences or specifications will make B's job difficult or impossible or degrade the larger system. Without continuing barter and exchange, there can be no optimal system.

They will be fighting an uphill battle. For obvious reasons, managers like to limit participation in decision making and retain, as much as possible, the power to make "their" decisions as autonomously as they can. As long as these decisions don't affect other groups, that exclusivity is fine. But in highly interdependent organizations, most real decisions have direct or hidden repercussions beyond the jurisdiction in which they were made.

Rigid rules of thumb and comfortable, routinized decision-making patterns can be a major handicap in coping with the incredible range of uncertainties and unpredicted events in modern business. Leaders need a broad, flexible repertoire of leadership styles—but based on a realistic understanding of an optimal decision process.

11

What Senior Managers Can Do to Encourage Work Leadership

Criticisms of the performance of American business in the preceding two decades are criticisms of senior management, which tolerated (and even encouraged) mediocre quality, poor service, slow development of new products and processes, and high costs. Current efforts to prune bloated central staffs, reduce the number of hierarchical levels, an "lean" the organization are simply reflections of past indifference to the growth of corporate fat. The following example is drawn from a key production facility of a very large, well-regarded, and technologically sophisticated corporation.

> *Interviewer (after being given a tour of the facility by the plant manager)*: In our walk around the plant, several times you pointed out how you and your engineers have been able to reduce scrap, and thus waste by a consequential amount in the past several years. I think you said that for some operations, almost 20 percent of the output previously had to be recycled because it didn't meet quality standards. Wouldn't those savings have been just as important to the bottom line five or ten years ago? Why did you wait to do all of those things you just described?
>
> *Plant manager*: To be honest with you, there were just no pressures to improve. We were efficient, we were a source of substantial profit for the corporation, and our division [of which this was one of a half-dozen facilities] has been an industry leader for more

than a decade. Top management was pleased with our performance, and there were just no pressures on us to do even better.

Interviewer: If I understand you, all of these engineering modifications could have been made much earlier and would have contributed consequentially to your overall profitability, but no one was
motivated to do all that extra work?

Plant manager: I don't think I would have put it that way. We have
always shown initiative in putting new products into production.
Extreme efficiency just hadn't been one of our high priorities. And
remember, even small changes require a lot of people to come to
a consensus—in our case, including the union for many things—
lots of meetings, and often some hard feelings. We felt that we
were more than meeting the standards and performance targets
we were asked to meet. And this whole quality thing has come to
be a high-priority item only in the past few years.[1]

The exchange illustrates what many have noted before, compla-
cency derived from success and the relative absence of consequential
challenge.[2] But more important, the comments of the plant manager
illustrates the modest incentives senior management has provided for
working leaders to keep improving their operations.

WHY SENIOR MANAGEMENT DOESN'T FOSTER WORKING LEADERSHIP

Why this apparent indifference to the bottom line? Why did American Business Products (chapter 3), led by a demanding CEO, maintain a culture that destroyed managerial initiative to take control of
its operations? The answer is more complicated than mere compla-
cency. It may well relate to senior managers' deeply embedded concepts of management and leadership and the unanticipated consequences of what appear to be logically sensible practices.

Working Leadership Is Undervalued

In many U.S. companies, top management does not appear to place
a high value on strong leadership in the ranks of middle management. This is not to say that it wants weak or inept managers; rather,
they want managers who are strong willed, forceful, and able to
commit themselves and their units to meeting ever higher performance standards. But they are not sensitive to the potential benefits

flowing from activist managers who are adept at building effective operations.

Big Decisions Are Overvalued

Many senior managers exhibit a building-block view of their organizations. As top managers, they perceive that it is their decisions that are critical to performance, and these decisions are embedded in a set of blocks that they seek to arrange optimally. The blocks are top management's decisions about what businesses to be in (or to leave), what organization structure to employ (and what to centralize and what to decentralize), what technologies to employ, and who should occupy the most important senior posts.

Parenthetically, it is interesting to note how Japanese senior executives appear to place much less importance on the specifics of structure:

> Why don't Japanese multinationals use organization charts? The reason is that they prefer to keep boundaries minimal and permeable, not only between units, divisions, and departments within the company, but between the company and its legally separate suppliers, distributors and subcontractors. . . . The borderless structure helps to ensure open communication and a strong, continuous information flow.[3]

In contrast, U. S. executives undervalue the contribution of implementation and overvalue the contribution of astute plans and sensible policies.[4] Getting the right choice from outside consultants and experts seems more attractive than internally generated, incremental results.

> Allen Company was in consumer services, and it acquired a company with a similar product line. The organization it acquired, Bates, has a highly effective middle manager. With his own internal programmers and using his own knowledge of the operation, he facilitated the design and implementation of a unique state-of-the-art information system. It integrated a variety of accounting, marketing, and service functions in a system that decreased the size of the clerical staff by more than 50 percent. Bates had spent four years fine-tuning the system and adding a number of enhancements growing out of experience in its day-to-day application.

Allen, however, had developed a relationship with a very well-known information services consultant, who had sold Allen top management on developing a system from scratch that would do many of the same things that the Bates manager's system was doing. As Allen and Bates middle management evaluated the consultant's proposal and the Bates working system, however, it seemed clear that the Bates staff had thought of many more fine details that allowed them to be more efficient and more accurate.

Allen top management decided that it would move forward with a seven million dollar contract to the consultant to build this new system. The decision was made even though most managers know that even the best of new systems take some time to debug. Further, the new system would not be maintainable by the existing technical staff; who would be dependent on the consulting firm for all enhancements and fixes. Allen was spending millions to acquire an untried system that at best would be somewhat inferior to a system it could obtain for nothing!

But top management finds it hard to believe that middle managers can be that technically expert or creative. Further, it is more comfortable with major technological decisions endorsed by externally legitimated experts than with having to comprehend and assess what insiders may have accomplished by way of implementation. And senior managers seem to hold the naive view that the most important part of acquiring a new technology is deciding which one you want and who is best at providing it.

Operations Are Undervalued

Senior executives appear to have little understanding of how difficult it is to develop and implement finely tuned human and or technology systems that accomplish all the objectives of a business in a cost-effective way. Even with all the well-publicized failures of new, complex systems—particularly business automation and complex computer-based management information systems—most executives still believe that the quality of the plan (and planners) determines the outcome.

In a similar vein, they don't really believe that consequential profit increments come from superior operations (that is, superior execution and implementation), from being able to do the basic work of the company better. For them, profitability is largely the product of superior strategic decision making (and, of course, the state of the economy.) Below is an excellent overview of the fallacy:

> Strategy, its high church theologians insist, is about outflanking competitors with big plays that yield long-term "rents" from a sustainable advantage. . . . The competitive scriptures almost systematically ignore the importance of hustle and energy. . . . [in this industry successful] companies don't have long-term strategic plans with an obsessive preoccupation with rivalry. They concentrate on operating details and doing things well. Hustle is their style and their strategy. They move fast, and they get it right. . . .
>
> Many wholesale banks have the same cost of funds, offer similar products and services and use the same kind of sales forces to reach the same customers. Yet some are more profitable. . . . They "get it right." They make fewer credit mistakes and don't suffer large write-offs. They get a higher share of corporate cash balances because their account officers get and stay close to their clients. They know their clients so well that they make suggestions before the clients know they need them. They provide accurate and revealing statements. "Lost" wire transfers are found promptly. They're informed, fast, and available. [5]

Don't these seem like obvious strengths that should be easy to duplicate by competitors? Yet recent data suggests that many large banks, for example, that invest heavily in automation and other new technologies do *not* gain increased economies; instead, their operations become more costly.[6]

Apparently, many Japanese senior managements also believe in hustle, in contrast to strategic coups: "Planning [in Japanese companies] is seen as a process of continuous experimentation and improvement, rather than as a discontinuous process of developing 'grand' strategies. . . . It is from the interplay of . . . committed individuals that strategy emerges."[7]

CORE COMPETENCIES AND MANAGEMENT CAPABILITIES

It is not surprising that senior managers believe that business success is derived from those leadership decisions that seek to identify what are likely to be high-growth businesses and providing these with adequate resources (often derived from squeezing nongrowth businesses).[8] In sharp contrast, this book and the studies it cites place emphasis on the strategic value of effective day-to-day management. Superb performance in the execution of critical activities may provide much more leverage than skill in making astute product choices. Below are some examples of excellence in execution derived from a recent review of the interrelation of strategy and operating effectiveness.

> The enormously successful retail chain Wal-Mart discovered it could move ahead of the competition by improving the handling of its merchandise inventory. It developed an extraordinarily swift system of replenishing individual store needs by expediting shipments from suppliers to distribution centers to individual stores.
> The system works as well as it does because of extensive interaction between Wal-Mart and its vendors, a company-owned trucking fleet, and a unique distribution-center mode of operation called "cross docking." Truckload lots of merchandise are broken down on the warehouse dock, where they are then repacked and shipped off to individual stores without ever going into inventory. Daily point-of-sale data from stores goes directly to vendors, who can then initiate shipments based on how goods are selling. Combined with the dedicated truck fleet, this allows for new supplies to be received twice a week in each store.[9]

> Honda has been able successfully to move from motorcycles to automobiles (including luxury vehicles), lawn mowers, and the like in part because of being able to *execute* superb dealer management, learning how to "train and support its dealer network with operating procedures and policies for merchandising, selling, floor planning and service management."[10]

These capabilities sound mundane and obvious, except that apparently few, if any, of Honda or Wal-Mart's competitors equal their effectiveness in these targeted management process areas. These are skills in execution, in hustle, as opposed to skills in selecting the right business. It is worth repeating that these competencies are *not* the result of management finding, copying, or adopting a new technique such as cross docking (at Wal-Mart). These techniques are simply examples of the numerous (and usually unnamed) operating break-throughs that occur when on-the-scene involved managers find ways of integrating into work systems countless numbers of microdecisions.

If they weren't so much an integral part of a superb day-to-day management process, competitors would simply lift the techniques and make them their own, because there are no secrets here or patent barriers. There is a vast gulf separating a description in a business magazine of a new procedure and the ability to make something that facilitates work happen routinely and effectively. The only thing that can span this gulf is adept manager-leaders who are focused on operations.

Different but also similar competencies can be focused on more explicitly technological skills. Although at first glance these may appear not to involve leadership skills, quite the reverse is true: they require parallel excellence in management in the perfecting of another kind of competence. Highly successful Japanese companies like NEC, Sony, and Canon have grown powerful and profitable by focusing on the development of core competencies that could then be leveraged to produce a stunning array of ever-changing state-of-the-art products.

> The real sources of advantage are to be found in management's ability to consolidate corporate-wide technologies and production skills into competencies that empower individual businesses to adapt quickly to changing opportunities. . . .
> Core competencies are the collective learning in the organization, especially how to coordinate diverse production skills and integrate multiple streams of technology. . . . The theoretical knowledge to put a radio on a chip does not in itself assure a company the skill to produce a miniature radio no bigger than a business card. To bring off this feat, Casio must harmonize know-how in miniaturization, microprocessor design, material science and ultrathin precision casting—the same skills it applies in its miniature card calculators, pocket TV's and digital watches.[11]

Thus, core competencies represent an intermix of managers, professionals, and technology. Managers and their professional subordinates can't afford to be satisfied with the superficial knowledge of how things work that is typical in organizations. They must devote energies to exploring the intricate nuances of operations that go substantially beyond what is necessary to make plans and hit budget targets.

Process Innovation

Senior managers who view the organization as being nothing more than the sum of its decentralized parts (and the profits and cash flow they generate to provide dividends and additional investments) are not likely to understand these core capabilities or competencies. As an astute British researcher who compares Western (that is, U.S. and European) to Asian companies has observed, it is much more consistent with Western Management principles to think in terms of discrete products and inventions that will be developed and managed separately.

> Process innovation lies at the roots of product innovation. . . . Process innovation is "bottom up" rather than "top down." More consistent with Western individualism is the creative unit invented by the creative individual and then manufactured as cheaply as possible . . . if necessary in low wage countries abroad.[12]

Having managers and workers really learn how things work is the heart of process innovation. A great deal of knowledge about internal functional interrelations and the critical parameters of materials, components, or software is required when confronting the task of making things smaller (in other words miniaturization), lighter, faster, with more features, of more consistent quality, or more adaptive to a wide variety of and/or changing user preferences.

It is process knowledge that leads to product innovations. More precisely, it is through an in-depth understanding of how things work, derived from seeking to make them work better, that alert managers and professionals can identify new product and service possibilities. Further, these new products are more likely to be implementable in a cost-efficient manner than those that are "parachuted in" from the outside. The latter are often rejected in a fashion not too different from how the body rejects transplanted organs.[13]

Process innovation requires close and continuing interaction among managers, workers, and skilled professionals. Each needs in-depth knowledge of the work and the underlying technology, and they need to complement each other in the continuing effort to attain mastery of technique and of the interrelating of techniques (that is, managing interfaces).

CORE INCOMPETENCIES

For years, American managers tolerated what used to be called Rube Goldberg or jerry-built designs with excessive and clumsy components that were difficult to assemble and vulnerable to failure, as well as having embedded high costs, because there were no inducements to do things better.[14] In brief, American management, (and its management principles embodied in GAMP) have ignored systems. The same needlessly complicated, obtuse methods injure the provision of services both inside and outside the firm.

> In some service operations a clerk has to look through five different files, coded in diverse ways, and then undertake a series of manual calculations to give an answer to an inquiry from an adjacent department or a worried customer. Also, some inquiries may be passed back and forth among a research function, a technical service group, and a customer service group.
>
> This occurs because no manager has bothered to think through the process. Instead, some executive has pronounced the need for a job titled "service" and a number of other jobs with titles like "systems analyst," "data bank supervisor," and "technology specialist" (to decide what computer terminals to buy). Each employee does his or her job "correctly," probably in widely separate organization compartments. But these building blocks don't lead to service or quality or efficiency; they lead to cumbersomeness and a system prone to breakdown and to worker-management disputes over productivity. In addition, these building blocks represent very costly manpower and overhead.

Unique Managerial Skills That Create Company Treasures

Core competencies usually represent interdisciplinary, cross-functional capabilities. Thus, managers have to be willing to reach out to other areas, both to learn what they do and to be responsive to their needs for change. Only through collaborative efforts and mutual understanding is it possible to integrate multiple streams of technology, just as the Japanese company Casio learned to marry miniaturization and microprocessor design. For this to occur, middle-level managers must be close to technology, earn the confidence of subordinates, and be willing to listen and learn, as well as be able to direct people to try out a number of "experiments" that will test the limits of their knowledge.

In Japan, great artists are often referred to as "national treasures." Senior management needs to be able to identify and encourage its "organizational treasures." These are managers like Eliot Felix and Mary Coel (in chapter 8) who were able to counter the centrifugal forces in the organization, devote endless hours to negotiation, and integrate a coherent strategic thrust around a core competency. Such working leaders become "company treasures" for the following reasons:

- They recognize and constantly work at gaining an in-depth knowledge of technologies, markets, and people. They are continously probing and learning and are not satisfied with the organization's conventional wisdom or written reports.
- In the same way, they stretch their people by getting the latter to see the contradictions and gaps in their knowledge that need to be resolved.[15]
- They are willing to keep working the interfaces between their unit and other units, between one specialization (or specialist's jurisdiction) and others that are relevant to a given competency. They don't retreat into a well-bounded turf, even though it is more comfortable and less risky and assures looking good on traditional control measures.
- They know the "good idea" is just the very beginning of accomplishment and they have boundless energy and optimism.

EVALUATING AND MOTIVATING MIDDLE MANAGERS

If senior management comes to understand the significance of core competencies for long-run viability and growth, it will also need to be more familiar with the critical role of working leadership. This can be another kind of capital worth building: managers who strive for in-depth understanding and improvement of technology and work methods and who thereby motivate their people. Such understanding would represent a major change in the way many senior managers view middle management and the relative importance placed on implementation skills.

But this will only occur if senior management believes that such basic competencies represent the organization's claim to a promising future and then seeks to design a supporting culture. As has been noted. U. S. senior executives often do the opposite. They overlearned both the power of decentralization to motivate executives and the ease with which capital allocation formulas can be applied when the independent variable is return on investment. It is not much of a challenge to be a CEO when only one or two numbers speak for themselves. But such a role also has little to do with exercising leadership; it has more to do with setting hurdle rates and whipping up internal competitive emotions.

Similarly, senior management is likely to dispose of assets that could be a critical element in a new technological thrust for "not earning their way." This simplistic market-price decision strategy ignores the tougher managerial trade-offs in such decisions that take into account when and where internal units need all the business they can get to develop a critical competency. Obviously, traditional accounting can militate against giving any weight to the longer-run gain from not contracting out.[16]

Senior management exercises an enormous influence over management styles and practices through the reward system it constructs. Obviously, managers are very sensitive to who gets singled out for consequential bonuses and promotion (and what has been done to deserve this recognition). It appears as though many senior managements encourage a style of management that is inconsistent with accepting responsibility for systems effectiveness.

Promotion Criteria

Many managers believe that getting ahead in their companies depends more on looking good than on actual effectiveness. Such managers, in our interviews, give these as promotion "tips."

- Avoid, as much as possible, confronting your boss with bad news. Withhold that kind of information and seek to "improve" the data or hope that something will arise that will allow others to get the blame if the data do not improve.

- Don't put your boss in the position of having to champion positions that are unpopular to senior management, even though these might represent major savings or improvements.
- Agree with the boss, even if plans are flawed or requests are unrealistic or even injurious to performance.
- Maintain a "clean desk" work style—that is, don't get involved in or become encumbered by the work, except in crises. Don't show too much interest in the details of technology; leave that to the staff and your professional subordinates.
- Concentrate on presentation skills, looking good at meetings and in one-on-one sessions with bosses, where you can demonstrate poise and style. Avoid showing emotion or intensity, which are signs of being too involved.
- Buffer your area from other departments. The more autonomy you can obtain, the easier it will be to meet your budgets and targets. Cooperation is a good talking point, but acceding to others' requests will likely injure your own short-run efficiency, and there is little credit to be had.
- Treat the organization as a playing field where your challenge is to demonstrate an intense desire to win career advancement and to best your peers.[17]
- Look for one activity in which you can excel and get visibility, even if it is unrelated to work responsibilities. For example, running a charity drive in the organization or undertaking an assignment to research a proposed venture or acquisition might provide more visibility than anything that could be accomplished internally.[18]
- Keep moving. A manager who isn't being promoted every couple of years (at the longest!) won't look good; it is important to have as steep a promotion trajectory as possible. Thus, you should expend work time looking for the next rung up.

Senior management appears to have only modest interest in how well the manager manages. This perception gets reinforced by a variety of top management decisions. For example, across-the-board budget cuts usually decrease the resources of highly effective managers just as much as those who have been slack and inefficient. Many recent downsizings have offered early-retirement packages arbitrarily on the basis of age or some other impersonal criterion, again ignoring enormous performance differentials among managers.

There seems to be little recognition of how valuable and unique are those managers who are truly committed and effective, who minimize self-seeking gamesmanship to further the performance needs of the larger organization. There is little recognition of managerial leadership (particularly at middle levels of the organization) making a significant difference. And there is positive encouragement of norms emphasizing peer competition rather than cooperation, encouraging the ability to show up and best other managers, tournament style. In some organizations, particularly those in consumer-packaged goods, the rapidity of promotions for those considered high fliers, guarantees that a manager will never attain or seek to attain any in-depth knowledge. Not only is time for learning lacking, but managers focus on their next job instead of the current one.

Subjective Performance Appraisals

For the most part, it appears as though overall appraisals of managers by top management are based primarily on two factors: "character" and "making your numbers." Underlying many of the factors that managers believe are important is the variable of personal character. Good character is defined in terms of being cool under fire, unemotional in meetings with peers and bosses and when criticized, articulate in presentations, and driven by an intense desire to get ahead.[19]

The other critical element is making one's numbers. There are almost limitless possibilities for destroying organizational effectiveness in the quest for meeting or besting individual numerical targets. To name a few, managers can ignore longer-run issues such as investing in personnel development and product development, manipulate numbers to hide problems and distort performance, be unresponsive to legitimate requests from peers to modify their routines for a larger goal, and hoard scarce resources. Both this and the issue of character avoid the need to comprehend and assess how subordinate managers manage.

ORGANIZATIONAL CONSEQUENCES

Without intending it, the beliefs and practices of senior management often lead to the very results executives confronting a highly dynamic, competitive world seek to avoid: fat, bureaucratic organizations. As described above, managers are encouraged to be inflexible in responding to external requests from peers. They are encouraged to wall themselves off from the larger organization.

> *To an adjacent department:* We can't modify our schedule and meet your needs for quicker data on that program; we are not set up to do that sort of thing. And we can't change the format either, even for a one-time use; our existing format was approved by the division head.
>
> *From a staff department:* Although that procedure [or form or policy] may not meet your needs, that is the one we have standardized for all units of the business. And we don't make exceptions, even though this may create inefficiencies in your case.

The Deceit of the Bottom Line

The most widely used evaluations give little or no credit for understanding and responding to the needs of systems or for flexibility and change. Managers are encouraged to look backward to procedures and budgets, not forward. It is better to lose a customer or push through a known defect than endanger a targeted "key measure." Some years ago, I watched a contractor complete a faulty component for a large hardware project because the accounting system would have penalized them for any delays and the defective component would be part of a larger system that wouldn't be tested for some months. Here are some other examples:

> The marketing group in a large organization complained constantly that its new product introductions were being sabotaged by the operations people. The latter absolutely refused to modify their procedures to take into account the unique requirements of some of the newer products. But since operations was meeting all of its goals, top management ignored the complaints.

> A large pharmaceutical company, eager to reduce the cycle time for new product introductions, began utilizing cross-functional teams. Top management's indifference to the needs for organizationwide cooperation, however, made most of these teams impotent. Members of the team would seek to get their "home" functions to adapt their

support schedules to that of the new product team. Anything a function did to facilitate the work of one team, however, was so resented by other product groups that there were constant mutual recriminations over favoritism. Top management saw no contradiction between its constant use of internal competition among units and its effort to decrease the time required to develop a new product.[20]

In contrast, Japanese companies encourage and reward loyalties to the larger organization and, of course, collaboration.

> The Japanese business leader is like the conductor in an ensemble of traditional Japanese instruments. He sits inconspicuously on the end of the last row of musicians. . . . From the rear, the conductor can see if the group is functioning well together. . . .
> Appraisals evaluate their [managers'] loyalty and commitment to the family and their entrepreneurial ability to build productive bridges between family members.[21]

Cycles of Fat and Lean

In much the same fashion, layers of excess management get built up that increase overhead and lead to predictable periodic cycles of cutting out fat and downsizing, then building up the head count again. Not being able to evaluate what is being done effectively, senior management tolerates increasing numbers of staff and line managers to deal with imperfections in work systems.

Two departments are in constant conflict over work standards and schedules. The division head, therefore, adds coordination personnel and additional staff controllers to improve the flow of work. The alternative would have been to get involved and work through the source of the problems.

Given the strong rewards associated with making targeted sales quotas, many product heads begin doing things that inflate short-run sales but either misstate real sales or injure the company's longer-run position in the market.

Rather than reevaluate the traditional incentives being used, additional staff auditors are used to double-check the procedures and data produced by product units.

As these staffs proliferate and produce requests for more reports and more explanations from line managers, those managers begin to employ more staff themselves to help do the analytical work that is now being requested. When combined with the staff first added to deal with excessive internal competition and deceptions, staff size can double over a few years.

The trend toward adding managers to cope with the problems of a defective organization continues until competitive pressures cause top management to institute major cutbacks. Then, over the years, the same trends are likely to reassert themselves.

In these same organizations, departments and divisions that are aggrandizing themselves in terms of power usually politick with impunity. Of course, the power produces more than psychological satisfactions; it also produces higher salaries and easier executive jobs. The jobs are easier because more powerful managers have greater autonomy to do things their way, as well as fewer demands on them from peers.[22] Executive salaries, meanwhile, increase in proportion to the number of subordinates.

Managing from Afar

Senior managements seem to believe that they need little or no information about their organizations. Their job is to set direction, set goals and targets, and provide the appropriate rewards and punishments. In fact, there may be a real aversion to getting into the real work of the organization. Some executives feel that they had their fill of messy people/technology issues when they "served their time" in earlier years; they now deserve to work in splendid detachment.

Such isolation, however, can be very dysfunctional. One of the world's best managed banks, Deutsche Bank of Germany, seems to be moving in the direction of more hands-on management (as do some U.S. companies).

[The new Deutsche Bank organizational structure is seen as] a radical bid by top management to reassert control over the bank's operations by knuckling down on largely autonomous regional managers. . . . Under the new plan, each board member will be in charge of one product area, with a vertical responsibility dropping from the board room down to the branch counter. . . . [Before,] as long as their numbers were good, the board wouldn't pry into individual operations.[23]

ALL THE WRONG SIGNALS

Top management often signals to the rest of the organization that it is not able to distinguish good from bad in terms of day-to-day management. There are many of these not-so-subtle cues that guide managerial behavior. In some companies, frequent reorganizations are designed to "shake things up" in the hope that better management will result. This is a rather blunt, crude instrument for obtaining change. It implies that senior management really can't separate the effective from the ineffective; therefore, almost any change is preferable to the status quo.

Similarly, many senior managers are passive as long as the "numbers" are reassuring. During good times, their organizations often grow fat and unresponsive to customers and technology changes. The lassitude and indifference to how well things are really going leads to growing ineffectiveness, and at some point—usually long after the organization has ceased being alert and adaptive—the numbers crumble, and then there is a bloodbath of cuts and discharges. In a few years, the cycle repeats. Thus, senior management here is either slothful or vengeful, depending on the stage of the cycle.

Across-the-board budget cuts hurt those who have been running a tight ship much more than they injure those who have plastered over their inefficiencies with redundant people. They also warn farsighted managers that if one really achieves high efficiency, there may well be a penalty down the road. Maintaining buffer stocks of people (like inventory) cushions one from such shocks.

> Ameritech (including the Michigan and Illinois Bell companies) announced in a downsizing that there were only eight hundred of their twenty-four thousand managers to whom they were unwilling to offer some incentive to leave. What does this say about building an organization of valued managers who really know

operations and have the confidence of their subordinates?[24]

As recent downsizings testify, senior managements, except when the economy (and profitability) turn sour, seem to have ignored the growth in hierarchy, increasing numbers of levels, and increasing bureaucratization. Because these encrustations inevitably hurt the flow of work and impair easy coordination among peer groups, top management in effect is saying that it does not understand the importance of coordination at operating levels.

> The top management of a billion-dollar division of a major corporation recognized that its success in future years depended upon a major transformation of its product line and the adoption of some very new and difficult technologies. The division president initiated a yearlong series of almost-monthly meetings with his direct subordinates, many of whom had to fly in from overseas. Almost all of the meetings were devoted to getting a consensus on a series of slogans and strategy "visions" that would encapsulate the future thrust of the business. Little time was devoted to what would turn out to be the extraordinary implementation challenges. Many of these would profoundly change the roles and relationships of the key players as a team and would also drastically change the jobs and functions they would have to create and manage within their functions.[25]

At least some senior managers signal their indifference to operational issues by their time away from work. Although there are critical public relations commitments to be fulfilled and useful contributions to the community, particularly for more visible companies, many senior managers at least give the appearance that they have little interest in the business as such.

These senior managers are saying with their "body language" that the day-to-day work of their companies is either not very important or very challenging, and that it is far removed from their purview. It would appear that "financial engineering," buying and selling companies and parts of companies, strategic decisions, and deal making are all much more appealing and exciting to many executives than handling "inside" issues.[26]

ADAPTIVE INTERFACE BEHAVIOR

In evaluating managers, more companies now consider their competence as team players, i.e., their systems interrelationships. Coordination that means higher quality, efficiency, service, and more rapid adaptation to innovation grows out of the lateral interrelationships of managers. To repeat, only the most standardized, static processes do *not* require adaptive responsiveness among managers. There is almost always the need to get a peer to modify her procedures, timing, or specifications to facilitate response to an unexpected problem or opportunity in an adjacent department.

An important component of performance appraisal and an important indicator of a systems problem (or systems effectiveness) is the willingness and ability of laterally interrelated managers to be responsive to one another's needs. This doesn't mean that a good manager always defers to requests for aid. Some requests will be too costly to adopt or represent a needless shifting of a technical burden from one executive to another (what used to be called "balloon squeezing," getting costs to show up in the other person's jurisdiction). Good managers demonstrate reciprocity, however, helping others in exchange for the obtaining of help.

A clear sign of managerial ineptness is unresponsiveness to other managers' requests on the basis of political criteria. The following are typical political fears in evaluating an "outside" request to change:

- Accepting the idea would suggest that the outsider has greater status or power and is able to make us defer to them.
- Accepting the idea implies that our work or procedures are in some way inferior, and theirs superior.
- My colleagues will consider me disloyal if I agree with the outsider group and accept one of their ideas.

Thus, senior managers, in appraising the effectiveness of their subordinates, need to undertake the following:

1. Conceptualize the system interrelationships that exist among their subordinates (who should be doing what with whom, when, and how).
2. Evaluate how their managers "stack up" in terms of fulfilling those systems requirements. How much mutual responsiveness, teamwork and open communication exists?
3. Examine closely the quality of the trade-offs subordinates make when negotiating with their peers (their balancing of legitimate needs of their own areas against legitimate needs of their peers or the larger organization). Recognize that an important criterion for managerial effectiveness is the capacity to deal with uncertainty and inconsistency. Thus, subordinates need to be aided in recognizing that there are legitimate conflicts and contradictions between what they want and what their peers need and want in terms of technical decisions.
4. Assess the alertness of subordinates to early warnings of system failures—their ability to maintain a broad network of contacts and relationships in order to assess when things are not working or when other groups are planning changes that will be deleterious to the manager's own operations.
5. Provide adequate listening time to hear out their subordinates' coordination issues.
6. Provide a mechanism to help "make whole" those managers who injure their own performance in order to aid the performance of others.

Nonleaders observe and appraise subordinates as though each is operating in a watertight compartment. They frequently get fooled by managers who are able to perform well by being unresponsive, inflexible and focused only on what makes them look good.

TIMELY AND TAILORED INTERVENTIONS

Reciprocity has its limits, however, and there will inevitably be highly ambiguous situations in dynamic organizations when it is not clear who needs to concede, change, or defer. Such situations may result in costly stalemates characterized by endless meetings, reviews, audits, and efforts to pass the buck. It then becomes important for managers to intervene swiftly to regain momentum and get the system operating. In the field, one observes managers who never learn about these stalemates that are impeding effective operations because subordinates have learned that the boss's interventions can be too costly.

> Increasingly, Bill and I are having difficulty cooperating, and it often means that work almost stops because we can't agree how it should be done without hurting his or my product. But I am afraid to mention this to Henry, my boss. Whenever he hears of problems, he comes running in like the fire department and feels he has to decide in the next minute who or what is right.
>
> Most of the problems we get hung up on can't be dealt with that easily, and I am concerned that his nervous trigger finger will result in a terrible decision. If he is going to be useful, he has to take the time to get involved and learn some of the nitty-gritty we are coping with, and help us think it through to a sensible resolution.

There is a broad range of downward interventions senior managers need to be capable of undertaking to ensure that the basic coordination requirements of the organization are being maintained. At times, these can bypass intermediate levels to allow upper-level managers to assess directly what is happening at the work level. There can always be concern over "uncertainty absorption"—that is, lower-level managers screening out uncertainties to reassure upper management. By not relaying negatives, of course, they hope to avoid upper management pressures. Many astute managers want to get a personal feeling for operations, undiluted by the perspectives of their subordinates. There are also times when their direct intervention appears necessary to override sluggish or inept performance.

> A large company's most profitable product was dependent on one industry. An unexpected change in government regulations imposed a new requirement on that product. Existing customers expected that the company would expeditiously install a modification in their installed base that would allow their existing equipment to meet the new standard. Senior management did not learn until rather late that the modification program was moving quite slowly, and that as a result many customers would not be able to use their equipment in the short run. A senior vice president moved swiftly then to take over the

technology modification program. He leased aircraft to
fly modification packages to customers and added an
extra shift to make sure that those packages were
completed before the holidays. Had he not gotten
involved, it is likely that many customers would have
been lost.

Also, the broader experience and perspective of senior management can be utilized to assist lower-level managers in making better technical decisions. Intervention can provide impetus, stress urgency, and thus energize a lagging program. High-status people who make occasional visits to the work level clearly have a major symbolic impact.

It is important to note that getting involved, getting close to the work or operations level, and having inputs need not mean that these managers are telling employees or subordinate managers how to do their work. This is vital not only from the point of view of motivation, but also because those closest often know the most about how the work should be done.

BUILDING LEARNING ORGANIZATIONS

For the most part, senior management has neglected addressing the requirements for building organizations that learn, in contrast to helping individuals learn. In a future characterized by rapid changes in technology and markets, this learning capability will be essential. One can surmise that this same future will require career lines to be shaped by this need for organizational learning as much as by individual growth. For example, Smith will be encouraged to move into department Z in order to allow Cohen's work to be synthesized with Smith's. Over the longer run, both Smith and Cohen will benefit from the additional corporate strength that comes from this synthesis, but the short run may be less personally rewarding in terms of obvious career advancement for Smith.

In chapter 5, the Ames case provided a very concrete example of some very important issues usually not addressed by senior executives. Both product groups represented critical technologies for Ames's future market strength. It was tempting to the respective managers to play "beggar thy neighbor," because the company had not provided the appraisal and reward systems that would encourage sharing. In fact, severe competitive pressures on the corporation had encouraged top management to be more threatening to those who were not able to show clear-cut performance superiority.

It was, therefore, very difficult for the two managers to make the trade-offs that were required by their technologies; each concession appeared to be an act of partial self-destruction. But the organization's capacity for continued learning in the technology and markets spanned by those two managers was dependent on their ability to find ways to marry their two products and resolve the technical contradictions. Those solutions, in turn, would represent a growing in-depth understanding of the underlying parameters of their work. And it is senior management's responsibility to make restitution to managers who sacrifice their unit's short-run performance for the needs of other units and/or the larger organization. It should not be punishing experience.

As many of the cases in the preceding chapters illustrate, know-how does not reside solely within nonmanagerial professionals. Managers also need to be sophisticated and to have an in-depth knowledge of the processes for which they are responsible. Leadership requires not only a commitment to the future, but also the patience to undertake a small number of key programs that will pay off over many years in an ever-changing array of products. The contribution of senior management is in identifying those future-oriented competencies and to provide the organizational systems that support continued investment in relevant human and technical resources.

This is a far cry from supervising a competitive race among the heads of decentralized units, in which senior management's role is limited to deciding who gets how much (given the results) and selecting among creative financing alternatives. It is also far removed from the comfortable assumption that one can tack together an acquired product line and technology with one that has been developed within the organization—that the sum of the two, in fact, will be greater than the parts. The reality is that the summation is likely to be *less* than the sum of the parts because of the misunderstood interrelationships that never get worked through.

Avoiding Careless Downsizing

Top management is responsible for getting human resource policies aligned with these technological realities. Investments in human capital are required if the work force is going to learn (and learn how to

210

learn) about technology and systems. But such investments go beyond training and providing incentives and careers that emphasize in-depth mastery of a field, whether it be a marketplace or a technology. The investments also must fund greter career stability. In many cases, American executives have overreacted to the need to be cost-conscious by breaking what tenuous bonds there were that tied employees to the organization.

The ceaseless "churning" of people created by cascading reorganizations, acquisitions, and deacquisitions, and the continued threats of work force reductions provide a poor environment for in-depth mastery.[27] Quite the contrary, in this increasing turbulence everyone learns that there is little reward for growing competencies and for reaching out to interrelate one skill or technique to another with which it needs to interface. Employees absorbed in polishing their résumés search for the same kind of quick fixes and easy wins that earn brownie points with their superiors.

They are also likely to assume more rigid postures toward other departments or functions who want to resolve an interface complexity of malfunction. With insecurity normally comes self-defense, and adjacent departments and the larger organization are the worse for it. Under these circumstances there is no increased learning or competence, only increased factionalism. Senior managers, of course, can be blinded to this because individual unit short-term performance may be enhanced as the incentives to look good are increased.

CONCLUSION

Ironically, while senior corporate executives demonstrate substantial interest in encouraging leadership capabilities in their managers (witness the amounts of training money invested), their actions often belie this interest. Inadvertently, they may be encouraging the very behavior they decry: narrow, turf-conscious gamesmanship and bureaucratic behavior in contrast to leadership.

Top management has great faith in the organizational efficacy of three levers to insure competitive excellence: astute plans, continuously rebalancing centralization and decentralization to find the "right" organization structure, and high annual performance hurdles. They do not appear to understand the vulnerability of both coordination and teamwork in highly fractionated organizations. As a result, there is little appreciation of the capital value of the development of core competencies and core technologies.

As previous chapters have sought to emphasize, managers need an in-depth understanding of how things work—the complex interrelationships of people, work routines and norms, communication linkages, and technology. Only then can they truly improve quality and efficiency and keep adapting and innovating products and services.

Unanticipated Consequences of Advancement Policies

Senior management often appears not to value those managers who take the initiative to facilitate the work process by integrating their work with peers and forcing change and modification in plans and routines to get something up and running. In the process, they fail to reinforce the personal courage and risk taking involved when a manager really assumes responsibility for making things work well and integrating his work into larger systems. Instead, they devalue these capabilities by excessively rapid promotions and transfers that do not reflect experience. (One major consumer goods company took pride in sometimes promoting effective managers every six months!)

Also, the emphasis on one or two quantified targeted performance measures tempts managers to "beggar" their neighbors. Many managers believe there is little to be gained (in credits or recognition) from being accommodative and flexible in responding to requests from peers. There is more to be gained by using political skills and accumulated power to strong-arm support groups and others upon whom one is dependent in any way. Powerful, prestigious groups and their managers expect to get other departments to defer to their needs quite aside from the merits of the case.

The result is often a predictable spiral. In the effort to hit their targets, managers injure systems and coordination. Further, they are indifferent to all costs that don't count against them. Over time, this leads to various excesses (including redundant resources) and interdepartmental conflicts. Then increasing numbers of staff and line managers are needed to deal with the resulting conflict and minimize its costs. These management "patches," added to the wasteful practices that were tolerated, lead to the accumulation of managerial fat and excessive overhead. At some point, there is a day of reckoning and subsequent cutbacks (called "downsizing" or "becoming lean and mean").

In these target-dominated managements, however, there is little interest in seeking to deal with the source of their problems. The incentives are too strong for managers to be competitive internally and to ignore the larger systems needs. These result when top management primarily evaluates people on whether they did or didn't make their numbers and has little interest in their ability to lead the accomplishment of work objectives.

Gresham's Law: Bad Leadership Drives Out Good

Working leadership is a perishable commodity because it is high risk and requires great energy, commitment, and courage. Continuous improvement is a very tough management task that demands enormous managerial energy and skill. There are many easier ways for middle managers to get ahead in most organizations. Unless senior management recognizes the value of leadership and can effectively identify its practitioners, the number of real leaders in the organization is likely to be very small.

Inadvertently, many companies encourage the very kind of gamesmanship that injures performance. Managers get rewarded who are good at career management in contrast to work management. Managers who are working leaders inevitably ruffle feathers at times they challenge their superiors, and they are usually contentious. This is because conventional wisdom can be wrong, and those closer to the realities of operations have unique insights.

In addition to recognition and reward for working leaders, senior managers need to provide them with support at those levels that determine resource allocations. To make things work, they will need representation for their strategy initiatives and for what will often be unconventional and ingenious improvisations. Often a supportive senior manager, with knowledge of how his or her colleagues think and conceptualize, can develop rationales and persuasive models, even slogans, that serve to sell the initiatives of her middle management. At higher levels of the organization, there is often less tolerance for detail and greater need for these incisive presentations.

In addition, senior managers need to be sensitive to the time and energy pressures that are self-generated by these leaders. Continuously reworking interfaces and introducing change, with all the required negotiations with peers, can constitute an imposing work load. When a boss then asks for still more reports or gives some special assignment while the subordinate is being overwhelmed with threatening work crises, the insensitivity shown is demoralizing.

The hierarchy is not dead; top management does have great influence. It is only when that influence recognizes the importance of leadership to effective performance that these organizations can meet the high standards of the coming decades.

But we have to introduce a critical postscript. Top management's power to enforce cooperation and coordination has limits; sometimes unexpectedly large limits. In the summer of 1992 when the distinguished and prestigious CEO of Digital Equipment was dismissed by his Board of Directors, Kenneth Olsen, Digital's founder, admitted a profound organizational failure. He said that he had been unable to get his engineering functional managers to work closely with Digital's product and marketing managers![28]

Regretably, top management has placed too much faith in the "right" organization structure and the "right" plan to solve its market and technology problems. Usually these solutions have been ephemeral; one major course correction follows another with enormous internal disruptions and confusion. Perhaps those managerial values are about to change, at least in more astute companies. Professors Bartlett and Ghosal confirm our findings in this conclusion drawn from their extensive research in multinational corporations: "Paradoxically, as strategies and organizations become more complex and sophisticated, top-level general managers are beginning to replace their historical concentration on the grand issues of strategy and structure with a focus on the *details of managing people and processes.*"

Top management talk about wanting more teamwork is cheap and easy. Getting it requires them to rethink their conception of the core of managerial work.

12

Finding Leadership in Management Research

EXPLAINING BEHAVIORAL STUDIES OF WHAT MANAGERS DO

There are greater needs for management involvement, not less, as coordination becomes more problematic in complex modern organizations. In fact, this conclusion may explain the otherwise puzzling behavioral data that appear when academics actually go out and observe managers at work.

It is interesting that there has been quite a long-standing discrepancy between professed management doctrines and theories and the findings of behavioral studies of managerial work. The doctrine (what I have called GAMP) would suggest that the behavior of managers would look like that of other professionals: rather slow paced, with substantial emphasis on isolation to allow planning and thoughtful decision making. Instead, a succession of observation studies of executives, even at quite senior levels, shows a frenetic life loaded with interaction. Managers seem to be forced to spend only brief periods on one subject or with one person and must hasten to redirect their attention to other issues and other people. On average, three-quarters of their working days are spent in impromptu contact with people, and most of these are outside of scheduled meetings.[1]

A Couple of Hours in the Life of a Manager

The description below* of a portion of a managerial workday reveals a dynamic patterning of activities that is in sharp contrast to the

---

*Reprinted with the permission of and copyright by McGraw-Hill. Leonard Sayles, *Leadership: Managing in Real Organizations* (New York: McGraw-Hill, 1989), pp. 29–36.

215

static view inherent in traditional management principles. In this case, we observe a woman who heads a product service department handling short-run contingencies at the same time she seeks to improve operations and the work system for which she is responsible. She "works the hierarchy" and fields a variety of lateral relationships with peers while endeavoring to motivate subordinates. Many of these things occur almost simultaneously, and the pace is fast. It is this almost frenetic pace, the diffuse pattern of relationships, and the simultaneous juggling of many issues that give managerial work its unique character among the professions.

Jane Rao heads product service for the Elgard Company. Elgard sells insurance, produces a variety of industrial equipment, and has recently begun selling a small number of consumer items derived from their commercial lines. Rao has several hundred employees, about half of whom work in the head office, fielding phone calls and letters requesting product information or registering complaints. The other half are in geographically dispersed repair centers. Some work there is done on the premises, but a field repair staff works on-site for large corporate customers.

One afternoon Rao decides to sample one or two of the numerous pink slips that her secretary has placed on her desk in a folder marked "Unsolicited Customer." There is no reason for Rao to talk with customers; her service representatives are well trained, and there are half a dozen supervisors to deal with difficult problems. However, Rao's name is on the company stationery and occasionally a persistent or impatient customer will try to reach "the boss." She knows that responding to a few of these will give her some feeling for how the reps are doing, what they're up against, and how well they're handling the pressure-packed problems.

As luck would have it, the first call Rao places turns up a totally unanticipated issue. She expects to reach a corporate office but is instead connected to a residential number. The customer has recently purchased the #36 model electronic typewriter, which has some features of a stripped-down word processor. The customer is angry. In response to his first complaint, he was told ("rudely," he says) that there was nothing Elgard could do about his malfunctioning machine because the warranty had expired. The customer claims that at the store where he purchased the machine and on the guarantee slip in its packaging, he was assured of a twenty-four-month warranty, and he wants the machine fixed or his money back. He is prepared to mail it wherever appropriate, but he is not prepared to wait any longer.

Rao assures him that she or one of her people will look into the matter and get back to him within a day or two. Immediately she calls one of her supervisors to inquire about the 24-month warranty. When the supervisor agrees with her that the normal company warranty is for twelve months, Rao decides to go out on the floor herself to one of the computer terminals used by telephone-response personnel in order to find the most recent information on the #36 model. Though she finds no mention of a 24-month guarantee there, she is delighted to see that the new hardware and software have greatly expanded the amount of information a clerk can access and that the system is working smoothly. (In fact, one of Rao's reasons for going out on the floor was to work the terminal herself, and to see the new system in operation.)

The efficiency of the new system aside, Rao's problem remains. Perhaps the 24-month guarantee is one of those new promotions that marketing has undertaken without informing service. Rao vaguely remembers hearing something about an extended warranty being offered as a part of a promotion package that marketing was considering "to jazz up" flagging #36 sales. In fact, just weeks before, she was involved in a minor skirmish with marketing over another promotion. They had developed a rebate procedure that required the customer to return the store receipt, part of the packaging, and a questionnaire that dealt with some market research data. Not only were the requirements for getting the rebate complicated (and easy to misconstrue), but the rebate was being handled by a vendor known for slow service. As a result, Rao's people had been flooded with calls from irate customers who wanted to know either why they hadn't received their rebate or how to handle the application. Her staff had had trouble handling the questions properly because marketing had failed to provide them any advance information as to what was being done, how, and when.

At the time of the trouble, Rao had gone to her boss to complain about marketing's failure to coordinate their plans with her department. But Green hadn't given her much support. In fact, he had indicated that marketing might be inclined to avoid working with service simply because Rao was always finding fault with their proposed campaigns, always pointing out how this or that feature would be troublesome from a service point of view. Rao had been stung by that criticism, because she thought service was now a high-priority value at Elgard and that their involvement up front was essential to make sure that high service standards were upheld. When she tried to say something about how important service was in retaining the customers that marketing might attract, Green had brushed it aside, saying that he expected his managers to be "team players."

Remembering all of this, Rao is not surprised when she calls Brown, her counterpart in marketing, and learns that they indeed have implemented an extended warranty on the #36. When Rao duly registers her complaint that her department has not been informed of that fact, Brown tries to pacify her with the information that the new guarantee has not created extra sales and that "no more than two or three thousand units" have been sold under its terms.

Rao's next call is to Gil Trump, liaison between service and marketing systems. She tells him to be sure that the systems people add to the data supporting the #36 screens the fact that some units are now being sold with a 24-month warranty.

It isn't long before Rao receives a call from Green asking her to have her staff keep track of the number of complaints received about the #36 units. Apparently, Rao infers, there are problems here, and Elgard, anxious to make it big in this competitive consumer business, is touchy.

To find out what's really going on, she calls Al Cohen, her friend in engineering. From Al she learns that engineering is already aware that there are problems, and that the problems are centered in a small auxiliary motor. The motor is a new, low-cost component that was added when the #36 was developed from the very successful #821 machine. The #821 had been designed for high-volume commercial use, and because it was assumed that the #36 machine, designed for the typical "at home" consumer, would be used much less intensively, it was produced with less robust components than its predecessor. Al also tells her that they are now making the more powerful motor available to their sales and service centers around the country, and if a customer "really complains," the more durable motor is to be substituted.

Al has a suggestion: "You know, if your service clerks could get some idea of what kind of users the #36 complaints are coming in from, we might find out whether these machines are getting into the hands of commercial firms that are just beating them to death, or if they are really failing in normal 'home' usage."

As she hangs up, Rao wonders whether she should tell Green that she is thinking of undertaking this informal survey for engineering. And she thinks again of a plan she has been considering for some time—that it would be very useful for service to have some kind of direct access to engineering. There would be many advantages to having her service personnel in direct contact with an engineering representative. At times there are technical questions that her people can't answer; at other times the literature displayed on their video monitors is out of date. Direct contact with engineering would clear up a lot of questions—and would also add to the prestige and visibility of the service jobs. Rao knows that over the years the reps have developed increasing technical competence, but she hasn't been able to get their salaries to increase correspondingly; management still thinks of them as just a telephone-answering service.

Rao's reveries are interrupted when Trump calls to say that despite his best efforts, systems can't do anything about updating the #36 screens for at least a month. The software, which had recently been redesigned at some significant cost, lacks the flexibility to add different or extra warranty data, flexibility no one had thought of in the design stages. It's the third time in the past two weeks that Rao has heard that the new upgraded software is more rigid that she had been led to believe. Apparently, it can't display multiple prices or show rebates either, although both are important factors in Elgard's marketing efforts and she had asked for that capability. She wonders how much of this is due to Trump's ineptness and lack of prestige in systems and how much is due to the fact that systems likes to think they know it all.

Rao calls systems herself and asks that all screens for their consumer products henceforth display one line in caps across the bottom of the screen: CHECK CATALOG FOR ADDITIONAL PRICE, REBATE AND WARRANTY DATA. This will alert the clerks that the screens are incomplete and that they should look elsewhere for the information. The systems manager she speaks to is informed: "That request will have to go into the queue and take its turn," she tells Rao, but Rao knows a reasonable amount about programming and systems and she is sure her request could be honored in five or ten minutes by an experienced programmer. But there is no way she can get it done without a good contact, and that's where Trump stands in her way.

She's also sure that systems is not anxious to start fussing with bits and pieces of their support software when it looks as though marketing is initiating a major effort to get new product features, many of which will call for systems support. Rao knows that systems isn't getting much more notice than she about what's coming down the pike, and their tactic might well be to wait until the dust settles and then deal with as many changes as possible at one time.

Both because she needs to relax and because she struggled to get the appropriation for the hardware through, Rao now goes back over to the telephone area to watch the clerks use the new video monitor that allows them to access six different databanks simultaneously, bringing up materials for display in separate windows at the same time. Her supervisors have said it's working well, but she wants to see for herself and get the feel of how the work flow is being affected. She also knows that being out on the floor and talking with the clerks helps cement relationships; they seem delighted when upper management cares enough to watch and question them.

Being on the floor also gives Rao a chance to watch Jane Atchley in the process of fielding calls. The customer whose complaint has prompted all of this had made some reference to having been cut short of time to explain his story. Rao knows that Jane has been criticized for curtness before, and while she may not have been the clerk involved this time, she still bears watching.

Indeed Jane's supervisor, Alice, had been reluctant to stay on top of personnel problems. Besides, Alice should have picked up on this #36 problem. Rao has told all the supervisors that during this break-in period when customers request information not available on the new equipment and software she should be informed. But not a single item has yet been brought to her attention.

Rao's mind wanders; someone could spend a dozen hours getting Jane to be a more considerate clerk and Alice to be more alert, more energetic supervisor, but there are so many other things to do. And what are the solutions anyway? Some might be tempted to let Alice go. She's made a number of mistakes in the past, but she's a long-service employee. Her departure would only hurt morale. Actually, there's always the chance of encouraging Alice to accept a job in accounting. She worked there when she first joined the company and they liked her—and there are openings in that growing area.

But Rao quickly puts aside the temptation to move Alice out of her department. She is concerned with adding staff, not fine-tuning its quality. Elgard's push into consumer products is adding to service's workload beyond the levels anticipated. Her budgeted staffing levels were developed on the basis of a long-standing formula relating number of units sold to service calls. In fighting for personnel at the last budget go-around she failed to anticipate what seems obvious now. Consumers, less sophisticated and less pressured for time than commercial customers, were much more likely to call in miscellaneous requests and complaints. Her performance indicators which Green watches like a hawk (e.g., how long a customer has to wait for an answer) are already trending down. And there's worse to come. She fears that marketing is about to encourage a number of new "knock-offs" of existing commercial products to be sold to consumers—although, to be honest, she recognizes that since she has not been included in strategy discussions, that presumption is more guesswork than anything else.

Her boss, to this point, has little sense of the crush of new service calls. All he sees and judges by is a single weekly number: average customer waiting time before call answered. That "average" hardly gives an accurate picture. Certain hours on Monday and Friday are very busy, but those long delays are covered up by quick response times during the slow hours and days. Further, the standard her boss likes—a response under twenty-five seconds—is "helped" by the number of consumers who simply give up, either because they get a busy signal or because the phone rings and rings with no answer. (These "abandoned" calls are not counted in the average.) Rao has often wondered whether she should risk sending up some "bad" numbers to make her case for some kind of relief.

Now as she leaves the floor to go back to her office, Rao runs into Jim Kit, one of her best supervisors. Kit has a problem. The mainframe is down, and without it he can't finish the monthly report service has to prepare for headquarters. One of the major items headquarters looks at is monthly service costs, an item that relates regional labor and parts allocations to centralized refunds and parts and unit shipments. Rao tells Kit that he should be able to do the whole thing on his minicomputer, given the software Rao has had developed for her people. "But," Kit explains, "we're supposed to match every expenditure with the data-entered case-disposition material, and with the mainframe down I can't do the matching." In a split second, Rao makes her decision: "Just don't announce that to anyone. The most important thing is getting in a report—any reasonably accurate report is better than none."

Though Kit wonders what will happen (and to whom) if anyone finds out the data hasn't been cross-checked, Rao placates him. She will deal with that problem, if and when it arises; in any event, it is a lot better to be found lax in following a procedure than to miss a deadline on a closely watched report.

Rao looks at her watch. Almost two hours have passed since she talked with the dissatisfied customer. It is now 3:45; she has to get some charts ready for a meeting with the divisional VP in the morning, and there is still a lot of correspondence that has to go out before 5. As she mulls this over, she sees her secretary waving; that can only mean that there is an "important" call waiting. If she's lucky, she can dispatch it in five minutes. As she moves to her office to take the call, she asks her secreaty to call the customer with the complaint and reassure him that the company will repair his machine.

Explaining the Behavior

But why should the managerial day be this fragmented, diffuse, and hectic? In terms of this study, the explanation seems clear. Managers are inevitably required to cope with a multitude of coordination issues. Work elements—the contributions of various other managers, products, and data—all have centrifugal tendencies. Managers are the ones upon whom much (although surely not all) of these integration problems focus. They are running figuratively from one "hole" in the plan (prescribing what should be working synchronously) to another in an endless quest to plug leaks. They are seeking with their energy and ingenuity to keep the systems intact that are constantly threatening to collapse into chaos.

At the same time, if they are indeed effective, such managers are seeking to innovate, to respond to an unfilled need of an internal or external customer, or to take advantage (as Kay Cohen did in chapter 9) of some new technology. But even a minor change unleashes a cascade of obstructions; what is usually a painstakingly built system of interlocked pieces threatens to come apart. Endless negotiations and then renegotiations will be required to construct a new routinized work flow.

Usually managerial issues that involve purely "people" problems require relatively long, uninterrupted contacts. These are necessary because it takes a good deal of time to develop mutual understanding of these subtle and emotion-laden problems, to delegate new responsibilities, or to work through career issues. No satisfactory resolution of a consequential personal issue comes about through a fleeting exchange of words, and managers who tend to give these short shrift are perceived as poor bosses who are indifferent to people.

Therefore, the large number of short contacts that are very typical of managerial work and fill much of the day are likely to be largely coordination issues: routines breaking down. In organizations with any amount of specialization, this will be a very frequent occurrence, for as we have seen work systems are very vulnerable.

The bureaucratic-style manager, of course, doesn't do much running around because he has stock answers to most questions (derived from standard operating procedures and what he perceives as written-in-stone agreements with other departments as to who does what and how). He refuses to budge from these routine methods and answers in spite of crises and unanticipated needs of other parts of the work system.

When a supervisor comes to such a manager to complain that another department is sending them nonstandard materials that are creating quality problems, the bureaucrat's response is, "Don't worry; if our quality declines, they will be responsible."

When an employee complains that he is wasting a lot of time and energy because a work table is too low, his bureaucratic boss answers either that others have been able to do it without complaining or that work methods are out of his hands.

And when an employee spots a leaking pipe that could cause an explosion, this kind of manager may well respond with, "We've spent our repair budget for the month already" (or, equally irresponsible, "Maintenance is supposed to check those periodically; it's their job").

In contrast, working leaders continuously improvise and innovate. They seek to overcome built-in barriers to getting things done right by creative solutions and agile footwork, negotiating quick agreements among all the interested parties. Lots of people need to be nudged, pulled, and pushed to do their jobs and make their choices in ways that will cause all of these to be mutually consistent and add up to effective *systems* performance. Others have to be linked and interlinked. The manager/leader needs to act as a catalyst, continuously building and rebuilding interrelationships among the far-flung elements of the work system.

Bargaining, consulting, and persuading are continuous activities for these leaders, because they recognize that there are an almost infinite number of uncertainties and vulnerabilities in their work systems. Many diverse interests have to be reconciled to cope with both new opportunities and old problems if *real* decisions are going to be made and *real* satisfaction achieved.

Even information is, for the most part, a product of interaction. Managers need to be able to anticipate problems and move quickly on opportunities (such as a customer who is dissatisfied with her current vendor). Such alacrity depends upon the ability to work the system, gaining the confidence of potential informants. Formal reports are usually too little and too late and many contain inaccurate or massaged data.

Importantly and obviously, leaders have to devote substantial energies to data and people management. That is never in question. But the cases discussed here suggest that managers have tended to undervalue their action role and their need for direct, personal involvement in the work process.

The Contrasting GAMP View

This highly active, almost peripatetic role of the manager is a very different conception of leadership than the attributes traditional GAMP principles suggest: passive, analytical, and thoughtful, punctuated by rare interventions devoted to explaining and justifying change. The world of the manager imposes this activist role now that there are few fixed elements in the work situation. Technology, at least in competitive companies, is always in flux, customers are requiring special services and modifications, new products are entering the work stream, and upstream and downstream departments are changing what they are sending or expecting.

This is very different from traditional mass production, where success came from meticulously following absolutely fixed routines, often for years, in order to wring out all the economies of scale. In today's organizations, the latchkey to profitability lies in hustle—in contrast to the big decision, the carefully worked-through strategy, and fixed routines.[2]

MANAGEMENT MODELS THAT DEAL WITH UNCERTAINTY

Of course, many organizational researchers have observed the tendency for organizations to become more compartmentalized and for individual managerial units to become less responsive to the needs of the larger organization. It is called "suboptimization" in academia and "turf consciousness," or just politics, in the real world.

And what are the solutions or cures for the gradual disintegration of organizations? Better planning or better controls are typical consultant and MBA course "solutions." But they can't be part of the solution; they're part of the problem. More careful and hard-nosed planning and tighter controls give the comforting illusion of predictability, of management having things tightly locked up. The annual plans and the numbers that are regularly collected for variance analyses always look as though management has created a highly predictable system that is very much under control, but their real impact is often "paper efficiency": reassuring reports and numbers that flow up the line with little connection to the actual situation.

What other prescriptions are senior management given to build organizations that maintain their integration in the face of increasing uncertainty, change, and difficult coordination problems? The usual ones are detailed below.

1. *Create the right organization structure. Include under a single manager those functions that are most highly interdependent.* This very sensible tactic tells management to avoid the usual temptation to cluster by functional title or responsibility, and rather to put those people and jobs together who are most interdependent, who have to engage in reciprocal give-and-take.[3] Companies should try to build teamwork by using structure to give people a sense of common identity. Essentially, this model is the familiar one that promotes decentralization.

2. *Use integration mechanisms.* One of the prescriptions is to add liaison staff, project coordinators, and other intermediaries to facilitate communication and the making of mutually consistent decisions in departments that are interdependent. Another related prescription for coping with high uncertainty is to encourage subordinates to engage in more direct exchanges with their counterparts in other parts of the organization. This allows quicker adjustment by bypassing the manager and also contributes to improved decision quality (because those who are more knowledgeable are negotiating).[4]

3. *Push down the locus of decision making.* As uncertainty increases, many research studies suggest that managers should become less involved with work issues. Instead they should delegate more fully, giving more leeway (that is, more autonomy) to employees. High-uncertainty organizations usually are staffed with professionals, who are trained to cope well with unpredictability and lack of structure.[5] Certainly in the extreme case of very professional organi-

zations like R & D laboratories, where individuals need to have a great deal of autonomy and there often are few if any interunit linkages to worry about, managers can step back from the work.

Thus, work leadership requirements are minimal at both ends of the uncertainty continuum: in settings similar to R & D and in traditional, truly rigid mass production settings. In the latter, the work is, or ought to be, well programmed. But most organizations today are not at the ends; they are in the middle.

4. *Increased differentiation.* Another structural intervention that appears in the academic literature on management to help cope with uncertainty is increasing the organization's heterogeneity. Senior management needs to encourage (or allow) work groups and departments to develop their own distinctive norms and values. This allows these units to be more sensitive to and more responsive to differences in technology and markets and increases the likelihood that there will be a good fit between the function the group is expected to perform and its modus operandi.[6] This presumes, though, that these differentiated units don't have much mutual adaptation to do.

5. *More use of teams.* In recent years, there has been an outpouring of literature on teams and teamwork. Recognition of the importance of teams is a reflection of a key factor in some of the cases in this book: high uncertainty threatening coordination. Small, mutually interdependent, and cooperative work groups provide an excellent mechanism for a continuous dynamic adjustment to changes in what needs to be done. When A and B can see each other's work problems, share a common loyalty, and have learned to work easily with one another, it is highly likely that each will be willing to adapt to job content changes needed by the other.

As noted in chapter 10, the only limitation here is that most teams are not and cannot be self-contained. Not only does their work affect other groups but higher levels of management and powerful staff groups also have an impact on what they are doing and how they are expected to do it.

LEADERS AND LEADERSHIP

It is ironic that leadership has been little addressed by researchers as a critical factor in getting work integrated and making systems effective. In much of management research, managers are perceived as planners and strategists if they are higher level, or scorekeepers and human relations facilitators if somewhat farther down the hierarchy. But there is little or no attention to their responsibility for coordination, technology, and systems.

Leadership is primarily viewed as a vitally important skill to obtain commitment and motivation and to energize people to accept the worthwhileness of a new strategy or other major change. But in organizations with highly interdependent and dynamic parts, all of which are in flux, accomplishment takes more than commitment. It is not that commitment is unimportant; rather, it too is dependent on the leader's ability to build a system worth committing to.

Unfortunately, too few leadership research studies have sought to observe managers *in situ,* doing their day-to-day work. It is not surprising, therefore, that they fail to identify the critical role of work leadership. They don't observe the heavy proportion of time consumed by work/technology problems.

13

The Leadership Solution

You will have to transform yourself from an overseer into a
doer.[1]

S ince the early 1980s there has been a steady stream of stories
concerning U.S. businesses—most financially healthy, with sophisticated, well-trained management—that are having serious
problems producing timely, quality, customer-responsive products
and services in an efficient manner. Heavy investments in automation
and new computer-based information systems frequently fail to deliver promised benefits. American management just seems to have a
difficult time managing operations. Why is it apparently so hard to
make things work well?

An easy answer has been that American management had not
really been challenged until recent years; management had grown
complacent, even sloppy. And many companies found it convenient
to argue that American workers lacked the work ethic (and respect
for authority) of the Germans and Japanese. The studies presented
in this book suggest that it is the traditional American conception of
management that needs to be questioned. The managerial skills that
were thought of as solutions are often a part of the problem.

The management of work (in contrast to the management of finance or of strategic planning) has suffered from benign neglect in
American business in the past decades. This may well be one of the
major reasons for the sorry competitive performance of many firms
facing hard-driving Japanese and European companies. The reputation of U.S. companies has declined precipitously in the same period;
after once being thought of as producing some of the best products

in the world, many of these same companies are now scrambling to play catch-up.

For the most part, the response of management has been to grab for one "magic bullet" or another. Thus, we have seen a series of disjointed, disconnected improvement programs headlined in the business press and featured in academic executive programs. Each of these usually calls for costly consultants and a cumbersome management overlay of new procedures and new staff roles. Unchallenged and unchanged has been the major paradigm, the worldview of organizational leadership established almost a century ago, based on command and control.

To be sure, "command and control" has been much softened over the years to where empowerment of subordinates and gaining acceptance of a shared vision (a commitment to the mission) has subdued the autocracy. (Regrettably, the improvements have not penetrated very far upward in the management hierarchy.) But the problem of work was and is still perceived as getting *workers* to do what *they* ought to do. Ignored are the legitimate ambiguities and inconsistencies among both tasks and managers, as well as staff experts. But work itself got short shrift, of course, as finance and strategic decision making absorbed most of management's attention span.

Regrettably, too, the psychologists and sociologists studying management and seeking more humanism in business bought into GAMP's traditional dualism: the belief that work and people represent quite separate universes. In the process, they ignored or wrote off the most challenging and critical leadership problems in modern business. They ignored the application of leadership to the accomplishment of work, of coordination and integration. Getting the basic operations of the business performed effectively was not perceived as a serious enough problem to cause management much concern. Senior managers were to be absorbed in planning and decision making, and their subordinates would handle the motivational issues. And it was assumed that the operations were programmed to work well automatically.

WHY LEADERSHIP NEEDS TO FOCUS ON WORK

Both America and traditional management principles excelled when highly routinized, volume-oriented product was the rule. Getting people and units to work diligently and properly, to stick to what they were supposed to do and give a day's work for a day's pay, produced comfortable profitability when combined with capacity output.

Contemporary change-based technology doesn't work that way. In fact, for many companies it hardly works at all. Much more management is required, and a different kind of leadership. Why?

- Because the interrelationships among jobs and functions are much more complex, with a very large number of subtle and often unspecified and interdependencies. It is extraordinarily challenging to get these interlocked so that the work system actually works.
- To make matters worse, most jobs and functions have a great deal of inherent play, particularly for managerial and professional work. They can be performed in widely diverse ways, and the elements can expand or contract from the original conception of the job. (What does it really mean for marketing's relations with operations to have as stated responsibilities that it will "coordinate new service initiatives with appropriate operating personnel"?)
- And these jobs and functions keep changing as managers respond to problems and opportunities, seek to innovate, or defend themselves.

Put together, these factors make it unlikely that any work system will work well without substantial mangerial inputs. *This is the leadership challenge for contemporary managers, to make things work and work well.*

Given their inherent complexity and dynamics, the parts of work systems don't smoothly synchronize for very long—if ever—in any work system. New innovations fail and quality and service are uneven, largely because of integration and coordination issues. For high performance, middle managers need to learn to continuously "rejiggle" or reconfigure the interfaces among jobs and functions. No work structure can stay static for long in a dynamic organization.

No matter how much emphasis is devoted to decentralization, managerial leadership will be required to coordinate work flows that cross jurisdictional boundaries. It is a reassuring myth for most managers that some time soon, they will directly control everything they need to accomplish their objectives. Then their authority will at long last be equal to their responsibility, and everyone who works for them will be loyal to their strategy and objectives.

This almost never happens; when it does, the decentralization is short-lived. At some point, a needed support or service function will be recentralized for the sake of efficiency, or a new, powerful staff group controlling access or permissions will emerge, built around a newly imported expertise.

In addition to these internal dynamics that create coordination challenges, there are frequent external changes buffeting the manager. Customers are more demanding, and new processes and products get introduced. Then shorter innovation cycles are demanded, government regulations change, and external sources of data and services and supplies keep elaborating their procedures.

If clumsy and costly "patches" are to be avoided, managers have to be as creative in integrating these changes as in responding to internal disturbances. And the challenge becomes greater as business units are urged to improve their performance and accept change. Each improvement and change in one group is likely to create challenging discontinuities for other work areas and functions.

These work, technology, and systems issues have similar impacts in service and manufacturing. Both have work flows and operations as their primary activity, and coordination is the critical factor in performance. Historically, highly routinized manufacturing, with invariant methods and models, represented a lesser management challenge to managerial acumen than did most service-based companies; the latter involved more customized and differentiated work activities. This is no longer true. With frequent model changes, constantly improving technology, and the need for quicker responses to customers, the distinctions blur. Not only is technology so dynamic, but almost every output is a "fashion good."[2]

THE INTERPLAY OF PEOPLE AND TECHNOLOGY

The managerial challenges that have been described all are amalgams of people and technology problems. It takes sophisticated, involved, and extraordinarily skillful and committed managers to know when, where, and how to persuade all the key players to do their jobs in ways that are mutually compatible (in other words, that make the system work).

In the PAE case (chapter 4), competitors could never match an innovator's product modification because the managers didn't understand the need to modify *simultaneously* all the interacting elements of their work systems. Instead, they sought to tack on the new element or component of the equipment as though it were an autonomous, self-contained module. Change was limited to the work and methods in the immediate vicinity of the new technology.

The vicissitudes of Kay Cohen (the product manager described in chapter 9) and Eliot Felix and Mary Coel, the managers described in chapter 8 provide a realistic description of the relationship issues that confront a manager seeking to be a working leader. The daunting number of negotiations could have seemed overwhelming. The job consisted of large numbers of widely dispersed interactions requiring finely tuned adaptations. They involved personality, turf, and status issues, and all required great skill as well as perseverance (and self-confidence). Significantly, they all were amalgams of technical and interpersonal issues and could not have been dealt with as merely one or the other.

It is these work-based "people problems" that are the focus for managers who are successful in building efficient, adaptive and innovative organizations. They then become working leaders because they both understand in-depth and are willing to tackle the multitudinous human relationship challenges that are embedded in the work and technology.

A NEW PARADIGM FOR MANAGEMENT
AND LEADERSHIP

What is needed is a new paradigm or worldview for leaders that reflects the realities of contemporary technology and markets.[3] Most managers are not managing mass-production—like operations in which almost everything is fixed for some substantial period of time, and profits come from pure volume. Instead, contemporary managers face everyday, persistent turbulence. Adaptability, flexibility, very frequent product or service change, and very short "runs" are the rule, not the exception.

As a result, the most critical performance issues for the organization revolve around *implementation, execution, operating capabilities and competencies, coordination, and systems issues.* Who does what with whom, when, and where in order to get quality, market-responsive work done effectively all have to be continuously reworked.

It is middle managers that need this competence, this concentration, and this initiative. Ironically, in the past, business has recognized the need to empower workers and work teams, but not these managers. They were still expected to accept the technology and the systems as given, as fixed, and as perfect. But turbulence in products and markets is forcing change.

The management of the past focused on a small number of critical decisions concerning markets and products, and these gravitated, sensibly, to top management. Today's and tomorrow's performance issues confront middle managers, who need a set of quite different behavioral skills to deal with a never-ending array of technology and systems issues.

As the cases in the previous chapters have sought to illustrate, this turbulence and change place enormous demands on work leadership. The challenge is not only to get subordinates to follow the leader with zest and commitment, but constantly and skillfully to work interfaces where legitimate contradictions, inconsistencies, and dilemmas confront both managers and workers. But finding solutions allows (or, better, forces) managers to become *real* leaders in that they can then influence simultaneously four critical and defining variables in the work setting:

- strategy
- employee motivation
- core operating competencies
- a leader-based microculture

Further, this emphasis plays to the strength of American managers raised in a culture that stresses individual initiative, challenging the status quo, improvisation, and risk taking.

Strategy and Core Operating Competencies are Complementary

In traditional organizations, strategy and operations are at opposite ends of the management continuum and have little relation one to the other. That situation is changing in a competitive world in which operating capabilities are both consequential and difficult to attain.

Significant strategic initiatives can evolve out of the solution of the challenges of operating work. In part, these are the result of new and powerful competencies that evolve and can be leveraged over new products, processes, and services. The managers who are close to the scene and who comprehend the elusive and subtle nuances of technology and markets are best able to create new strategic initiatives. Unlike those imposed from the top, often with little insight into the problems of execution, these strategies should have a lower mortality rate. This is not simply because people work harder for goals for which they feel ownership, but because the objectives are more realistic.

Motivation and Culture

Conventional business wisdom is fatalistic about organizational culture: if senior management isn't enlightened, there is little room for alternative norms and values. But employee motivation increases in an environment of high performance and continuous problem solving as described in chapter 7. Motivation can be the *result* of effectiveness, perhaps more so than its cause. Employees identify with managers who can take initiative in modifying the decisions and norms of both bosses and peers, particularly powerful staff groups. These working leaders demonstrate organizational courage, as well as commitment to performance (as opposed to career enhancement).

In the process, such managers can create "microcultures" within a large organization. Within this world, there can be productive zestfulness and work pride on the part of employees, as well as confidence in management. Its values and norms that stress continuous problem identification and solution, and continuous improvements in quality and service, may be quite different than those of other units of the larger organization. A determined, skillful middle management leader creates a special world by force of personality and work effectiveness.

Work-Level Competencies as the Foundation of the Business

The generally accepted management principles (GAMP) emphasized that the most important management activities are those involved in planning, which represents the "real" leadership of the organization. It is top-down leadership—top management telling the rest of the organization what they can do. In sharp contrast, the growing emphasis on the comparative competitive advantage of excellence in execution turns that seemingly obvious management principle on its head. Many future products, services, and responses to the marketplace can grow out of the foundations, the bedrock of the organization; its operating competencies.[4]

These are created by a very different kind of leadership than was conceived by the most students of management and organizational behavior. It is leadership that becomes expert in the nuances of what it takes by way of managerial microdecisions to make a technology work and continue to evolve. And such leaders are also able to translate that expertise into influence with all the key participants in the work process because they have the requisite behavioral skills.

Murphy's Law and the Japanese

Many managers have learned to blame the engineer's favorite whipping boy for problems on development projects. Murphy's Law asserts that if there is a chance of anything going wrong, you can be sure it will (but you can't know in advance what "it" will be). These same managers are likely to feel that there is something unusual and perhaps even cultural (and therefore unattainable by Westerners) about the Japanese obsession with perfection.

> In the early 1980s, I recall listening to some American customers for Japanese semiconductors laughing about how Japanese suppliers would not sell parts in which the lot number or company name on the part was blurred or off center, even though that lettering had no relationship to performance.

But small mistakes, oversights, and little blunders can be devastating in tightly coupled systems. Huge, multimillion-dollar software programs that may take years to implement (such as those for sophisticated new management information systems) often don't work because of a trivial embedded programming error. Nuclear plants can be shut down because a small valve malfunctions, and an entire industry is threatened with extinction. Oil refineries explode, requiring a billion dollars of repairs, because of a small leak from a rusty pipe.

Involvement in Work Is Misperceived

Most senior managers (and students of management) have little real understanding of how much managerial skill it takes to make thing work well with high levels of efficiency, adaptability (or flexibility), and quality.[5] Managers who have this working-leadership capability are rarely celebrated. Quite the contrary, until very recently American senior management not only tolerated, they actually encouraged organizational incompetencies. Managers were told that they should not get involved with work or technology issues, because it would smother subordinate motivation. It would be "micromanaging" and would keep the managers from doing "real" managerial work.

American management has been taught to look back and to look forward. In companies, middle managers spend an inordinate amount of time worrying over (even manipulating) the acquisition and appropriate display techniques of data that will appear consistent with plans, budgets, and commitments. In a similar vein, a great deal of time is expending preparing and seeking to gain acceptance for future plans covering various time periods. Managers learn that one of their most important functions is developing visual and oral presentations that "sell" in order to obtain reasonable resources and hurdle rates for what they will be expected to accomplish in the months ahead.

But managers, to add value and not overhead, need to be involved in improving operations and in operating work, because contemporary technology requires managerial interventions. Less effective is managing at a distance through results, reports, and a hands-off style of delegation. Without real involvement, many middle-level managers function primarily as checkpoints, as hierarchical clearance centers. Rather than expediting work, they impede it. (Many of the reorganizations and downsizings that have taken place in the 1980s and early 1990s were prompted by the multiple levels of checkpoints for decisions that frustrated those managers seeking to introduce change.)

Paradoxically, knowledge of and involvement in the realities of work systems by middle managers does not demotivate supervision and employees, as traditional theory predicts. Quite the contrary, these leaders gain support and responsiveness because they understand the realities their subordinates face and are helpful and constructive in shaping the organization to facilitate work objectives. By solving problems and improving work performance, they are perceived as vital participants, in contrast to being perceived as bosses who simply reward and punish from a distance.

All the systems, coordination, and adaptation problems discussed here were defined away by traditional management principles. There were no interface or systems issues because jobs and functions and business units had clear, unambiguous boundaries, just as staff and line executives had perfectly compatible roles. There were no conflicts and no inconsistencies, because everything was designed to add up (if done properly and energetically) into the planned, coordinated whole.

Also, where there is little top management appreciation of the vulnerability of coordination, specialist groups multiply and procreate, further complicating the job of attaining high performance. For many years, management experts really believed that there was nothing problematic about having staffs proliferate and requiring line managers to get clearance for most of their decisions and "buy" their expertise and services. Taylor even believed that there could be eight separate supervisors over a given work operation (one for efficiency, one for quality, one for safety, and so on).[6]

Traditional Binary Management Principles Still Encumber Leaders

It was traditional management principles, with their mechanistic, top-down view of organizations, that saddled management (and management education) with this logically correct, but spurious *binary* view of leadership and work. They neatly separated managerial work from subordinate work; there was a clear line of demarcation, just as in the charts. Motivation and people problems had little or nothing to do with technology issues, and vice versa. And handling change was supposed to be very different from handling routine and stability, just as planning was separated in time from implementation in reassuring serial fashion.

The same binary philosophy underlay the simplistic views of decentralization and leadership. Give a manager an activity to manage so that there were no ambiguities surrounding which resources were hers and which belonged to some other manager, the theory said. Then responsibility (for results) would nicely equal authority (control over needed resources). The result, however, was a group of uncooperative fiefdoms whose rulers neither gave nor received any of the advantages of belonging to a common organization.

It was also binary thinking that shaped the widely accepted view of delegation. The superior's job was clearly separable from the work of the subordinate; therefore, by involving oneself in work, systems, and technology issues, the manager was crossing a clear boundary and infringing on the subordinate's work and responsibilities. The result inevitably was a diminished sense of managerial responsibility, as well as motivation on the part of the subordinate.

Rediscovering the Obvious

Ironically, if one had surveyed the management field in the 1950s, there were many business courses and books being written about the very subjects that resurfaced as *new discoveries* in managing work roughly forty years later. Below are just a few examples from MIT's offerings (in their then-nascent business program) circa 1950.[7]

- *Techniques and usefulness of statistical quality control.* Managers learned sampling and charting techniques and the importance of quality to both cost and customer satisfaction.
- *Continuous restudying of jobs to improve efficiency* (in those days called "work study" and "work simplification"). "Question everything" was the challenge then—as Toyota would gain credit for rediscovering fifty years later. Almost the same terms, in fact, were used as today. (For example, managers learned to list all the steps required to complete a report or assembly operation and assess which were unnecessary or could be combined or could be accomplished with less effort, including the search for things done "just because they had always been done that way" and for redundant approval procedures.)
- *The usefulness of worker-management committees to surface and gain acceptance for worker-initiated improvements in work methods.* In the late 1940s, it was frequently noted that participating, involved employees not only felt better about themselves and their jobs but contributed more energy to their tasks. Supervisors were taught how to run meetings to encourage this participation.
- *Interviewing and relationship-building skills* to help managers learn the real problems and issues confronting employees on the job, as well as the often hidden realities about the technology.

Of course, these insights probably will be lost again and be rediscovered as "new truths" as long as a focus on work performance is not central to the manager's world.

CAN MANGEMENT BE TAUGHT? DO MBA'S LEARN TO LEAD?

Are young managers taught to be work leaders? Probably not, unfortunately. MBA students get superb training in making presentations to their bosses and surrogate bosses (their instructors), and they also learn to do first-rate analytical work. The great emphasis on business cases serves to convince them that the toughest job of managing is to work through and carefully weigh the "facts" that have been presented, emphasizing what is most relevant and excluding the superfluous. Then they learn the importance of crafting a persuasive, concise set of arguments that will justify the "correct decision."

To be fair, they also learn that there are often problems of selling the solution to an anachronistic boss or shortsighted employee or obstinate union leader. The decision, arrived at by tough-minded, rational thought and removed from passions or politics, may be right but unacceptable.

What they don't learn from most Harvard Business School–style cases are the more subtle skills of being a manager in a real organization who needs to be concerned, not only with making things work, but with making them work well and work better. For real managers, data doesn't come in little, nicely tied-up, easy-to-handle packets, nor is there often just the one decision. There may well be countless small choices along the way of solving a problem, and the real results usually don't come in clear-cut victories or losses that can be toted up at any given point in time (and graded by the boss or the instructor). Successful work managers expend great effort making incremental improvements by slight changes in what goes on below them, as well as getting peers and bosses to accept slight changes in plans and standard operating procedures that were assumed to be fixed in the short run.

Further, the impact of the total array of incremental choices shows itself over time (although it is obscured by the fact that lots of other things are changing at the same time). Managers don't get the neat, reassuring classroom-type feedback: they made the right choice and everything works. In the real world, not everything is working at the same time; some things are going very well, whereas others are improving and others slipping. Management is an iterative process in which one is constantly seeking to learn, to tease out the relevant parameters with an obscured field of vision because so many things are changing at the same time. It is difficult to distinguish cause and effect.

Real learning doesn't occur easily; it requires painstaking observation, interviewing (of good informants, both supervisors and employees), and reading of reports. A manager can only learn the inner workings of the technology/structure/people work systems by patient efforts over some period of time. Experienced managers are surprised continuously by insights they obtain by observation and talking with supervisors and employees down the line.

> I never knew until we had a major failure that our people were having trouble mating the module we make with the one that comes from that subcontractor. I had always thought that the interface design was unambiguous, and everything had worked so well for the past six months.

What business school instructors (particularly those in pit-shaped auditoriums) favor, however, is the student who thinks and speaks well under fire and can make balanced decisions (that is, they can function well dealing with the tough question from the instructor combined with the competitive eyes of fellow students). Some instructors give the impression that they are emulating law school faculty; they prepare students to face a world somewhat like a courtroom with a judge who says "right" or "wrong" and a jury that will be persuaded by verbal pyrotechnics and tight logic.

Students primarily learn to look in their packaged cases for the cleverly hidden problems that cry out for the textbook ideas and solutions. They perceive management not as a voyage of discovery, but rather a trip on a well-marked course. They are prepared to deal with storms, to be sure (that is, the dullards and the obstructionists who don't or won't understand their mission). They are not prepared to keep learning.

Published Critiques by MBA Faculty

Some years ago, a Harvard Business School professor bravely echoed some of these criticisms of MBA education:

> On the one hand, problem solving and decision making in the classroom require what psychologists call "respondent behavior." It is

this type of behavior that enables a person to get high grades on examinations. . . .

On the other hand, success and fulfillment in work demand a different kind of behavior which psychologists have labeled "operant behavior." Finding problems and opportunities, initiating action, and following through to attain desired results require the exercise of operant behavior which is neither measured by examinations nor developed by discussing in the classroom what someone else should do.

Instruction in problem solving and decision making all too often leads to "analysis paralysis"[8] because managerial aspirants are required only to explain and defend their reasoning, not to carry out their decisions or even to plan realistically for their implementation. Problem solving in the classroom often is dealt with, moreover, as an entirely rational process, which, of course, it hardly ever is.[9]

They [MBA students] study written case histories that describe problems or opportunities discovered by someone else, which they discuss, but do nothing about. What they learn about supervising other people is largely secondhand. Their knowledge is derived from the discussion of what someone else should do about the human problems of "paper people" whose emotional reactions, motives, and behavior have been described for them.[10]

In a more current critique, professor Henry Mintzberg has very similar reservations about the utility of MBA leadership training:

It [the typical American MBA program] attracts students who generally have only the barest understanding of what goes on organizations. . . . [and] accepts them on the basis of tests that measure their ability to answer closed-ended questions. Then it subjects them to analytical courses, almost none of which pertain to the calculated chaos of management. When management itself is broached, it is usually through case studies. . . . All these managers-to-be sit neatly arranged in a classroom, ready to debate what the kingpins of Detroit must do. No one can claim ignorance—lack of understanding, no firsthand knowledge, no "sense" or "feel" of the situation. Because good managers have to be decisive, good management students must take a stand.[11]

More Internships Instead of Canned Cases

A better model for management education would be medical school training. Doctors learn that a careful examination of the patient is a good place to begin. Jumping to conclusions on the basis of an "obvious" symptom or superficial similarity to a textbook description can be dangerous. Many times a variety of tests will be used, and there may still be the need for careful observation over some period of time. The physician learns to make tentative judgments about a test or a treatment, but she is prepared to learn more on the basis of gradually emerging data that may shift her diagnosis. Even though the patient understandably wants a crisp decision in contrast to a restrained "maybe this, or maybe that . . . but it is too soon to tell for sure," the doctor knows that the complexity of the human body (and psyche) makes quick decisions both rash and dangerous to patient health.

Of course, if managers were trained like doctors, they would also intern under supervision. Then they could learn the painstaking skills of careful examination and avoiding decisions for decisions' sake. They would learn how to listen to what patients say and also to observe them under a variety of conditions and after a variety of probings. They would learn how to test their hypotheses: if the patient is suffering from X, it should show up in Y (usually) or, if not there, in Z (if I know how to look at it properly).

Experienced managers and good doctors also are always on the lookout for anomalies and inconsistencies.[12] In particular, they are looking for what they did not correctly predict they would see or would occur. Managers carry around in their heads the "maps" of their world that provide them with causalities and explanations: "Jane is a fine worker and can cope well with stress"; "Our new computers can handle all X type problems"; "My boss supports me when I have an idea that will improve customer service even if it is quite costly"). When something occurs that contradicts these convenient predicors, a sensible manager seeks an explanation. This search is not motivated by idle curiosity, but to see if there is a new factor in the situation that will affect the manager's world and that he or she must, therefore, take into account in the future.

THE SYSTEMS CHALLENGE

As noted in the discussion of GAMP, managers appear instinctively (and regrettably), to ignore or misunderstand work systems as a result of traditional management training. Their managerial actions suggest that this is how they see the challenge of getting work accomplished:

1. The primary challenge is getting people to do their individual tasks.
2. Jobs and technology are fixed for the most part, and when they are changed, it is usually under the direction of staff technical people or some higher management task force. Technology is certainly not the manager's responsibility.
3. Technology and people problems are quite distinct.
4. If everyone does his or her job properly, the sum total of everyone's performance will add up to effective work (efficiency, high quality, and so on). Where performance is inadequate, it is usually the result of laziness, ineptness, or some political maneuver.
5. Managers manage best who manage least, who delegate most and manage by results.
6. Managers are almost interchangeable, because the problems of managing apples are very similar to the issues that will be critical to managing oranges. There is no consequential learning time to get up to speed in a given area, because the details of how things work are not that relevant (except for a first-line supervisor).

Managers do need to know the intricacies of the work systems for which they are responsible. In particular, managers need to know the "innards" of markets, products (and services), and operations— and one does not tell you much about the other.

Almost Nothing Works by Itself

What makes these apparent truths anything but eternal verities is the fragility of coordination and integration, that is, the ability of the organization to convert tasks and functions into completed work that satisfies an internal or external customer. As the reader has seen repeatedly, most work systems are inherently unstable and fragile (that is, vulnerable to self-destruction). They don't really operate as systems in which the parts come together efficiently and effectively. In a dynamic world, the chances are better than even that external events will intervene with some regularity. Customer tastes and demands will change, a new government regulation will appear, a competitor or vendor will do something unexpected, or a new technique or piece of equipment will become available. The ramifications can then be profound on the internal work system.

There are also consequential problems of inadequate amounts of change. As was so profoundly evident in the data from the photo-lithographic alignment equipment (PAE) industry case in chapter 4, new methods and new products require an enormous amount of synchronized change among many parts of the system for a new module or modification to work properly. There is also great momentum and conservatism in work systems, so that it takes enormous managerial effort to get all the mutually reinforcing adaptations made by all the relevant groups and contributors. There are even greater vulnerabilities in tightly integrated systems, such as large software programs and highly automated telecommunications and manufacturing systems. In these, almost any slight deviation or defect ramifies and amplifies as it works its way through the system. And the result is that these systems usually represent highly unstable equilibrium; it doesn't take much of a push (or mistake) to throw the system into disarray. The analogy to what mathematicians (and lots of other people) are now calling "chaos" seem evident. [13] Very small perturbations, such as the proverbial butterfly flapping its wings in some far-off place, have a profound impact on the effectiveness seen in a work process in another part of the globe.

BUT WHY MANAGERS?

Managers have to get involved in these pernicious systems issues because they are the only ones with the very specific information and established organizational relationships that are required to keep things together (that is, integrated and mutually compatible). Regrettably, many managers believe that the systems are working just because they are designed to work, to have the parts fit together congruently and compatibly. The opposite assumption would be a much more useful one, namely, that most systems are either not working well or are close to some kind of collapse. Managers thus have real work to do; they are not simply planners and appraisers. [14] On their shoulders falls the responsibility of keeping the system going and putting it back together again when it fails.

Typically, middle managers are more mobile and more informed than their nonmanagerial and supervisory subordinates. Both their organizational position and their experience should have given them contact with a wide range of specialists in other functions and in staff roles. Many times these lateral peers (or almost peers) control critical authorizations. They are thus able to engage in direct negotiations with people who can make needed changes in work parameters. For example, human resources staff can help approve a salary increase to keep a critical employee, and the head of engineering can modify a standard that is holding up a product approval.

Just as important, these middle levels of the organization should have a much greater store of knowledge. They occupy obvious crossroad positions in which large numbers of people casually and intentionally see and interact with them and pass along vast quantities of information. In fact, managers with good social skills get inundated with information, and it takes a great deal of skill and discipline to make adequate use of it.

Good managers are constantly evaluating and filing away things they learn almost accidentally, as well as through direct questions by them and direct initiations by others. These storehouses of personal knowledge often contain more current, accurate, and relevant operationally detailed information than one can find in carefully massaged and tailored reports. Managers have learned to place more credence on these direct, verbal accounts than on the written word (because they are probably more current, are certainly richer in detail, and are probably more valid).[15]

As we have seen, employees and managers must make countless choices and trade-offs every day regarding how their jobs should be performed. Their manager, who can't make these decisions for them, needs to be sure that those choices reflect the manager's current strategy. Thus, in the Ames case, the general manager over the two managers (who each are both customer and vendor to each other) has to stay close to their exchanges. It would be easy, given differences in personality, skill, or perseverance, for one to make concessions to the other that would injure the general manager's strategy for developing these several products. After all, most of the issues that they will be negotiating on have no easy right or wrong answers.

PERSONALITY ISSUES

These managers must obviously be flexible and be open to new learning. What was good practice or worked yesterday may turn out to be flawed today. George Bernard Shaw was right (as with so many things) when he observed wryly, "Consistency is the enemy of enterprise."

Managers also must have extraordinary personal skills to work these interfaces, to keep taking initiative, and to persevere in the light of a problem following every solution and others ready to grab defeat from the jaws of victory. And they require substantial self-esteem to weather the criticism and the anxiety associated with their "rocking the boat." In trying to make things work and work well, others have to change, particularly bosses and peers. But everyone has some reason for doing what they are now doing, not the least being that it has been authorized and probably has shown some reasonably positive results in the past. Thus, the manager is always negotiating change within a broad network of interdependencies, because no system works without an extraordinary amount of fumbling, trial and error, and rejuggling.

U.S. MANAGERS, U.S. CULTURE, AND THE FUTURE

The functioning of semiconductor materials depends on the presence of certain impurities. These minute quantities are very consequential, although they are nonetheless impurities. By analogy, the "impurities" in work systems are the heart of the manager's job. Teasing out their source, finding remedies, and responding to internal and external customers in ways that keep the system going are an enormous but often unrecognized challenge. Changing to another analogy, American managers are going to have to relearn the basics of blocking and tackling if American business is going to thrive in a fast changing world economy. The "basics" that they learned in less competitive days for more stable technologies just aren't useful for the way the business game needs to be played today.

But most important, it is the ability to do the basics of working leadership, the building of robust work systems, that should be most recognized and most rewarded. For too long, senior managers have assumed that their traditional control and appraisal systems worked to inspire managers in ways that built the business. Instead, they have inspired managers to build walled-in empires and their own careers.

The Lure of the Big Decision

Management, understandably, is tempted with the lure of solving problems through big decisions. General Motors suffered the indignity of having its dominant position in the U.S. auto market decimated by the Japanese; it must have believed that it was courageous and farsighted to commit sixty billion dollars to revamping its manufacturing and creating the "factory of the future." Spending big dollars and taking big risks represent the epitome of traditional management action. Regrettably the much tougher job of working through the minutia of work systems and the interplay of technology and the people is less appealing and less prestigious. Current texts on management stress the importance of the energizing the organization through creating a vision of the desired future state; less attention is given to everyday implementation.

Leadership and Control

For the most part, when management (and students of management) have sought to deal with involvement in the work of the organization, they have been concerned with control. Managers who probed work issues usually were seeking to check up on subordinates, lacked confidence in their subordinates, or had anxieties about the loss of control. Managers hung up on control sought to limit the discretion and autonomy of their subordinates. They would often insist that all contact with outsiders (such as peers in other departments or customers) either be conducted by the manager or, at the least, be cleared with the manager. They hoard external contacts and deprive their subordinates of both developmental opportunities and organizational visibility.

In contrast, managers who are working leaders facilitate the work of the levels below them. For them, involvement means continuously increasing their understanding of the functional relationships and parameters that explain the intricacies of the work systems: the dynamics of tecnology, of the marketplace, and of their internal and/or external customers. (This is why managers who only want to spend a year or two on a current assignment before promotion must have limited ambitions for what can be accomplished in improving work effectiveness.)

Need for a Counterculture

The irrelevancies of management principles are no accident, nor is their repeated "validation" in the writings of business experts. Both are products of American culture. Americans find it easy to adopt a strongly individualistic, atomistic, compartmentalized view of business organizations, as of political life. Standardization, not allowing for managers to fine tune a technology, is very appealing. And the transference of this broader culture to business worked quite well until the last quarter of the twentieth century.

American managers, unlike many of their Asian competitors, do not get much training or experience in thinking in terms of whole systems and larger wholes. Their education stresses "facts," compartmentalized knowledge, and clarity of boundaries—not only between jobs and functions but between church and state, family and business, courts and legislatures, and the mind and body. In addition to perceiving these watertight compartments, Americans learn the importance of opposing forces: free-market business managers versus government regulators, environmentalists versus business interests, and so forth.

That jurisdictions and issues overlap, that interests can be harmonized through skillful negotiations, and that cooperation, competition, and conflict can coexist is not much appreciated. Until very recently it was never questioned, for example, that companies should keep their vendors at arm's length. The legalistic relationship was limited to a written contract, usually for a limited period of time. Now management is learning the true complexity of the interdependencies between what is purchased and what is produced inside, and the usefulness of extensive collaboration.

In America, the cowboy is still idealized—after all these years of urban life—who, like the entrepreneur and deal maker of today, is not beholden to anyone and who seeks to beat the system, not work it or improve it. But modern technologies require closely orchestrated, coordinated efforts among many interlinked managers.

America's Comparative Advantage

If American management can shake off the vestiges of old and binary GAMP, there is substantial hope for the future. After all, American culture produces strong individualists who show their willingness both to stand up and be counted and to take risks (at least before they get acculturated in traditional corporations). The case examples included in previous chapters have as a recurring theme the potential contribution of this kind of individualism to working leadership and to organizational effectiveness. It is leadership that combines involvement with work systems, integration, and coordination issues with a sensitivity to and skill in persuasion, negotiation, and accessing information.

These leaders were always looking for "surprises", unanticipated problems and opportunities that did not fit their current understanding or theory of the case. This sensitivity and alertness and willingness to take responsibility for shaking things up are all indispensable requirements for managing in fast-changing world (in terms of both) markets and technology.

Many Americans are inherently improvisational, iconoclastic, and irreverent of the past. Combine that with an understanding of markets and technology and leadership, and one has the ingredients for a significant competitive advantage. It is an advantage based on individuals and individual ability and ingenuity, *not* on better forecasting or planning, more rationalism, new forms of organization (or theories X, Y or Z), or new procedures or techniques, homegrown or imported. Ironically and surprisingly, individual leadership capability has become more, not less critical, in this age of increasing technical specialization and sophistication.

American business is now quick to adopt solutions to its performance problems. It is much slower to ask why they occurred in the first place.

Why did American companies become fat and tall, so hierarchical? Answer: Coordination failures and work problems created the need for more levels and more staff to check and control. Why did these same companies find it difficult to produce high-quality goods and services and customer satisfaction and to introduce quickly and efficiently new designs and new services? Answer: Work systems didn't work very well; teamwork was faulty and lots of things "fell between the cracks."

Placing a tough new CEO in charge may help, just as some new technique may help, but the long-run solution to improved performance is managers oriented to work and operations and able to manage the real coordination issues, able to deal with those answers by effective work leadership.

Research Appendix

With justification, the reader should ask for the sources and validity of the generalizations contained in the preceding text. In the past, the data for those research-based monographs have come from field-work, primarily extended and intensive case studies. The methods were derived from social anthropology: observation and open-ended interviewing. For both, I always took prolific notes, usually after each encounter, that I later expanded on when transcribing them. At a still later point in time, I did a content analysis and sought to identify recurring patterns or regularities in the data.[1]

Of course, such methods are castigated with some regularity as anecdotal, and even erroneous. In this regard, I was struck with a recent recounting of a critic's putdown of Piaget, the distinguished French child psychologist: "But why should one take his work seriously? he only spoke with children."[2] I hope that critics will say the same of me, that I only spoke with managers. I didn't give them survey questionnaires, and I didn't even ask a series of carefully contrived questions based on one or another well-known organizational behavior theories. Instead, I listened to them talk about their work, their problems, their tactics and strategies for accomplishing their objectives, and their hopes and fears.

Thus, this work has made use of some case study and field interviewing methods but in a much less formal and systematic manner than my previous research. Reflecting the forty years I have studied and taught about organizations, it is more an interpretive essay than a research study. The cases and examples are illustrations of various phenomenan; they are not offered as "proof."

Almost a decade ago, I began working through the concepts and some of the ideas that are now in this book. This work stemmed from a sense of dissatisfaction with how management and organizational behavior ideas were communicated in MBA classrooms and with what I was reading in books and speeches by consultants and managers seeking to tell others "how to do it." Much seemed to represent a fix-it mentality, various kinds of palliatives that a manager could learn to apply (or, at the least, to use the jargon). None addressed what seemed to me to be basic flaws in the underlying or implicit theory of the core of managerial work or what was most problematic about being a manager.

I could not understand why so many of the distinguished researchers in the organizational behavior bought into the traditional principles of management unquestioningly. Their prescription for delegation and decentralization, for example, seemed not to reflect the inevitably blurred boundaries between boss and subordinates and between one organizational unit and another. I later decided, perhaps with some prejudice, that they accepted this deductive and unrealistic framework (or paradigm) for organizations and hierarchy because they did not go out and look at the functioning of real companies and didn't watch what managers had to do in order to get something done effectively. And when they did go into the field (usually with an instrument), it was with a clear hypothesis in mind that would brook no interference from the anomalies and imperfections of the real world.

I tried outlining my preliminary analysis about five years ago, and wrote a half-dozen chapter drafts. On rereading, these seemed simplistic and inadequate and had to be discarded. These chapters are a kind of distillation of work I have been engaged in for some years. They represent an effort to tie together and integrate a number of themes and issues that have always seemed to indicate discrepancies, frictions, or inexplicable discontinuities in management doctrine.

The basic theory also reflects the anthropological perspective of William F. Whyte and Eliot Chapple. Organizations need to be understood, and the structure and controls built upward, from the flow of work. It is the technology that shapes the critical factors that constitute the organization.[3] It is an erroneous maxim of the traditional field of management to think of organizations in top-down terms, with an emphasis on the top of the pyramid and the delegation and accountability processes that transfer the authority of the chief executive eventually to those who do the work. I think I failed to see the full significance of this simple, but powerful precept until I began working on this book.

The data from which I draw my conclusions thus are not derived from systematically undertaken case studies. Rather, the specific case examples are derived from very scattered sources. First, I reanalyzed my own research notes from previous field studies. Second, as a staff member of the Center for Creative Leadership, I participated in two significant field studies that worked within four very large corporations; one with Wilfred Drath (focusing on delegation issues), and the other with Marian Ruderman (focusing on promotion criteria). I also was privileged to have access to some of the data collected by Dr. Barry Gruenberg, who was working on several organization development projects in another major U.S. corporation during 1990 and 1991. These gave me access to a number of case examples of managers at work.

Third, I seek to read the business press systematically. I am aware of the limitations of journalism, but I believe that their more descriptive articles represent a useful and usable source of data. Fourth, and perhaps least systematic and most suspect, I am also an inveterate interviewer. Wherever and whenever I find a line manager with whom to carry out a discussion, I take advantage of the opportunity to probe his or her recent work experiences. Modestly, I think I am able to get most such informants to discuss their jobs and their organizations freely. (It is important to repay their confidence with complete anonymity, which is why all of the examples in the text for which there are not attributions have been disguised by slight changes in context as well as names.)

I did have the opportunity to obtain some systematic case materials. As indicated in previous chapters, I found Dr. Rebecca Henderson's intensive study of changing market leadership in the photolithographic alignment equipment industry invaluable. Her detailed case studies, which included behavioral data, allowed me to undertake a reanalysis using the framework of this study. In addition, in 1990 I participated in a field study of a major operating division of a major corporation, findings from which are described in part in the Ames case in chapter 5. With the exception of Henderson's published data, I have changed the technology and names in every example in order to protect the anonymity of informants and organizations. I felt this was necessary, because many people have knowledge of the organizations in which I have worked or for which have information.

In sum, this does not comprise the kind of more traditional case study–based research I have done in the past. In contrast to the other studies, this has been a much more deductive kind of research project. Based on earlier work I developed certain hypotheses, and I sought to test them by the kind of data I could collect using the sources described above. One obvious limitation was research staff; the staff was limited to one—that is, myself. As compensation for this disadvantage, however, I had the advantage of being a member of the research community of the Center for Creative Leadership. This has been the most supportive setting for research I have known as an academic researcher.

It should be noted that all company names, with the exception of those included in previously published sources, have been contrived. The included case materials are from the author's field research notes, and names as well as some other identifying characteristics have been changed to protect the anonymity of both people and organizations. Thus American Business Products, Ames, Ajax, Allen, Bates, First, Process Chemicals, and Eclipse are not real company names. Similarly, the manager names—Coel, Felix, Cohen, and Rao—are not the real names of executives we interviewed and observed.

Notes

1. Waltz Faster—They're Playing a Tango

1. The CEO of one of America's best managed companies recently said that he was considering selling several businesses that had been part of the corporation because he personally could not add much value to their management! (Interview with the author, January 9, 1992; because this was not public information, the name is being withheld).

2. Fred Bleakley, "As Big Rivals Surge, Citicorp's John Reed Is at a Crossroads," *Wall Street Journal,* August 16, 1991.

Chapter 2. A New Leadership Perspective

1. James McGregor Burns introduced these now widely used terms. See his *Leadership* (New York: Harper & Row, 1978), p. 4.

2. See Michael Piore and Charles Sabel, *The Second Industrial Divide* (New York: Basic Books, 1984).

3. David Halberstam, *The Next Century* (New York: William Morrow, 1991), p. 59.

4. In the 1950s, particularly in France, there was growing sentiment that U.S. companies—in part because of the training provided by a U.S. academic invention, business schools—would dominate the European economy. See J. J. Servan-Schreiber, *The American Challenge* (New York: Atheneum, 1969).

5. Halberstam, op. cit., p. 73.

6. See Paul McCracken, "The Big Domestic Issue: Slow Growth," *Wall Street Journal,* October 4, 1991. The specific figures McCracken cites are these: from 1900 to 1973, real income after taxes per person at work rose at the average rate of 2.2 percent. From 1973 to 1990, the rate of increase declined to 0.5 percent.

Chapter 3. U.S. Management Principles

1. David Garvin, "Quality on the Line," *Harvard Business Review,* Vol. 61, No. 5 (September–October 1983), pp. 65–67.

2. Sidney Schoeffler, R. Buzzell, and D. Heany, "Impact of Strategic Planning on Profit Performance," *Harvard Business Review,* Vol. 52, No. 2 (March–April 1974), p. 137; and R. Buzzell and F. Wiersema, "Successful Share-Building Strategies," *Harvard Business Review,* Vol. 59, No. 1 (January–February 1981), p. 135.

3. Informal remarks by John Neuman. Meritus Consulting Services, Coopers & Lybrand, Boardroom seminar, New York, September 26, 1991.

4. This is a summary of a news report that appeared in the *Wall Street Journal,* December 24, 1990.

5. *Wall Street Journal,* January 5, 1989.

6. These conclusions are mine, derived from reading Frank Wayno, *The Road to the Baldrige Award: Human Resource Aspects of the Strategic Transformation of Xerox* (Ithaca: New York State School of Industrial and Labor Relations, Cornell University, 1991), p. 36 (typescript).

7. Many cuts in employment levels, of course, were also accompanied by asset disposals, but I am referring to the many examples of announced reductions in the work force that do not cite accompanying changes in the business.

8. Tom Peters and Robert Waterman, *In Search of Excellence* (New York: Harper & Row, 1982).

9. This description is based on several interviews with consultants who work for the company and who wish to remain anonymous.

10. Personal communication. His former employer's CEO was quoted in the business press (about the time of this interview) asserting that managers will have to mend their ways and learn to be more effective at introducing new products in a timely fashion and to be more responsive to the market.

11. See John Kotter, *A Force for Change: How Leadership Differs from Management* (New York: Free Press, 1990).

12. James McGregor Burns, op. cit.

13. Middle manages are managers who may have two or three levels of supervision below them and often, but not always, are general managers (that is, they have most of the functions reporting to them necessary to manage a product or service).

14. See the classic volume by Melville Dalton, *Men Who Manage* (New York: John Wiley, 1959). Dalton provides many persuasive examples of managers "winning" by hitting their targets through injuring the performance of others. For a number of more recent examples of how playing by numbers distorts the organization and leads to ineffective real performance, see Robert Jackall, *Moral Mazes: The World of Corporate Managers* (New York: Oxford University Press, 1988). Jackall describes one case in which one division manager sells a critical product line needed by another division, creating a string of problems.

15. Most of the training future managers receive from their people-oriented human behavior course deal with issues of motivation and leadership legitimacy. There is no mention of the management issues associated with obtaining effective work performance and facilitating coordination. Words like *production, operations, coordination,* and *work flow* rarely appear in text indexes.

16. See Harold Leavitt, *Corporate Pathfinders* (Homewood, Ill.: Dow Jones-

Irwin, 1986), pp. 3–4, 26–27; and Daniel Katz and Robert Kahn, *The Social Psychology of Organizations* (New York: John Wiley, 1978).

Chapter 4. Efficiency, Quality, Service, and Innovation

1. The next chapter deals with the source of integration and coordination problems.

2. Eliot Chapple and Leonard Sayles, *The Measure of Management* (New York: Macmillan, 1961) pp. 18–45. See also Leonard Sayles, *Redefining What's Essential to Business Performance: Pathways to Productivity, Quality and Service* (Greensboro, N.C.: Center for Creative Leadership, 1990).

3. *Wall Street Journal,* January 14, 1991. What is especially surprising about this example is that this cable break took place less than two months after another accidental cable cutting had taken place in the same state.

4. This exmple is derived from detailed accounts that appeared in the *New York Times* and the *Wall Street Journal,* September 19, 20, and 23, 1991, and the *Wall Street Journal,* December 12, 1991. The two newspapers carried almost identical descriptions of the event, but it should also be noted that AT & T reported that it was still investigating the incident and could not give a complete explanation. Further, some of the description is based on union and employee statements, and the facts that are uncovered with more time for research may differ from this account.

5. John Keller, "AT & T Management of Backup System Led to Network Outage, State Panel Says," *Wall Street Journal,* December 12, 1991.

6. *New York Times,* September 19, 1991, p. 19.

7. AT & T made the additional mistake in its first explanation of the source of the failure of blaming employees who, contrary to instructions, had not been monitoring the audible bell warning system or the visual control board. In later explanations, they apologized and instead referred to management failures.

8. *Wall Street Journal,* September 23, 1991.

9. See Charles Perrow, *Normal Accidents* (New York: Basic Books, 1984). Perrow includes a number of cases illustrating the vulnerability to failure of large, complex systems.

10. "Nuclear Agency Blames Nine Mile Point Accident on Design Error, *New York Times,* October 19, 1991.

11. William Carley, "Artificial Heart Valves That Fail Are Linked to Falsified Records," *Wall Street Journal,* November 7, 1991, p. 1. Early in 1992, Pfizer announced it was "ready to spend more than $500 million to settle all lawsuits and claims" arising from the use of this product (*Wall Street Journal,* January 27, 1992).

12. The leadership issues of reconciling the need to have substantial technical knowledge with empowering subordinates will be assessed in chapter 6.

13. As usual, the name and identifying technical details have been changed to preserve anonymity. Thus, some of the information will appear technically vague.

14. The cases from which this composite description are derived were observed at IBM (Leonard Sayles, *Managerial Behavior,* New York: McGraw Hill, 1964), and in the new ventures unit of an anonymous large U.S. conglomerate (Robert Burgelman and Leonard Sayles, *Inside Corporate Innovation,* New York: Free Press, 1985).

15. The managerial issues involved in leading this kind of cross-functional work team are assesses in chapter 10.

16. Placing functional specialists together who must closely coordinate was a subject of substantial research thirty years earlier. See Chapple and Sayles, op. cit., pp. 25–26.

17. Around 1980, Xerox learned that its Japanese competition could produce a high-quality copier in Japan, pay for shipping to the United States, allow markups for distributor and dealer and a profit for themselves, and have a selling price that was below Xerox's own internal manufacturing cost. Frank Wayno, *The Road to the Baldrige Award: Human Resource Aspects of the Strategic Transformation of Xerox* (Ithaca: New York State School of Industrial and Labor Relations, Cornell University, 1991).

18. David Halberstam, *The Reckoning* (New York: William Morrow, 1986), pp. 499–500. High-level finance executives believed that the cost/reward ratio was unfavorable given the need to write off existing and still usable paint equipment and facilities (although these produced a distinctly inferior finish).

19. Personal interviews with managers in several software consulting companies.

20. The observations that follow are based on the research of professor Rebecca Henderson. See Rebecca Henderson, *A Failure of Established Firms in the Face of Technical Change: A Study of Photolithographic Alignment Equipment,* Ph.D. dissertation, Harvard University (Cambridge, Mass.: Department of Business Economics, 1988). Some of the findings appear in Rebecca Henderson and Kim Clark, "Architectural Innovation: The Reconfiguration of Existing Product Technologies and the Failure of Established Firms," *Administrative Science Quarterly,* Vol. 35 (1990), pp. 9–30.

21. Henderson (*A failure*) and Henderson and Clark ("Architectural Innovation") come to a similar conclusion, although they deal with only some of the coordination complexities that are described in the next chapter.

Chapter 5. Coordination

1. John Holusha, "DuPont Is Planning New Round of Cost Cuts," *New York Times,* December 5, 1991.

2. Personal correspondence with the author.

3. See Leonard Sayles, *Leadership: Managing in Real Organizations* (New York: McGraw-Hill, 1989), chap. 6.

4. Leonard Sayles, *Redefining What's Essential to Business Performance* (Greensboro, N.C.: Center for Creative Leadership, 1990).

5. Leonard Sayles, *Managerial Behavior* (New York: McGraw-Hill, 1964), chap. 7.

6. *New York Times,* March 1, 1991.

7. See Richard Cyert and James March, *A Behavioral Theory of the Firm* (Englewood Cliffs, N.J.: Prentice-Hall, 1963).

8. See Kenneth Arrow, *The Limits of Organization* (New York: W.W. Norton, 1974).

9. This example is drawn from the fieldwork of my Center for Creative Leadership colleague, Wilfred Drath.

10. Rebecca Henderson and Kim Clark, "Architectural Innovation: The Reconfiguration of Existing Product Technologies and the Failure of Established Firms," *Administrative Science Quarterly,* Vol. 35 (1990), p. 18.

11. Ibid., p. 17.

12. Alan Kantrow, *The Constraints of Corporate Tradition* (New York: Harper & Row, 1984), pp. 28–29. The Goldmark/CBS Records case is Kantrow's.

13. For a well-documented account of General Motors' myopia and its inability to perceive both changes in the U.S. market and the real threat of the Japanese fuel-efficient, high-quality car, see Maryann Keller, *Rude Awakening* (New York: William Morrow, 1989).

14. Henderson and Clark, op cit., pp. 24–26.

15. A former director of General Motors asserts that a very high price was paid for the British sports car manufacturer, Lotus, in order to obtain the know-how associated with suspension technology. See E. Johnson, "Corporate Culture and the Changing Environment," address to California Bankers Association, Palm Desert, Calif., May 1989. General Motors also invested a great deal to develop a joint venture with Toyota (the NUMMI assembly operation in California) in order to learn the latter's manufacturing and employee relations know-how.

16. See Paul Carroll, "How an IBM Attempt to Regain PC Lead Has Slid into Trouble," *Wall Street Journal,* December 2, 1991. Carroll describes difficulties experienced by IBM in the development of OS/2, a new operating system software for its PCs.

17. Christopher Bartlett and Sumantra Ghosal, *Managing Across Borders* (Boston: Harvard Business School Press, 1989), p. 148.

18. This is not to say that personality differences and the quest for power did not play a role here. What is often neglected, however, in these kinds of managerial conflicts is that there is usually a "ground" upon which the more personal factors play themselves out. And that ground, more often than not, is one of work, technology, and systems contradictions or conflicts.

19. See Charles Perrow, *Normal Accidents* (New York: Basic Books, 1984).

20. Bartlett and Ghosal, op cit., pp. 139–140. All of these observations on ITT are from their work.

21. *Wall Street Journal,* November 1, 1991, quoting Leo Thomas (the most senior Kodak executive for imaging products).

22. *Economist,* December 2, 1989, p. 5 (Japanese technology survey).

23. Thus, the *Economist* understates and misleads the reader in their praise of the Japanese company, Fanuc. The journal implies that it was Fanuc's wisdom or farsightedness in seeing the interrelationship among these three discrete innovations that was the source of success. That "vision" surely was helpful, but it was only the beginning. Leadership skills in implementing the fusion of the three distinct developments had to be just as important.

24. See the *Wall Street Journal,* February 3, 1992.

25. For a provocative discussion of the continuing management dilemma surrounding centralization and decentralization, see Charles Hampden-Turner, *Charting the Corporate Mind* (New York, Free Press, 1990), p. 139.

26. Herbert Simon, "How Managers Express Their Creativity," *Across the Board,* March 1986, p. 15.

27. *Wall Street Journal,* August 16, 1991, p. 1. Penske is credited with increasing that company's share of heavy truck engine market from about 3 percent to 28 percent in less than three years. The impact of such intense involvement on subordinate motivation is discussed in chapter 11.

Chapter 6. The New Leadership

1. Presentation at the Annual International Conference of the Strategic Management Society, Toronto, Canada, October 24, 1991. Mintzberg is a professor at McGill University's School of Management and has a worldwide reputation based on his many years of pathbreaking research.

2. See Thomas Steiner and Diogo Teixeira, *Technology in Banking: Creating Value and Destroying Profits,* (Homewood, Ill.: Dow Jones-Irwin, 1990). General Motors invested billions in new technology for auto assembly plants that apparently did little to improve performance. The *Wall Street Journal* reporters found quality and productivity far superior in an old 1960s GM plant as compared to a new 1.2 billion dollar factory (August 29, 1991). Maryann Keller's more systematic study of GM's 60 billion dollar investment found a similar lack of return on robotics and other improved technology. See Keller, *Rude Awakening* (New York: William Morrow, 1989).

3. For a description of the behavioral skills involved in convincing upper-level managers to change their views, see Leonard Sayles, *Leadership: Managing in Real Organizations* (New York: McGraw-Hill, 1989), pp. 135–148.

4. B. R. Schlender and M. Waldholz, "Genentech's Missteps and FDA Policy Shift Led to TPA Setback," *Wall Street Journal,* June 16, 1987.

5. See Joseph Moses and Karen Lyness, "Leadership Behavior in Ambiguous Environments," in Kenneth Clark and Miriam Clark (eds.), *Measures of Leadership* (West Orange, N.J.: Leadership Library of America), pp. 327–334. In one study in a large corporation, they estimate that three out of four managers cannot function in ambiguous working situations.

6. Alice H. Eagly, Mona G. Makhijani, and Bruce G. Klonsky, "Gender and the Evaluation of Leaders: A Meta-Analysis," *Psychological Bulletin,* Vol. 111, No. 1 (1992), pp. 3–22.

7. See Andrew Grove, *High Output Management* (New York: Random House, 1983), p. 61. Grove founded and became president of Intel. He describes how senior management evaluates requests on the basis of how well middle managers can answer highly specific questions.

Chapter 7. High Performance as a Source of Motivation

1. See George Farris, "Organizational Factors and Individual Performance," *Journal of Applied Psychology,* Vol. 53, No. 2, pp. 87–92; also George Farris, "Chicken, Eggs and Productivity in Organizations," *Organizational Dynamics,* Vol. 3, No. 4 (Spring 1975), pp. 2–15.

2. Danny Miller, "The Perils of Excellence: Some Self-Limiting Aspects of Success," (Working paper, University d'Montreal, Quebec, 1991).

3. See H. M. Lefcourt, *Locus of Control: Current Trends in Theory and Research* (Hillsdale, N.J.: Lawrence Erlbaum, 1982).

4. Jack Falvey, "Fix General Motors Now," *Wall Street Journal,* February 3, 1992. Unfortunately, the author does not provide the source of his data.

5. Leonard Sayles, *Managerial Behavior* (New York: McGraw-Hill, 1964), p. 161.

6. Christopher Lorenz, "The Birth of a 'Transnational'", *McKinsey Quarterly,* Autumn 1989, p. 76.

7. This material is drawn from Charles Hampden-Turner, *Charting the Corporate Mind* (New York: Free Press, 1990), p. 68. The interpretation is mine, however, and the case example has been rewritten.

8. Obviously, an important task of the leader is helping employees learn how to be successful in the tasks for which they are responsible. Such success increase self-esteem, a critical factor in motivation, and helps them get acceptance among their peers. See Robert Wood and Albert Bandura, "Social Cognitive Theory of Organizational Management," *Academy of Management Review,* Vol. 14, No. 3 (July 1989), pp. 361–384.

9. In a study of the U.S. space program, it was observed that scientists and engineers from various countries that had poor relationships with one another, or even where there were open hostilities, could often continue to have unemotional "scientific exchanges." Leonard Sayles and Margaret Chandler, *Managing Large Systems* (New Brunswick, N.J.: Transaction Publishers, 1993).

10. The term "challenging the process" is from J. Kouzes and B. Posner, *The Leadership Challenge: How to Get Extraordinary Things Done in Organizations* (San Francisco, CA: Jossey-Bass, 1987).

11. An obvious issue here is that such managers become controversial as there is a need for confrontation, for breaking away from what was a consensus. In many, conceivably most organizations, there is a bias toward those who don't "rock the boat," who are good team players.

12. Leonard Sayles, "Using Systems Controls to Boost Productivity," *National Productivity Review,* Spring 1982, p. 183.

13. Note that in this latter case, it also took managerial initiative to get the program behind the automated rating system reviewed and examined in fine detail. The program was controlled by an outside vendor, and the manager felt she had to move swiftly before other good customers were turned down. Without her status and contacts, the problem would have festered, and the systems error perhaps would never have been discovered.

14. Leonard Sayles, "Who Is Fat and What Is Lean," *Interfaces,* Vol. 15, No. 3 (May–June 1985), pp. 54–59.

Chapter 8. Strategy from Below

1. The first case is derived from Robert Burgelman, "Intraorganizational Ecology of Strategy Making and Organizational Adaptation: Theory and Field Research," Working Paper #1122, Stanford, Calif: Stanford University Graduate School of Business, 1991; to be published in *Organization Science*). An overview of the significance and dynamics of these "autonomous strategic initiatives" appears in Robert Burgelman and Leonard Sayles, *Inside Corporate Innovation* (New York: Free Press, 1986).

2. Burgelman, op. cit., p. 15.

3. Of course, this kind of major shift in responsibility provides a major development and growth experience for executives. See Morgan McCall, Michael Lombardo, and Ann Morrison, *Lessons of Experience* (Lexington, Mass.: Lexington Books, 1988).

4. Danny Miller, *The Icarus Paradox* (New York: HarperCollins, 1990), p. 109.

5. John Kotter, *A Force for Change* (New York: Free Press, 1990), pp. 21–30.

6. Ibid., p. 26.

7. Obviously such trade-offs favoring the longer run are likely to be made where senior management understands the work (see chapter 11).

8. Ibid., p. 27.

9. *New York Times,* September 29, 1991. These procedures and the extra equipment cost about 10 million dollars in the first year of operation.

10. Douglas Smith and Robert Alexander, *How Xerox Invented, Then Ignored the First Personal Computer* (New York: William Morrow, 1988). Also see "The Lab That Ran Away from Xerox," *Fortune,* September 5, 1983.

11. Stephen Roth and Michael Porter, "Bendix Corporation (A)," Harvard Business School Case 9-378-257 (Boston, Mass.: Harvard Business School, 1981).

12. John Markoff, "Abe Peled's Secret Start-Up at IBM," *New York Times,* December 8, 1991. Note that it was RISC technology that formed the basis for the strategic initiative of Kohn at Intel, described above.

13. *Business Week,* December 16, 1991, p. 118.

14. See Don Frey, "Learning the Ropes: My Life as a Product Champion," *Harvard Business Review,* September–October 1991, pp. 46–86. Former CEO of Bell & Howell, Frey describes the challenge of being a product manager at Ford.

15. It would be misleading to suggest that such managers are responsible for all successful corporate innovations. Joseph Wilson, CEO of what was then Haloid, sponsored and fought (with his board of directors) for patience and support to commercialize Xerography, which eventually became the basis for a new industry as well as the major product of the renamed Haloid (Xerox). See James Brian Quinn, "Xerox Corporation (A)" (Hanover, N.H.: Amos Tuck School of Business Administration, Dartmouth College, 1977).

16. Personal interview with James McSwiney, March 6, 1988.

17. A decade after their merger, according to the *Wall Street Journal,* the two technology companies, Burroughs and Sperry (now combined in Unisys) had still not resolved their cultural differences. *Wall Street Journal,* July 23, 1991.

18. Henry Mintzberg, "Crafting Strategy," *Harvard Business Review,* Vol. 65, No. 4 (July–August 1987), p. 70.

19. Ibid.

20. Richard Pascale, "Perspectives on Strategy: The Real Story Behind Honda's Success," *California Management Review,* Vol. 26, No. 3 (1984), pp. 47–72.

Chapter 9. Managing Stability and Managing Change

1. Task and technology names have been altered to preserve anonymity.

2. James Brian Quinn's work is most instructive in emphasizing the importance of what he calls "incrementalism" in pursuing innovations (in contrast to making

the right decision once and for all). See his *Strategies for Change: Logical Incrementalism* (Homewood, Ill.: Irwin, 1980).

Chapter 10. The Decision Process and Management Teams

1. For a careful analysis of how functional background shapes decision choices, see Richard Ritti and Fred Goldner, "Professional Pluralism in an Industrial Organization," *Management Science*, Vol. 11, No. 4 (December 1969), pp. B233–B246. Also see Danny Miller, *The Icarus Paradox* (New York: HarperCollins, 1990).

2. Leonard Sayles and Margaret Chandler, *Managing Large Systems* (New Brunswick, N.J.: Transaction Publishers, 1993).

3. A good summary of what the authors call the "thick," turbulent stream, the decision process that is behind most major commitments, is provided by Morgan McCall and Robert Kaplan, *Whatever It Takes: The Realities of Managerial Decision Making*, 2nd ed. (Englewood Cliffs, N.J.: Prentice-Hall, 1990).

4. Irving Janis and Leon Mann, *Decision Making* (New York: Free Press, 1971), pp. 129–133. Janis and Mann first introduced this concept of flawed, defensive decision making.

5. Danny Miller, *The Icarus Paradox: How Exceptional Companies Bring About Their Own Downfall*, (New York: Harper Business, 1990).

6. For some extreme cases, see the *Wall Street Journal*, July 5, 1991, p. 1. For a more systematic case study of a major commercial bank caught up in the lending fervor, see Gary Hector, *Breaking the Bank: The Decline of Bank of America* (Boston: Little, Brown, 1982).

7. Christopher Bartlett and Sumantra Ghosal, *Managing Across Borders* (Boston: Harvard Business School Press, 1989), p. 152.

8. Ibid. pp. 152–154.

9. See chapter .

10. Morgan McCall, Michael Lombardo, and Ann Morrison, *Lessons of Experience*, (Lexington, Mass.: Lexington Press, 1988), p. 48.

11. Nigel Campbell, "How Japanese Multinationals Work So Well," *Prism*, Fourth Quarter 1991, p. 63.

12. A good analysis of the source of these contradictions is Morgan McCall and Michael Lombardo, *Off the Track: Why and How Successful Executives Get Derailed*, (Greensboro, N.C.: Center for Creative Leadership, 1986).

Chapter 11. What Senior Managers Can Do to Encourage Work Leadership

1. The plant manager is rated excellent by top management.

2. See Danny Miller, *The Icarus Paradox* (New York: Harper Business, 1990). Miller's subtitle is relevant: *How Exceptional Companies Bring About Their Own Downfall*.

3. Nigel Campbell, "How Japanese Multinationals Work So Well," *Prism*, Fourth Quarter 1991, p. 62. In contrast, proposals for even minor changes in formal structure lead to consuming struggles among executives in U.S. companies.

4. One of the best critiques of this emphasis on a "one big decision" by top management is James Brian Quinn's study, *Strategies for Change; Logical Incrementalism* (Homewood, Ill.: Irwin, 1980).

5. Amar Bhide, "Hustle as Strategy," *The McKinsey Quarterly*, Autumn 1986, pp. 27, 30. Bhide argues that historically, strategy was based on astute investment decisions given the overhang of large fixed costs. But fixed assets are less important in a fast-changing and more service-oriented economy; therefore, strategy can change almost in a flash. But many companies still operate as thought they were in that earlier environment, placing great emphasis on key top management decisions that would determine most of what occurred for a number of years.

6. See George Bollenbacher, "America's Banking Dinosaurs," *Wall Street Journal*, March 18, 1992. The data is derived from his book, *The New Business of Banking* (New York: Probus, 1992).

7. Campbell, op. cit., p. 66.

8. Readers will recognize this as a simplified view of the so-called portfolio approach first associated with the Boston Consulting Group. Multiproduct companies were urged to distinguish their future high-growth "stars" from their "cash cows" (to be "milked") and their "dogs" (for disposal).

9. George Stalk, Philip Evans, and Lawrence Shulman, "Competing on Capabilities: The New Rules of Corporate Strategy," *Harvard Business Review*, Vol. 70, No. 2 (March–April 1992), p. 57.

10. Ibid., p. 66.

11. C. K. Prahalad and Gary Hamel, "The Core Competence of the Corporation," *Harvard Business Review*, May–June 1990, pp. 81–82.

12. Charles Hampden-Turner, *Charting the Corporate Mind* (New York: Free Press, 1990), p. 174.

13. See Michael Piore and Charles Sabel, *The Second Industrial Divide* (New York: Basic Books, 1984). Their analysis emphasizes why flexibility and quick adaptability are more critical in the current economic world than the economies of scale that were so eagerly sought in an earlier industrial era.

14. The cases in chapter 3 showing that some companies actually saved money when they had to reduce the quantity of pollutants and waste generated by their technology are relevant examples. They were forced to rethink what they did and why they did it and discovered numerous process improvements as a result of being pressured to do things differently.

15. Ronald Heifetz describes the leader's role as orchestrating tensions and challenging subordinates to come to understand the more difficult realities of the situation. This contrasts with the typical manager's temptation to maintain an excessive degree of comfort and composure. See R. Heifetz, R. Sinder, A. Jones, L. Hodge, and K. Rowley, "Teaching and Assessing Leadership Courses at the John F. Kennedy School of Government," *Journal of Policy Analysis and Management*, Vol. 8, No. 3 (1989), p. 542.

16. I am not saying that all contracting out is undesirable. There are many peripheral functions that can be dispensed with, saving dollars and managerial effort; however, the decision cannot be based simply on what looks peripheral. Often so-called service or support activities, for example, embody critical technical competencies that are or should be an integral part of the basic capability of the company.

They are or ought to be closely intertwined with other functions if management is going to be able to really learn the fundamentals of some activity.

17. There has been some concern expressed by women's groups that an emphasis on management potential being synonymous with an "intense desire to win" was also a gender-biasing promotion criterion. *Wall Street Journal,* December 30, 1991.

18. Dr. Marian N. Ruderman of the Center for Creative Leadership has been helpful in alerting me to some of these issues.

19. Dr. Robert Hogan believes that top management often favors executives who "talk a good game," are inherently selfish and self-seeking, and have no capacity to set demanding achievement goals for themselves. They have learned to get ahead by their articulate, chameleon ways; truly, the "dark side of charisma." See Robert Hogan, Robert Raskin, and Dan Fazzini, "The Dark Side of Charisma," in Kenneth Clark and Miriam Clark (eds.), *Measures of Leadership* (West Orange, N.J.: Leadership Library of America, 1990), pp. 343–353. David Riesman would have found them lacking in inner-directedness; see *The Lonely Crowd* (Garden City, N.Y.: Doubleday Anchor, 1953).

20. I am indebted to Robert Burnside for this example.

21. Campbell, op. cit., p. 64.

22. See Leonard Sayles, *Leadership* (New York: McGraw-Hill, 1989), pp. 113–132. Also see Jeffrey Pfeffer, *Managing with Power* (Boston: Harvard Business School Press, 1992). Pfeffer makes the acquisition of power not only appealing but the sine qua non of organizational survival.

23. Terence Roth, "Aim Is to Be Competitive," *Wall Street Journal,* January 18, 1991.

24. Data from *Wall Street Journal,* September 26, 1991.

25. The one significant exception was a series of team-building exercises that helped give a sense of greater camaraderie within the top management group of the division; however, these were not content or problem oriented.

26. I am indebted to Robert R. W. Wright, who has been a consultant to the senior managements of many corporations, for this observation. Wright has sensed a strong desire on the part of executives to shift their attention to issues that seemed more pliable, more easily and quickly settled.

27. See Hampden-Turner, op. cit., p. 175. See also Leonard Sayles, "Leadership for the Nineties," *Issues and Observations,* Vol. 10, No. 2 (Spring 1990).

28. *New York Times,* July 22, 1992.

29. Christopher Bartlett and Sumantra Ghosal, "Matrix Management: Not a Structure, a Frame of Mind," *Harvard Business Review,* Vol. 68, No. 4 (July–Aug., 1990), p. 139 (italics added).

Chapter 12. Finding Leadership in Management Research

1. See John Kotter, *The General Manager* (New York: Free Press, 1982); Rosemary Stewart, *Managers and Their Jobs* (Maidenhead, England: McGraw-Hill, 1967); Henry Mintzberg, *The Nature of Managerial Work* (New York: Harper & Row, 1973); Sune Carlson, *Executive Behavior* (Uppsala, Sweden: Acta Universitatis Upsaliensis, 1991); and Leonard Sayles, *Leadership: What Effective Managers*

Really Do (New York: McGraw-Hill, 1979). Mintzberg was one of the first to note the absence of a conceptual explanation of why managers had this fast-paced, almost chaotic, densely interactional work life. See his preface to Sune Carlson, op. cit.

2. See Amar Bhide, "Hustle as Strategy," *McKinsey Quarterly,* Autumn 1986, pp. 27–40.

3. See Eliot Chaple and Leonard Sayles, *The Measure of Management* (New York: Macmillan, 1967); Jay Galbraith, *Organizational Design* (Reading, Mass.: Addison-Wesley, 1977). I should note that there are vast differences in the kind of teamwork issues posed by autonomous work groups or self-managing teams comprised of employees and teamwork issues inherent in management teams. The latter obviously have members who are competitive and have legitimate differences that injure their ability to cooperate.

4. Galbraith, op. cit.; Charles Perrow, *Organizational Analysis: A Sociological View* (Belmont, Calif.: Brooks-Cole, 1971).

5. Tom Burns and G. M. Stalker, *The Management of Innovation,* (London: Tavistock, 1961). They began using the now well-established terminology: organizations with a great deal of uncertainty requiring more employee autonomy are *organic,* in contrast to the routinized, *mechanistic* organizations. See also Peter Blau and Richard Schoenherr, *The Structure of Organizations* (New York: Basic Books, 1971).

6. Paul Lawrence and Jay Lorsch, *Organization and Environment* (Boston: Harvard Graduate School of Business, 1967). This is the classic and most frequently cited research in this area.

Chapter 13. The Leadership Solution

1. John Huey, "1990's Survival Guide—Where Managers Will Go," *Fortune,* January 27, 1992.

2. Tom Peters, "Competitive Strategies," address to the 11th Annual International Conference, Strategic Management Society, Toronto, October 24, 1991.

3. See Thomas Kuhn, *The Structure of Scientific Revolution* (Chicago: University of Chicago Press, 1970). Kuhn demonstrated how paradigms that are no longer as relevant retain credibility for extended periods by various intellectual rationalizations. Eventually, of course, the whole structure crumbles, and a new paradigm gets acceptance that explains the phenomenon more parsimoniously.

4. See George Stalk, Philip Evans, and Lawrence Shulman, "Competing on Capabilities: The New Rules of Corporate Strategy," *Harvard Business Review,* Vol. 70, No. 2, pp. 57–69. The authors subscribe to the views I have expressed: companies are discovering that they can redefine strategies by relating them to key business processes that they have learned to manage effectively.

5. It may well be that the reluctance of professors of management to look at the functioning of real organizations as working systems may be responsible. Their views on leadership and management are based on surveys and questionnaires deduced from well-established academic-based theories, but they rarely step into an organization to see its day-to-day functioning or learn what managers are confronting, worrying, and doing.

Notes

6. Frederick Taylor, *Scientific Management* (New York: Harpers, 1911), p. 99.

7. The author was a student at MIT in 1950 and took courses in which these subjects were featured.

8. Some readers may note that this term, which struck a responsive chord in managers after its appearance in Tom Peters and Robert Waterman's *In Search of Excellence* (New York: Harper & Row, 1982), apparently fell on deaf ears when it was first used more than fifteen years earlier in this article.

9. J. Sterling Livingston, "Myth of the Well-Educated Manager," *Harvard Business Review* Vol. 49, No. 1 (January–February 1971), pp. 82–83.

10. Ibid., p. 84.

11. Henry Mintzberg, "Managerial Work: Forty Years Later," in Sune Carlson, *Executive Behavior* (Uppsala, Sweden: Acta Universitatis Upsaliensis, 1991), p. 118.

12. See discussion in chapter 9.

13. James Gleick, *Chaos: Making a New Science* (Penguin Books, 1988).

14. Henry Mintzberg said this best in his classic article, "The Manager's Job: Folklore and Fact," *Harvard Business Review,* Vol. 75, No. 4., (July–August 1975).

15. Ibid.

Research Appendix

1. For more complete descriptions of the data collection and analysis methods employed, see the research notes in my monographs:

Leonard Sayles and George Strauss, *The Local Union* (New York: Harcourt, Brace, 1967).

Leonard Sayles, *Behavior of Industrial Work Groups* (New York: John Wiley, 1957).

Leonard Sayles, *Managerial Behavior* (New York: McGraw-Hill, 1964).

Leonard Sayles and Margaret Chandler, *Managing Large Systems* (New York: Harper, 1971).

2. I am indebted to professor Seymour Sarason of Yale University's psychology department for this choice morsel of social science history.

3. Eliot Chapple and Carleton Coon, *Principles of Anthropology* (New York: Henry Holt, 1942).

Acknowledgments

Readers deserve to be spared whatever distress the author may have incurred completing his work. But it may be of some interest to know that this slim volume stems from more than a decade of research and the traversing of many blind alleys.

In the early 1980s, while a professor of management at Columbia's Graduate School of Business, I became troubled by my inability to interrelate our field studies of managerial behavior with the models of management used in most MBA classrooms and the increasingly apparent performance problems of American business. It was only after I joined the Center for Creative Leadership that I was able to find the missing link that related these three factors: a contrary view of managerial leadership. I am much indebted to the president of the center, Walter F. Ulmer, Jr., for encouraging my work and providing an extraordinarily stimulating environment. Dr. David DeVries, formerly its executive vice president, provided a contagious enthusiasm that frequently buoyed my fragile spirits.

The study includes some data shared with me by Professor Rebecca Henderson of MIT, Professor Robert Burgelman of Stanford, and Dr. Barry Gruenberg, for which I am most grateful. Of course, there is the usual qualification: the interpretation is mine, and they may not concur with how their data has been reanalyzed. I also worked with Bob Kaplan, Bob Burnside and Victoria Guthrie of the Center for Creative Leadership staff, whose unfailing stimulation was critical during a period in which some of these ideas were germinating. Peggy Cartner, the center's reference librarian, was a marvelous resource. At a later period, Dr. Walter Tornow and Martin Wilcox were most helpful.

Old friends and mentors always provide seminal ideas to be recycled by an author. In my case, Professor William F. Whyte of Cornell, Dr. Eliot Chapple, and Robert Wright have filled that important niche, as they have for many, many years. My colleague at Columbia Univeristy, Professor James Kuhn, some of whose interests in leadership parallel my own, has been a steadfast friend and a source of stimulating ideas. Martin Edelston, the indefatigable publisher and editor of Boardroom Publications, has goaded me for years to address the performance problems of business. Dr. Alvin Mesnikoff, psychiatrist and former senior health services administrator, has generously shared his management insights with me.

My administrative secretary, Debra Nelson, provided consistent and intelligent aid, critical judgment, and unfailing support over endless months and drafts. My own word processing is reasonably fast, but hers is more accurate. I did not have to displace as much anguish on my editor and friend at The Free Press, Vice President Robert Wallace, as Debra Nelson suffered. But the enthusiasm he conveyed, from our first discussions to the completion of the writing, was very meaningful to a fretful author.

Such acknowledgments as these usually close with emotional references to a spouse who performed one or all of such spousal functions as "keeping the home fires burning" (a traditional division of labor) or typing, editing (sometimes even spelling), or filing and reference services. Alas, Kathy Ripin was not much engaged by these, and most of the latter services were performed by the do-it-yourself-inclined author. (The sparse support functions characteristic of my university career did much to encourage the development of these skills.) Further, gender roles have evolved substantially since the former kind of expression was de rigueur.

But Kathy, my wife, did much more than fulfill a behind-the-scenes role. Her own superb leadership skills, honed in a large and complex business, combined with a rare ability to both describe and conceptualize her challenge-filled days provided continuing tests of my evolving ideas. In every way, her own working leadership mirrors what I describe in the chapters contained herein.

Dobbs Ferry, New York
August 1992

Index